SOOOOOO..... MANY CARS SOOO..... LITTLE TIME

A Memoir – one man's love affair of automobiles
and the industry that produced them

By:
Roger Paul Hilderbrand

Soooooo Many Cars
Sooo Little Time

Copyright © 2018 by Roger Hilderbrand

ISBN 1985038986

Printed in the United States of America

CONTENTS

"LADIES & GENTLEMEN, START YOUR ENGINES"

INTRODUCTION

Catchy little title, don't you think? I suppose I could try to impress you with something like, "My Purposely Driven Life..... Through Cars" (my apologies to Pastor Rick Warren) or maybe a bit more scholarly, something along the lines, "A Boy's Search for Manhood as Expressed Through Cars." Nah, that would never do.....way too wordy. Besides, you, my much appreciated reader, might fall asleep (I do that to people on occasion) before getting past the title! So I'm sticking with "Sooooooo Many Cars.....Sooooooo Little Time".

Let me cut to the chase with you. If books were rated as movies, this book would be rated "R" for sexual content, real or implied, and the use of language not acceptable on school grounds or church camps. But in all fairness, prepare yourself for the "earthiness" of several passages that sneak up on you from time to time, all intended to make you better appreciate the fun read that the book is intended to be.

You never forget your first one.....car, that is. Not a chance of that happening in my lifetime. That "first" put me on a path I could never have imagined. It is now inspiring me to write all about CARS, PEOPLE, and ME, but make no mistake about it, the "STARS" of this book are "CARS" (poetic rapture being experienced at this moment), whether expressed in narrative, photos or lists. We'll look at the industry and the people behind the scenes (winners and losers), the where's, when's and how's of buying or leasing cars and trucks, whether new or pre-owned. And on a lighter note, I briefly consider what changes I would make to automobiles, regulations I would modify or eliminate, factors to consider while traveling in an autonomously driven automobile, the scary stuff you have to be on the lookout for, how to minimize "road rage," and much, much more. You will also find the mother lode of all car lists for your perusal, and here comes that expression "last but not least", I provide you with a useful condensed dictionary or glossary that, hopefully, will help navigate you through some terms and words frequently misunderstood, never heard before, hope never to hear again, or the meaning of some words you have little desire to know in the first place. No matter what, I have a little something for everyone and, quite possibly, a few unexpected laughs might just come your way.

The PEOPLE and ME part of this book is where I focus on my friends, family and former teachers, who either nurtured, loved, guided me, or, just got in the way as I lived out my life through cars. I take a long look at myself and the memories that helped shape my life, laying out some biographical details in an attempt to answer some of the why's behind my love of cars.

Do you remember those feelings you had when you first met that special, "don't let my heart fail me now" one? One you spent as much time with as she would give you? As time wore on, the two of you became inseparable, like two blind porcupines making love in the dark. Then one night quite by surprise, she goes away for a time.....without you! You try desperately hard to sleep without her, but you can't as you fondly recall the many intimate moments you shared. You think about her ethnicity..... German, Italian, and you rapidly conclude that her true beauty is more than skin deep. Your eyes can't get enough of her as you lapse into a listless, lustful gaze while fondling her lines, your ears are gratified by the sound of her provocative whispers, all the while your heart races, reminiscing about the first time you were inside her! Well folks, that's just the tip of the iceberg as to how deeply and hopelessly in love one can fall for a gorgeous.....CAR!!

Yes, I could have been rightly referred to as a luster of cars, a.k.a., an unfulfilled love affair of automobiles. I could do worse, as some men take that practice to new heights by chasing after women. Not me.....I chase cars. It's safer, cheaper and morally appropriate. Just for the record, though, I survived boyhood in spite of myself, by keeping my heart occupied with a love of cars, ever in search of that yet to be discovered dream car. You'll come to see how my version of lusting became somewhat fulfilling, without quite ever getting there. This just propelled my passions all the more, which brings to mind a little sonnet I wrote for this occasion:

iv

'MY DREAM CAR'
(just one of them)

Ah, yes, it's not just coincidental
That I find myself dreaming about a
'1956 Lincoln Continental.

For many decades, including this
My passionate dreams are finally turning to bliss.

From a vision transcendental
To feelings not so metaphysical.

The Dow Jones agrees.....it's time
Buying a dream car ain't no crime.

So, I cashed in a handlful of stocks,
sold shares of Apple, Disney and Cox.

As a known speeder, I am aware of Sheriff Joe's jails.
places not designed for comfort, escape or telling tales.

Because of it, I cautiously make my haste to Tempe
Where my dream car is so impatiently waiting for me.

Heading out the door, consumed in my awaiting joy,
To lay my hardened eyeballs on this much sought after toy.

A much needed test drive calms my worst fears,
that puppy made for some unplanned tears.

Wow! This car is too good to be true,
With paint so gorgeously displayed in blue.

Bill, my master mechanic declares, "it's a sleeper"
Convincing me that this beaut is indeed a "keeper".

The deal done, my trip home, euphorically, begun
Driving that great classic ever so carefully, for fun.
While tooling up I-10, passed like a flash
Telling me that this car just had to last.

Loving this dream car is going to be a wondrous thing,
Most assuredly making my heart, now and forever, sing.

Well, folks, about now you might be wondering why you are reading this, or why you should care. I hope you seriously consider both questions because I see a little bit of me in each of you, and you are important to me, worthy of reading about. One more thing - please accept my heartfelt apology for so blatantly throwing my heart out there for all of you to see, especially at such an early stage in the book. Please understand my need to get this off my chest, add some ink, and get this onto a printed page, where it rightly belongs. On that note, our proverbial car's gas tank is full and ready to go, so let's do it. Fasten your seat-belts.....we are going for a literary ride!

MEMORIES

How, when and where did my love affair with cars begin? My earliest memories go back to the small town where my maternal grandparents raised me until my grandmother's passing when I was the tender age of ten. Our town was so small that it didn't deserve a name as there was little to do or see in this hole-in-the-road, pit-stop on the way to nowhere with the occasional farmer dropping in to buy some gas or groceries from my grandpa's general store. He sold everything from prophylactics to butchered meats, many of which he slaughtered himself. To this day, I can recall those little, helpless pigs squealing for their lives as Grandpa "did the deed" that so terrorized me.

Anyhow, I grew up in this burg of a town that became known as "Resume Speed," or, at least, that's what the sign indicated as you were leaving town, a town with a population bursting at the seams with all of 35 people. Heck, we had more pigs than we had people which presented a bit of a problem come Halloween eve when it could get a little iffy, trying to sort out one from the other. Actually, I'm pulling your leg (Hoosier-ese for innocuous exaggeration) a bit, as the town really does have a name, though not particularly recallable...New Bellsville...just as fer piece down the road from Nashville, in Brown County, Indiana. That area around Nashville offers some of the most scenic vistas for viewing autumn foliage you'll ever see...breathtakingly beautiful. If I can't get back there each October to experience this briefest of seasons, at least my heart is there.

So here I am, 4 years old in Resume Speed, getting an infrequent visit from my dad who lived some fifty miles away in Bedford, a.k.a. "The Limestone Capital of the World" (I have always sensed that that claim was not entirely justified as nearby Bloomington had its shares of limestone quarries). Anyhow, on one of Dad's irregular, unplanned visits (so it seemed), he would show up in this brand-spanking new 1947 Ford 2-door sedan, navy blue, with the thought in mind of taking me for a ride in that beautiful car. What a thrill that was, as I can remember it to this day. What I most vividly recall was my dad picking me up by my waist and depositing me atop the front fender, facing a ready camera being focused by my grandmother. Boy, I must have been an alright kid to rate that kind of treatment coming from that demigod who answered to the name of Daddy Paul. What made that memory stand out so dominantly was Dad didn't come around with any expected regularity, making it all the more special when he did. And, sure enough, each infrequent visit would bring him to my grandparent's doorsteps sporting, yet, another new car. Seeing this slow moving parade or flow of new cars with each visit sort of paved the way, so to speak, for developing a mindset that new cars and a budding relationship with Daddy Paul were mutually intertwined. That myth got shattered by the time I became a teenager, but for a time, it was a grand illusion.

My next memory involving cars took place sometime around the age of 5, so I was told. As infrequent as my dad's visits were to Resume Speed, they weren't any more frequent than the ones I had going back to Dad's apartment in Bedford where he introduced me to my cousin Gary, youngest son of dad's older brother, Uncle Chloral. Separated in age by 6 months, boy, did we ever hit it off. As much as I was developing this love of anything with four wheels on it, low and behold, so was Gary, as we later on became known as quite the car "nuts." It must have been in our gene pool! For you neophytes out there, car nuts do not grow on trees; they come into this world as an offspring and grow into something recognized as being "car crazy." That would be doubtlessly, certifiably...Gary and Roger Hilderbrand.

How vividly I remember the two of us playing with match box cars for hours on end, racing across the living room floor of dad's apartment, crashing into each other at will. We finally broke that habit a bit later in life but, at the time, it was great fun and a precursor of things to come like "Dodgem" cars that were so eagerly driven at the local county fairs where one could hone up on one's "crashing" skills. Thereafter, no trip to Bedford was complete without playing with Gary and cars always seemed central to anything we did together. As the years passed, our relationship deepened, taking on a life all of its own, as some people believed us to be brothers, something not lost on me.

Now, in the course of a couple of paragraphs, I have ripened into the age of 6, where I find myself sitting alongside a dusty old country road just outside of Resume Speed, delighting in counting the number of cars that would go by, as well as naming their make, model, and, sometimes, their model year, names like Hudson, Willys, Nash Rambler, Studebaker, Packard, DeSoto, Kaiser, Frazier, and Crosley, to name a few. Was that ever a sneak preview of things to come, cars that, for any number of valid reasons, lost their way with the American car buyer. So sad. Some of those makes didn't deserve their untimely death, having the styling, features, pricing, and local service availability. But, it wasn't enough to overcome their inability to keep up with their mainstream competitors...Ford, Chevrolet, and Plymouth. To my simplistic way of thinking at that tender age, many of those cars were undeniably, without question, "butt ugly." Even to this day, I reserve the use of that expression in my description of very few cars who richly deserve to be called butt ugly. No finer example of that would be the 2001 Pontiac Astek (much, much more on this maligned piece of sh##, later in the book).

Next at age 8 while I'm still living with my grandparents, I ventured out into my grandpa's garage where he stored his Reo brand, gasoline-powered lawnmower, thinking it would be great fun if I were to crank up that beast. As if it were meant to be, that puppy started right up with one swift jerk of the engine cord, like there was no tomorrow. I mean that mower came to life, purring like a kitten. With a smile on my face that could have competed with a Cheshire cat, I reveled in what had just happened, and, without Grandpa's permission. Exciting as it was, I couldn't quite bring myself to a place where I was totally comfortable with this exhilarating experience because, conceivably, my little a## might soon be turning to grass, itself, and my grandpa would become the lawnmower, for this boldest of moves coming from an 8 year old. Not wanting to delay relieving my heightened anxiety any longer than necessary, I decided the recipe called for me to meekly (or "monkly" for you Catholics out there) approach Grandpa and 'fess up and get this probable a## kicking session in the books as history! Well, well, looky what happened as Gomer Pyle once pronounced, "Surprise, Surprise" and that one word best sums up my Grandpa's reaction to this gut-wrenching confession. He just sat there taking all of this in without as much as saying a word. It was as if he knew a good thing when he heard it. That is to say, his lawn-mowing days were over, no small thanks to Roger Paul. So, I began mowing that rather large yard almost every week, all the while fantasizing that lawnmower was an Indy 500 race car and I was behind the wheel! No one was about to pass me! How's that for an over-active imagination? I mean to tell you, I was mowing that yard nearly every week without fail. Strangely enough, Grandpa never once offered a word of thanks. It was as if he expected me to mow that lawn and, by golly, that was perfectly alright with me. Lest I forget while I'm on the subject of lawnmowers, even to this day, I fantasize over owning a John Deere or Club Cadet riding lawnmower. Only one little insur-mountable problem has to be dealt with here. Humans do not ride lawnmowers in the desert! I suspect rocks, sand, and cacti are a bit difficult to mow, not to mention disturbing our rattle-snake inhabitants! With remorse, I had come to grips with the realization that owning a riding lawnmower is right up there with a fish needing a bicycle!

My grandmother passed away when I was age 10, at which time, it was decided for me that I should go to live with my dad, who lived in Brownstown, Indiana, some twenty-five miles from Bedford, a town where dad became the local Ford dealer with the financial backing of my Uncle Chloral. As I had a lot of time on my hands, I would ride my little red J. C. Higgins bicycle from our house down to the garage (maybe a mile) to spend more time with Dad and familiarize myself with a car dealership. What fond memories that created for me. Trying my best to stay out of Dad's way while being naturally curious about anything and everything having four wheels on it and a Ford label to boot, I spent much of my time checking out parts catalogs, product brochures, reading the "Ford Times" and visually .checking out our new and used car inventories, noting exterior/interior color combinations. For some reason I never quite grasped, I noticed Dad didn't seem to get too swayed about my opinions and what I considered to be beautiful colors for a particular 1953 Ford Victoria. I knew beauty when I saw it. Apparently to my little mind, Dad didn't. Nearly fifteen years later, I learned from my

4

Uncle Chloral how nervous and unsure of himself Dad became when ordering new cars from the factory.

As you might imagine, I was soaking up product knowledge like a sponge in water. I even knew what optional equipment was in vogue at the time, some of which surprises me to this day, things you had to pay extra to get like rubber floor mats, and turn indicators. They didn't become standard equipment until the 1956 model year when a whole host of safety-related options were being introduced i.e. padded dashes/sun visors, and recessed steering wheels. When I look back, it amazes me that seat belts weren't being introduced in the same timeframe as they certainly were considered safety-related. Thirty years later, we have the Japanese to thank for making so many add-on items, formerly considered as options, now included in the base price of the vehicle as standard equipment. It amazes me what a little competition can do...and did! Just think, if the previous American view of what constituted a standard product hadn't been forced to keep up with the competition, and if they, also, manufactured toilets, a toilet seat could very well have been an option!

Age 11 is knocking on the door, and I'm still all in one piece. As was my dad's custom in those days, we went to visit one of dad's six brothers nearly every Sunday, as a family, so it seemed. One such visit was to see Uncle George (now age 95). Anyhow, Uncle George and Aunt Martha lived on this farm with their two sons and four daughters. The boys and I are within a couple of years of each other in age and I found they were far more advanced in the knowledge and exposure to things that alters one's perception of farm life than I would ever get exposed to. That included how they routinely drove an old 1948 Ford, 8N tractor out in the fields just for kicks and giggles. Well, on this one particular visit, Vernon and Jerry offered to teach me how to drive this tractor. So, off we go high-tailing out into the pasture, shifting gears on that monster as if it were related to a slot-machine. How fun!! I later learned that the 1948 Ford tractor was the first tractor to feature a four-speed, manual transmission. What a hoot it was to be driving this form of a Ford convertible...Oops... there goes my overactive imagination, kicking in again. Scratch that reference to a convertible and return to earth with me as I correctly identify this four-wheeler as a tractor... again. As a driving experience, you have to admit a tractor beats the mucus out of a lawnmower and, as you may recall, I was fantasizing the mower belonged in Indianapolis on a race track!

Survivor that I am, I make it my 12th birthday unscathed, ready for more adventures. Now having lived with my dad and stepmom and two half-brothers, for nearly two years, Dad sells the dealership in Brownstown and returns to Bedford (always his home away from home) to rejoin my uncle as sales manager of the Ford dealership that Uncle Chloral owned. It was at this time and age that dad gave me my start in the car business by duly installing me as the official car-washer...to refresh the looks of a used car destined for parking on the used car lot located across the street or getting a new car all gussied-up for delivery to its new owner. Water-soaked shoes were the badges of my job while the chamois and sponge were the tools of my trade. What fun! I got so good at it that I felt like I was one of the full-time employees working for a weekly paycheck. I could pound out washing a used car in thirty minutes or less while earning a whopping 25 cents per car. Not bad for a 12 year old in 1955. For the record, the mechanics back in the shop, who I smooched the occasional cigarette from, got to calling me the "MMCW" or "Mighty Master Car Washer!"

As a side note, I vividly recall some of the language I got exposed to back there in the shop, words that weren't being taught at the local junior high school. One such word started with the letter "f" and it was said with such gusto. Imagine that! But, coming back to the point I hope I was making...at 25 cents a car, that really wasn't so bad if you consider that I didn't have to wash or destreak the car's windows, inside or out (that always slowed me down on washing a new car) and I wasn't particularly artful in chamoising off a car, either. But the great equalizer was the 35 cents I got for every new car I washed. Although I necessarily washed a new car at a slower pace and more thoroughly, I always looked forward to washing that new unit, fantasizing that it was my new car that I was washing. Even at the slower pace, I still pounded out those puppies with glee, knowing the faster I washed a car, the faster I could place myself behind the steering wheel and drive this freshly laundered vehicle to his appointed parking spot just outside the building, along the curb. How my father ever came to trust me to crank up the ignition and put a

6

car into a moving gear is beyond me; I wouldn't have knowingly violated that trust for anything. That driving distance, probably, wasn't any more than fifty yards, distance enough for me to find my favorite rock station and chill out for all of five minutes (if that). All this joy heaped on a 12 year old!

Well, the much dreaded day of reckoning finally arrived signifying it was time to hang up the chamois and sponge. If chamois had numbers to retire like professional athletes, my last chamois would be have been high-numbered, hanging from the garage's rafters, long retired by now. Having outgrown the sponge and chamois act, I was now seeking an opportunity to prepare myself for the next automotive adventure that might beckon and whose call had to be answered, hopefully, for a better wage than 25 or 35 cents per car. Realistic or not, I set myself a goal to make $1.00 per hour. What a paradigm shift in attitude? Not too many sentences ago, I was reveling in making 25-35 cents per car which equated to 50-75 cents per hours. A 50% raise wouldn't be all bad, would it?

All of a sudden, I find myself at age 14. Imagine that...adding two more years to my life by merely typing one more paragraph. Life isn't quite that short or that simple! Anyhow, I'm still hanging around the garage like a lost puppy, giving flight to my mischievous schemes and dreams. For sure, one memory that pops to the surface involved this rather old, nearly broken-down Coke machine that must have made the trip over on the Mayflower, looking old and, true to character, acted as such. This much maligned monstrosity had one thing going for it...it worked most of the time and, more importantly as if part-Eskimo, the Cokes it dispensed were ice-cold at 5 cents a guzzle. Anyhow, this near antique-aged Coke machine had a habit of cannibalizing nickels...mine in particular. So, off I go to see the office manager to explain my tale of woe, expecting her to take pity on my grievous misfortune of having lost a nickel. In fact, I got into the habit of becoming a regular visitor to the office as a chronic complainer about losing nickels to that unrelenting beast of a machine. The office manager, bless her heart, not once, ever questioned my veracity as she freely gave me my nickel back. Without knowing for sure, I had this sneaky suspicion that Uncle Chloral was making allowances for my misfortune...better viewed as a case of bad luck than a repeated, questionable deed! My worse fear was Uncle Chloral might act on my complaints to the point that he might have replaced that machine with something a bit newer and more dependable. Thank God...that never happened. I never stayed thirsty for very long!

Earlier, I used the word "mischievous" and I selected that word with both care and kindness. Since it will be describing me in what follows. During my freshman year, my ole buddy Johnny Cooper and I played a little Halloween prank (if you don't treat, this is what you get) on our old maid Algebra teacher, Miss Mabel Brooks, always a "Mabel" unless she was within hearing distance. Now, this Miss Brooks is not to be confused with "Our Miss Brooks" who, as it happened, had a TV show named after her and she, as well, was a teacher. At that, all resemblances and comparisons stop! The Miss Brooks I had couldn't teach herself out of a bag if her life depended upon it. In fact, she should have been arrested for playing the part of a teacher. She was, in a couple of well - chosen words, a fraud, worthy of any prank we could concoct. Well, it turns out Mabel owned one of the ugliest 1949 Ford, 2-door sedans known to man, finished off in lizard green, a punishment to your eyeballs for having looked at it for more than five seconds. Just walking down the sidewalk seeing that beast parked at the curb in front of her house was enough to piss you off. Well, back to my story, Johnny and I had an idea. "Let's go over to Mabel's house on a school night during Halloween season and see if she is stupid enough to park that ugly duckling at the curb" as she normally did. And, if were got lucky enough to find her car unlocked, well...the fun would just be beginning. We tiptoed up to her car and gingerly tried opening what we hope was an unlocked door, and EUREKA...the Halloween demons were on our side...that door was unlocked! Oh goody, our fun could officially begin. One of us decides to wedge a three-foot long tree branch between the horn rim and the steering wheel. At the time, this little prank was referred to as "sticking the horn" and, stick it, we did. That beast's horn was blaring strong enough to compete with a castrated cat. Well, our fun was far from over. So, don't miss this. After we wedged the stick, we depressed the interior door lock button located on the window sill while simultaneously, depressing the exterior door entry button, which has the effect of locking the door without the use of a key. Getting the picture? Like Doublemint Chewing Gum, we were "doubling our pleasure" – not only was her horn stuck, her car was locked! Yea for our side for ingenuity! We are laughing our a##es off as we go scurrying off to find a safe hiding place for the fireworks that surely are about to happen. No sir, we were not about to be disappointed, After about ten minutes of this horn's wailing, old Mabel discovered that horn, that was so incessantly blowing, just might belong to her. She would be right! So, here she is in her housecoat (as ugly as the car), hair in curlers, with a cigarette drooping from her mouth, walking at a rather brisk pace towards her parked car, every step confirming that blaring horn belonged to no one but her. As she finally arrives at her curbside parked piece of ugliness, she lets out an extended string of words that would make a back-sliding sailor blush! Then, our little exploit was further rapturously rewarded as she discovered her car door is locked, thus, forcing a quick, unplanned trip back into the house to get her keys. Meanwhile, that horn is still blaring like there's no tomorrow but not quite with the same intensity as before. Finally, Mabel reappears, presumably with keys in hand, still cursing up a storm, walking at nearly a jogger's pace, when, as she gets about half way from the house to the car, the horn decides to die! Now our joy is replete with fullness beyond measure. Thank you, Mabel, for the memory!

It was at age 14 that I discovered my all-time favorite "to die for" car, taking a vow that I would one day own one...a gunmetal gray/red, 1957 Ford "Baby" Thunderbird. Words don't do justice for the instant love affair that had, so hopelessly, entrapped me. I dreamed about owning that most beautiful of God's creations, knowing that someday that dream would be coming true. It came true, alright...57 years later, in 2014. Yepper, it took me a mere 57 years to make a '57 Bird my own! So, the moral to this story is NEVER, NEVER give up on your dreams. If you can't fight to keep them alive, no one else will!

BTW, Ford outsold Chevrolet in model year 1957 for the first time since 1935. Totally unexpected, the 1957 Chevrolet Bel-Air, 2-door hardtop went on to achieve stardom as a collectible classic for decades to come, despite coming in second best at the time the cars were being sold as new. By contrast, where is the '57 Ford today? Here's a hint...it's not even in the same universe as the '57 Chev.

Totally unrelated to my dreams of a '57 Bird but at about the same time, I remember Dad talking to a sales prospect who was all decked out in bib-overalls, came into the garage about ten minutes before quitting time on a Saturday afternoon, wanting to see a new Ford we had parked on the showroom floor. You would have thought he, who appeared to be a farmer in his overalls, was a leper, as a couple of our salesmen were just hanging around watching the ticks come off the clock, making no effort to engage this sales prospect in a conversation (sales pitch). No clock for my Dad, no sirree, Bob. Acting as if it were a new day and, at the same time, showing some genuine appreciation for his coming into the dealership, Dad struck up a conversation with this man, demonstrating some of the features on this particular showroom model. In the course of ten minutes or less, Dad became convinced that this old farmer was not a "tire kicker", as he reaches down deeply into his jean's pocket and up surfaced a wad of bills, which he proceeds to peel off $2,500.00 in cash...buying that car on the spot. All this, while the two salesmen were just standing around biding their time. There's more than one moral to this story....pick the one you like. But here's mine...never take a person for granted. Never allow yourself to be impressed by appearances or lack thereof. Dad didn't and was rewarded for it. This was just one of the five hundred + new Fords that my dad sold over a ten-year period which works out to be about one car a week for ten years, all sold in a General Motors factory town! Yep, Dad had his ways.

Now I'm 15 and am getting seriously close to the big one, the one I have been waiting for since the day I learned how to spell the word "car." But, here I find myself on the cusp of good things to come that all started with dear old Dad asking me if I would be interested in driving a car to the automobile auction block located up in Indy, some seventy miles away. I guess driving all of those cars out of the washing stall at the garage along with learning how to drive my cousins' tractor (Vernon and Jerry) was beginning to pay off. Me, driving anything for seventy miles...you have got to be kidding ! I mean, does a bear go to the bathroom in the woods? After I gather myself up, giving my best measured response to such an idiotic question and once my euphoric outburst subsided, I meekly respond with a, "oh, heck yes" or something to that effect. I don't remember my exact words, but with some controlled discipline, I used language that was socially acceptable to parents of a 15 year old!

Driving that car up the highway towards Indy in the middle of the night was truly a delight, hitherto, never experienced. Of course, I was a part of a convoy, caravan of cars, if you will, with Dad, my stepmom and me, dutifully in tow, careful to stay together without allowing anyone to break into our lane where we maintained a steady speed. If there was a cop traveling in the same direction as we were, we would lift up a silent prayer that he would pass us and be on his merry way and that, actually, happened a couple of times. That will get your heart to "thumpin" in nothing flat. So, here I find myself sandwiched between my stepmom who is leading us up the highway as the alpha dog and my Dad who was bringing up the rear, offering him an excellent view of my driving skills (or attempts at). Depending on how the auction went the following day and whether a car went unsold, there was an excellent chance of getting to drive that car back to Bedford. Secretly, I wanted that to be the case and, sometimes, it was. Now, as I think back, I am amazed that Dad would trust me enough to do this without a driver's license and with his blessing. The pay was terrible, the experience...priceless!

Sometime in the same year, I became aware of some kind of, difficult to describe, odoriferous smell that permeated the air while down in the basement of the garage. On occasion, this smell made its way up into the showroom and parts department. This redolence had a boutique quality about it as far as my nose was concerned (probably not for others). This much I can tell you...I loved that olfactory delight, assuming the smell was unique to our garage's basement where large parts were stored i.e. fenders, door, parts used in the body shop (now known as a "Collision Shop".) Now, fast forward with me if you will, some fifty years later. Here I am visiting a local Mercedes-Benz dealer in Scottsdale, Arizona, where, low and behold, my nostrils, while firing on both cylinders, are immediately awaked to this very same, distinctive bouquet. Can this be? Sure enough. Not unlike gasoline, the smell is the same, wherever. Anyway, while at this dealership, one of their employees told me that smell was a combination of rubber, oil, and gasoline. Mix in a little musky, dirty air and...you've got it.

Again, about the same time, just short of my 16th birthday, which I never thought would ever get here, was new model year introduction time...a huge deal back then. My family would attempt to keep the new models a big secret until the official intro date by hiding them in friends and family members' garages. Even Uncle Chloral contributed to this secrecy by keeping them out of view at his farm, some ten miles out of town. That's what barns are for, right? Not to be excluded, Dad would sneak one or more of the new models into our storage garage at home. Now, I get to be the "heavy" as I was giving these cars a private showing to my friends. As the introduction date drew near, Dad and my uncle would bring these new models out of storage and returning them to their rightful place...the dealership. In an effort to build excitement for the new models, Dad would arrange to "soap up" the dealership windows with some kind of white chalky, window paint so that people couldn't see inside. Of course, it invited curiosity, if nothing else. But as a teaser, Dad would carve off just enough soap to create a "peek-a-boo" hole about the size of a baseball. People would see this "open" spot in the glass and would allow their curiosity to take full rein. The whole point was to build up interest for the new models, days in advance of its official introduction with the hopes that the lookers (possible sales prospects) would go out and tell their family and friends. Nothing earth shatteringly creative about this but it turned out to be a cost and time-effective means to getting the word on the street while avoiding the costly expense of advertising. Sadly, those days are forever gone. By way of contrast, auto manufacturers, today, have zero qualms about where, how, and when they introduce their new models. But, back in the day, it was always in September or October, a nostalgic time when the fall foliage was in full stage, along with attending Friday night high school football games and, least I forget, the annual Homecoming Parade with its convertibles used for escorting the "queen" and her entourage, and the Persimmon Festival over in Mitchell. Enjoying those Indian Summer days, short as they were, while taking in the beauty of those falling, beautiful leaves, is so typical of southern Indiana in the fall of the year.

Although I had officially hung up my sponge and chamois, I did, every so often, wash my dad and uncle's cars. Without further delay, allow me to introduce you to my cousin Gary's older brother, Tommie, who on one particular day needed his new 1959 Ford Galaxie 500 demonstrator washed. As demonstrators, those cars had to be clean, never knowing when they might need using for a prospect's test drive.

As an aside, who could ever forget Ford's bold claim, at the time, that their 1959 models no longer required waxing, thanks to their trademark-protected Diamond Lustre (TM) finish that came standard on all new Ford products. I have always wondered how many people bought into that claim. I know, I wasn't one of them. So, cutting back to the chase, here I am washing cousin Tommie's '59 Ford Galaxie 500, salivating at the bit to get that beaut washed up so I could drive it out of the car washing stall and park it at the curb, some fifty yards from the rear door of the garage or exit point. This driving washed vehicles out the door to be parked at the curb is something I had done countless times when I was the "car washer du jour". Well, this particular time, things didn't go per script despite my experience. At this point, let me tell you a little bit about the garage door mounted on the rear of the building (next to the car washing stall). It featured a pair of rounded concrete blocks (for lack of a better word), two feet high, out of the driver's view, where the concrete blocks met the cemented floor. The blocks were designed to keep cars from veering too close to the brick wall while exiting the building. Well, it usually works that way, but on this particular day...it didn't. It turns out I got a little too snug to the left side of the wall and somehow I managed to run Tom's nice, new, clean car over the concrete block that I was too blind to see. What I so artfully did, was run the left-hand side of the car up onto the top of the block where the car came to rest with a thoroughly damaged, concave-shaped rocker panel, extending much of the car's length. Well, now I have gone and done it – my perfect record of driving cars out of the washer rack, accident-free, were over. At this point, I suppose I should be thankful it was a relative's car and not a customer's new car that I could be readying for delivery; but, no, I was scared out of my wits, something akin to a cold cat on a hot stove. Eventually, my pants dried out, saving a needless trip to the men's john. So, with fear in my heart, I go searching for cousin Tom...to plead mercy for my life, not even considering how Dad was going to react to my little misdeed. Finally, I found Tom and started explaining what had happened. He didn't even let me finish giv-

13

ing him the details of this fiasco when he abruptly interrupts me in mid-sentence, saying, "I guess we will have to get that fixed, won't we?" spoken in a touchingly solicitous manner, not worthy of any further comment. And that, my friends, was the end of that. Even, Dad didn't get too outwardly upset but did warn me this better not happen again and I needed to be more careful the next time. The next time? That was thinly veiled enough to lead me to believe that this dog was going to live to hunt again. Presumably, insurance took care of the damages because I knew Dad would have had a lot more to say about the situation if that repair bill had to be paid out of his pocket!

Another of my less than favorite memories involved cousin Gary's older model Harley-Davidson motorcycle. It was a thing of beauty...bright red with tan saddle bags. Seeing that stationary beaut parked so innocently and unattended over in a corner of the garage, just ratcheted up my "Curiosity Meter" a notch or two. That puppy needed checking out. So, I helped myself onto the seat and with my right foot, I gave it one strong, downward, adrenaline-filled thrust and, low and behold, that bad boy came alive! Actually, that was the good news; the bad news, unbeknownst to me, was I had unintentionally opened up the throttle to FULL BLAST, totally seizing me in fear for my life. I was so frozen that my brain went dead and the best I could do was to try and manage me from having an unplanned panic attack, all set in motion by my curiosity working overtime! That engine was roaring sooooo loud, at a decibel level not known to man, that it could have passed for a tornado siren. To say I was scared, is to call the Titanic a fishing boat! Even today, I have an exceptionally strong preference for vehicles with four-wheels... all on the ground at the same time! Eventually, someone with more knowledge of motorcycles than I, which was zero, came to my rescue. I promised myself this would be a one time experience.

With my sponge and chamois fully retired, it was time to find that job that could pay me $1.00 per hour and do so without getting my shoes wet. Did such a job even exist? I would soon find out. Anyhow, I figured I needed to start saving money big time, the sooner, the better, if I was going to buy a car by my sixteenth birthday. At this age, all cars were dream cars to me, and if money were no object, I would have a garage full of them.

Fortunately, I discovered money (or lack thereof) had everything to do with my prospects of getting that dream car into my driveway. As an ongoing lesson in life, I learned that money figures into almost everything worthwhile. So, while pondering about my dream cars, I rapidly came to the conclusion that I needed to get some of that green stuff earned and put away. I came up with an acronym that succinctly describes CARS for me...Careful Accumulation Requires Savings. Remember, you read it here first, folks!

It was my good fortune when I learned about a new job that was opening up at a local eatery, Leonard's Drive-In, THE hot spot in town for cruising in search of girls, drag races, and admiring gawks that the coolest cars generated. This "new" job (in every way) had never existed at any restaurant in the history of Bedford, Indiana, up to this time. So, you could say I was a pioneer of sorts in my new role as a "car hop." I had heard about car hops out in California at Bob's Big Boy Restaurants featuring chesty girls on roller-skates, taking and delivering food orders to patrons in parked cars. Since I wasn't any of those things, I couldn't quite visualize myself as a teenage boy hustling after a $1.00 an hour job as a car hop; but, my daydreams of owning my own car, bought with my own money beckoned so strongly that, boobs or no boobs, I was going to make that job work for me! So, with some degree of intrepidation for what I anticipated would be a lot of teasing (mostly good-natured), I applied for and got that job. In short order, the teasing began in earnest, suffering through some of my classmates mockable questions like, "did someone hide your lipstick, honey?" or "did someone steal your skirt when you weren't looking?" Let me tell you, a little of that razzing went a long way towards helping me to decide this wasn't going to be any career move. In fact, I was ready to quit the first week that I was on the job but my instincts told me otherwise because my reason for taking the job hadn't changed one iota...I needed money to buy a car and buy it as expeditiously as possible (nearest the date of my 16th birthday) and that was doable. With this renewed inspiration, I was invigorated to new heights of enthusiasm and motivation to "get 'er done." I set myself the goal of becoming the best car hop known to man or, at least, east of California. The faster I served and delivered food, ALWAYS with a smile on my face and, in particular, to little old ladies, the faster my tips grew and grew and kept growing. I was raking in about $35-$40 a week in tips and another $25/week in hourly wage. A little quick math is called for here. I was working 6 hours per shift, 5 days a week or 30 hours per week. Now, divide those hours into an average weekly of $64 and you can readily see that my $1.00/hour goal had been met with ease as the actual hourly earnings, before tax, was just a shade over $2.00 per hour. So, I guess the heckling was worth it. And, although I didn't have a particular car in mind to buy as long as it was either a Ford or a Ford or, possibly, a Ford, I had a budgetary figure of $1,000...max! So, using my advanced math skills, tenaciously honed by sitting in Miss Brooks Algebra class, I quickly computed the timeframe needed to get me to the point of purchase, using the earnings model I had just developed. And, by golly, it was going to be on my 16th birthday, or possibly, a bit earlier. I can't remember for sure, but I do recall that I bought my car days before I got my driver's license, so, I had to be 15. Needless to say, I was sooooo ready to start driving that beast but had to settle on washing and waxing that car nearly every day until I got my driver's license. That car might not have been the best looking 1956 Ford, 2-door sedan in town but I am betting it was the cleanest!

Selecting my dream car was not entirely my doing. In Dad's role as a car salesman, he took in on trade this 1956 Ford Mainline, 2-door sedan, working hard at trying to convince me that this vehicle would make the perfect "starter" car. But the truth be known, Dad didn't want me to have some kind of a "speed machine," preferring something on the gutless side, mattering not that I was the one paying for this car not him. And, gutless it was. It had the smallest V-8 engine that Ford made, a 272 cubic inch dynamo, saddled with a 2-barrel carburetor and a single exhaust pipe that made its grand appearance by poking its little metallic diameter out from beneath the rear bumper...out where the big boys resided with their hot 265 and 283 Chevy's. Sure, I would have preferred a 312 or 352 Police Interceptor, but, right at that moment, I was so caught up in a euphoric bliss, realizing that this car, although not a hot car, it was going to be my own car and that was good enough for me (see the human nature in settling for second best when one has never experienced the best?). After a few more minutes of coming to grips with being on the threshold of being a bona fide car buyer and Dad looking at the stars in my eyes, clearly, the deal was done. So, Dad excused himself to go back into his office (a dozen feet away) to get some papers for me to sign, making this transaction a new entry into the young history of my life. As I waited for Dad to return, I stood there and sucked up the moment, visually taking in every square inch of that car's body, knowing it was mine. I slapped myself out of my reverie as Dad returns, comes up to me, and says these unforgettable words, "I believe these belong to you," as he hands me two sets of keys. Now, that truly made it official. And, to think that I got so caught up in the excitement of the moment, it never occurred to me to take that "less than a beast" out for a test drive, before making any firm decision (like most intelligent, emotionally-detached people). But, "I believe these belong to you" belongs right up there with, "Gentlemen, start your engines" – I hope I don't have to explain that, especially, if you're from Indiana.

Having achieved my earnings goal in less than a year, it was time to move on to some other kind of job that didn't involve taking the verbal abuse that I never got used to hearing and was so continuously being dumped on me. As the shepherd was overheard saying, "let's get the flock out of here" and that I did! My take away from that job was, it gave me a challenge to give it my best effort, especially, since I wanted the last laugh to be on me for putting up with all the B.S. and teasing. The result? I got what I wanted in spite of unfair ridicule...justice served! And, as a post note, I can tell you I have been working my little a## off ever since!

Well, the big day finally arrives...let's hear a drum roll and get those trumpets blaring! As you might be guessing by now, it's August 23, 1959, a day that will go down in history as the 16th birthday of Roger Paul Hilderbrand, the very one you have been reading so much about.

My big day was down-sized a bit in that I didn't have a valid Indiana state driver's license on the date of my birthday. I own a car that, at the moment, isn't doing me much good and won't until I can legally drive that puppy out of my driveway. It turns out that my birthday fell on a Sunday, the one day of the week when the local license branch is closed. Lucky me, huh? So, there was this gratuitous agony that had to be endured for another 24 hours, which shouldn't have been too big a deal. After all, I waited 16 years for this day to arrive! What's one more day? With contained disappointment, I make it to Monday morning at 8:00 where I find myself helping one of the clerks open up the doors at the license branch for business and their first duty of the day was to provide me with a written test that I had every confidence of passing and getting me behind the wheel of a car to demonstrate the necessary driving skills to a state-employed examiner who accompanied me through the driving portion of the test. Finally, after much waiting (I must be related to Job), I am told I have passed the written and driving tests and to make it official in exchange for a little cash, they proudly pronounced me as one of Indiana's newest drivers with a perfectly clean driving record (that would change, soon enough).

Although getting that driver's license and buying my first car were huge steps toward total earthly bliss, that much hoped for joy needed to make itself known. One such joy is, indisputably, being attracted to girls and, if it's meant to be, vice versa or is it versa vice? Girls, with their physical attributes available for viewing, were stoking the fires that made my dreams real for me. I mean, what good is a cool car without a cool (there are better adjectives) girl, especially, one who gushes all over herself about how great, good-looking and cool I am. Only kidding, she's gushing about my car, not me. Not a bad thing, I'll settle for that! Now, back to physical attributes some of which are exceptionally noteworthy...being expert at French kissing (practice makes perfect), dancing chest-to-chest where those bullet-shaped, wire reinforced bras (whatever happened to brassieres?) could take their toll, praying that some bruise marks would appear on one's chest, matching up, geographically, at the appropriate location, to show-off to your buddies. And to think, all this was possible without the enormously beneficial use of a modern-day GPS system. Imagine that! I will be describing some of these attributes in greater detail; so, don't go away. There are words to be read.

By age 16, high school meant a lot of things to me that had absolutely nothing to do with going to class or doing homework. One had to have an appropriate outlet for all that misdirected energy experienced in a classroom, drawing into clearer focus the things that really mattered: Fast/cool cars, dreamed-of sex, rock & roll music, the latest clothing fads, and sports...not necessarily in that order but it would be close. Anyhow, all of the above made it onto my list: a "To Do List" whose aging equivalent has become my "Bucket List". My, how the years change ones perspective on what needs doing as that biological clock keeps on relentlessly ticking away. Maybe a better choice of words could be "Get 'Er Done List"!

With so many possible school-related activities in pursuit of the things that really mattered, it's a wonder I found any time for studying and doing homework, and some of us didn't. Would you care to guess which camp I fell into? With a little more reading, you will become an expert on my academic achievements. Well, eventually, school won out, partly because cars could become and, many times, were costly propositions in terms of gasoline (even at 25 cents per gallon), routine maintenance, insurance, and the occasion repair bills. By contrast, completing assigned homework meant studying and diverting some of that normally used time devoted to driving my little dream car, hot in pursuit of the girl "du jour". Girls "du jour" had a way of not making it into the real world but it was still fun to fantasize.

As I ponder the subject of girls, it brings to mind one setting for an utopian scenario: Having a gassed-up, freshly washed car, with a sweet little thing, seated right next to me (thank God that I don't have bucket seats), close enough to help me read the speedometer! In order to save me needless embarrassment, she would express her heartfelt appreciation for my thoughtfulness at repeated attempts to be suave and debonair, while gently and delicately inviting her to park her beautiful little tush right there next to mine, knowing she had helped me drive within the posted speed limit. You know, learning how to correctly read a speedometer offers enormous benefits in the form of developing the obligatory skills associated with steering a car, one-handed. Looks easy, you say? Well, not necessarily so. Like all things involved with both driving a car and a relationship with a girl, it requires practice, practice, yes, you guessed it...more practice! Of course, it helps if you have a good teacher who is willing to share what she knows.

Appropriately equipped for the fun times to come with a

driver's license in hand and a car that belongs to little old me, I find myself at home one particular night with nothing else better to do (I must have ran out of money, gasoline or both), when, totally out of nowhere, dear old dad comes walking across the living room floor, towards me, holding "something" ever so daintily between his thumb and forefinger, almost as if, whatever he was holding, was diseased. With contrived authority in his voice, he asked me, "What might these be?" Shocked by the question, I reply, "Dad, those little things save lives and are commonly referred to as "rubbers." Not satisfied with my answer, he goes on to ask," How did they find their way into your car?" Getting testier by the moment, I blurted out, "They flew into my car from a foreign country for all I know, and, if you add a little water, like anything else, they will grow up to be healthy, productive rubbers, ready to save lives." Not to be taken in by my sarcasm and feigned scorn, dad asked, "Do you have any plans to use these so-called "life-savers?" Without missing a beat, I answered, "I have no set plans at the moment, but, maybe I should, now that I think about it and you were insightful enough to have brought it up in the first place." Without backing down, uncharacteristic of dad, he wanted to know if I knew how to use them. I told him, in so many words, that I did not, as there were no instructions included inside the sealed package; but, with my superior intellect, I was sure to figure it out. I mean, after all, thousands, if not millions, of those little life-savers have been in use long before I was a twinkle in my mother's eyes, carefully choosing my words, so as to create a thinly veiled inuendo that might encourage Dad to change the subject as I was growing more and more anxious about what his next question might be.

Having my fill of Dad's unending, embarrassing questions, I decide it is high time that I turn the tables on him with some questions of my own, such as, "Where did you discover those little life-saving jewels?" Finally, maybe after a full minute's hesitation (at least, it seemed that way at the time), Dad sheepishly says, in so many words, that he needed to borrow my car to go visit a prospect for a car he was trying to sell while his own car was in the shop for repair. Anyhow, he goes on to explain, when searching for a pen or pencil, he took it upon himself to rummage through my car's glove box when he, accidently, stumbles upon these pygmy-sized, little creatures. Not wasting a moment and in total disgust in an elevated tone of voice,

I flat-a## told him he had no business "nosing around" in my car where his eyeballs were not welcomed! I asked him if it was necessary for me to hang a "No Trespassing" sign on the door of my glove box. Where the courage came from to ask such a question...I don't have the faintest idea.

At this point, I am soooooooo thankful Dad hadn't yet asked me if there was an intended recipient that I might have in mind for bestowing such a magnanimous, thoughtful gift on and why did I have something as sensitive and objectionable in my possession to begin with, that could create the illusion that I had plans for this special-purpose "device" (see the Devil in that word?). Upon hearing this, I was ready to go with citing the Boy Scouts motto, "Be Prepared" which would have been a laughable response but I didn't feel much like laughing nor did Dad, I presume. Infuriated beyond words of any kind of intelligible measure, I flat out ask him if he was pleased at finding my little unused treasures and had he found more than he had bargained for when he opened up that glove box? As it turns out, I did have a secret stash of magazines (title started with the letter "P") hidden under the floor covering inside the trunk. The last thing I needed was Dad discovering these as well and was holding back, getting ready to pounce at the opportune moment. With Dad's superior "nosing" skills, it's no telling how easily he might have surmised that there were more goodies, ripe for detection.

And, what do you think I got for all this mental jockeying around...nothing!! Dad seemed to be dumb-founded, incapable of speaking. Was he having a stroke or were the words just not there for him? At that, I seized the moment by nearly yelling, "If you can't come up with a better response than that, it's pointless to answer yours! So, good night." With that said and with a triumphal pace, I hastily made my way up the stairs leading to my bedroom, my safe haven, a place where my feet couldn't get me to fast enough...all the while basking in my new-found courage in standing up to Dad and...living to tell it!

This, not soon to be forgotten scenario, though short in duration, was deserving of an Oscar, don't you think? I know I thought so as I was thumping my chest pretty good for having the gumption to contest Dad in a situation neither of us wanted to be in. I often wondered what ever happened to those little dwarfish-like, hermetically-sealed devils other than, I know for sure they didn't find themselves back in the glove box of my car, nor in the Smithsonian.

Now that I am all settled in, enjoying my new car (new for me), I thought it was time to bone-up on some of the 30,000 parts that comprised a typical car of the time. For instance, how do you gap a set of ignition points, when and how to replace a condenser, what was involved with changing spark plugs, when to change the oil, when to give the car some fresh grease (lube job) just to keep the car drivable? Things like that...things that the Bill Burford's of the world take for granted because they have the tools and the talent. I had neither then or now – just ask my wife, Sandi. I barely venture out into the hammer and screwdriver world for fear of making a fool of myself and/or the continued inflicting of pain on my thumb and its fragile thumb-nail (from being beaten on enough times over several decades). I eventually discovered that, if you smash your finger enough times, you'll learn which is which although I have to say, I have developed a bit of a love affair with the screwdriver. I screw bet-ter than I hammer, it's just so much more user-friendly.

Look at me now, basking in my newly-found freedom...with a personal passport for the open road! When I am behind that steering wheel, I am instantly liberated from all the crap being thrown at me whether it be parents, school, or whatever else is out there, working to get in the way of my fun. As you might have guessed, there ain't no controlling me, no sir. I am a free and happy camper in pursuit of fun times. "Oh Lord, don't let me run out of money now." Owning my own car was everything I envisioned it to be, at least, at that moment.

Now I have brought you to a place where I have to tell you a little something about the "first's" in my life beginning at age 16. To mention a few has to include the first date in my car, the first speeding ticket, experiencing my first French kiss, discov-ering the location of the "Passion Pit' inside a 1956 Ford, my first drag race, and the not soon to be forgotten, first "F" on my Report Card, an object I learned to abhor every grading period. No doubt about it, the periodic reading of my Card by my dad didn't bring tears of joy for either of us, or any need for exuber-ant celebration over at the Hilderbrand residence on Fourteenth

Street, where gnashing of teeth was commonplace during grade reporting season, no small thanks to Dad's lack of humor!

With that introduction out of the way, let's truly begin. My very favorite "first" was discovering the "Passion Pit", conveniently located in the rear section of a 1956 Ford. "Define the rear section," you asked? Well, if you have to ask, I guess I have to tell. But, then again, on second thought and before you think I am giving you some kind of blaze response, get out your dictionary and look it up. See it? In easy to read descriptive words, Mr. Webster defines "Passion Pit" as "the back seat of a parked car situated within the confines of a drive-in theater or a place susceptible to being found out about by "bush-whackers," a subject I will enlighten you on, momentarily. BTW, if you found that definition in Mr. Webster's book, you had better hang on to it...that dictionary is one of a kind, probably worth a million bucks...kidding can be such fun!

There are numerous sociological and health benefits available to willing, active participants to those who visit the Passion Pit. The one that stands out is the little recognized way it offers you to get to know your date better and onto a first name basis more quickly ("Getting To Know You" as the song goes.) That's particularly useful on a first date. Then, there's the unencumbered view of the movie screen, the reason you went to the drive-in in the first place, right? And, don't you remember how uncomfortable and needlessly burdensome those bucket seats were, if you were unlucky enough to have them? Yessiree, bucket seats were definite show-stoppers! Even without checking in with my doctor, I knew he would agree with my assessment that, just stretching out, alone, pays its own special health dividend, not available to our "straight-laced" classmates.

OK, next on my list of "first's" involves the fine art of "bush-whacking." This delicately performed activity is intended to disturb the natural flow of things when the Passion Pit is in play, typically in a very secluded, under-known location, involving a male and his favorite girl (usually.) When the "bush-whackers" or initiators decide to strike, the would-be helpless victims are entrapped inside the car while the bush-whackers special training for this occasion makes use of select tools that include a high-beam flashlight, possibly a mobile spotlight and some kind of device that creates a lot of noise when struck. And, when the whackers light source zeros in on a set of eyeballs staring back, the hapless "bush-whackees" don't know what to do although they have definite options that includes praying, crying, screaming, or combinations thereof. C'mon, use your imagination. More times than not, the whackees abruptly discontinue their playful activities and, as a shepherd was once overheard saying, "let's get the flock out of here." That usually holds true for the whackers as well. Not knowing how the whackees are going to react, they many times, take off, as well. After all, they have had their fun for the night knowing they have destroyed someone else's recreational possibilities for the evening. This much I do know...nobody I knew ever got hurt physically, emotionally, or sexually. If they did, they weren't telling! But by the end of the evening, one party should be laughing pretty hard, the other, pissed! However, they shouldn't be too pissed because the whackers could very well be someone besides fun-seeking classmates i.e. parents, police, security guards. I'm sure there are some interesting stories floating around out there where the whackers daughter is whacked by her own father. Stranger things can happen!

And, how could I ever forget that "first" date in my own car. Trust me...I didn't. My first recollection was going over to pick-up my date when she was thoughtful enough to introduce me to her father, who reminded me of a fish; they don't talk, you know, they just look. And look at me, he did. With the fewest of words, I am reasonably confident I correctly deciphered his unspoken words which went something like this, "don't even think blah, blah, blah"...you fill in the blanks! By George, it worked and I have her father to thank for that.

Another "first" that I joyously discovered was another art form...French kissing, At this particular time, I was dating this gal (whose name will remain nameless) who attended the Free Methodist Church there in Bedford. Very early on in our relationship, she returned my facial kisses by sticking her tongue inside my mouth without a thought to the bacteria we might possibly be exchanging. Wow!! Was I ever enjoying this! Since this quick course in "kissology" was being perpetrated on me by a "good" girl, I was left to naively assume most girls kissed that way...wrong! Was I ever in for a rude awakening! By dating others, I quickly learned that not all girls French kissed; but, nonetheless, I sure was impressed with this one particular gal. What a teacher she turned out to be! I often wondered if more girls who attended the Free Methodist Church shared the same proclivity for kissing. You don't suppose they teach that over there in Sunday School, do you?

And then there was my first speeding ticket so ingloriously given by a state cop who wasn't the friendliest guy in town. How unlucky was that? One thing for sure, that pric## was going to write me a for-real ticket...no pass card for me. Anyway, I'm getting a little ahead of myself here and need to back up and give you some details behind my blunderous, stupid act. As it was turning dusk, I was traveling with my lights on, westbound on Sixteenth Street at, shall I say, a "healthy clip" when I took notice of Larry Ikerd, Indiana state trooper, who had somebody pulled over, presumably, giving this hapless soul an early Christmas present. Being a bit distracted by Ikerd's flashing lights that he chose not to turn off, I made a spur of the moment decision to continue driving past Ikerd but taking the time to hit my horn while driving past him at the same "healthy clip". For added pleasure, I waved in the friendliest of gestures. Unbeknownst to me, I learned later that there was another state trooper's car, that I did NOT see, parked and hidden from my view, directly in front of Ikerd's cruiser with his lights turned off. Had I seen him, I would have slowed down and taken a pass on hand gestures and the rest of it. But, no,I was giddy with excitement about passing a preoccupied state trooper who I presumed couldn't do anything about my speeding except make a note of it and set his radar to nail my axx sometime in the immediate future. Well, less than a minute after I passed Ikerd, all of a sudden I am attracted to looking into my rear view mirror, just to see a set of flashing lights beckoning me to pull over, which I dutifully did. The trooper who pulled me over was Sam Cruse, a good buddy of Larry Ikerd's and the author of my first of many speeding tickets.

Of course, Dad learned about the speeding ticket, but not from me. This second-hand information didn't set well with him for some reason. So he decided to exact some memorable punishments that, foremostly, relieved me of two sets of car keys for thirty days. Do you know how long thirty days is in the life of a 16 year old boy? Well, I do and it might as well have been for eternity. And, I got that speeding ticket within thirty days from the day I bought the car! You talk about a double whammy! Naturally, no punishment would be complete without me paying the fine for my dastardly act of stupidity. And, no, this is not the end of my tale of woe. It's now time for some humiliation at the hands of the Bedford City Police Department, who cordially invited me to sit in on a Driving School class. From my perspective, I think the whole point for me was learning how to better detect the presence of police officers, intent on writing speeding tickets to poor, unsuspecting teenage boys. It was a painful lesson to get exposed to, but it didn't figure into my future speeding exploits one iota.

One of my favorite things to do at the time was watching, or better yet, actively participating in "drag racing." How drag racing ever got its name is beyond me; it's right up there with being "pi##ed off." Who makes up these words? What, exactly, does this act entail? For openers, there's no "dragging" of anything in drag racing. It's entirely a matter of getting from Point "A" to Point "B" faster than the competing car racing down the highway in the lane next to you. Dangerous? You betcha. Fun? You betcha.

One of our favorite drag-strips (stretch of highway) was located down in the "flats", midway between Bedford and Oolitic, surrounded on opposing ends by a fairly steep hill, allowing for early detection of any incoming traffic coming from either direction. That, of course, included the uninvited presence of a state trooper who might stumble upon our stretch of road while traveling with his headlights off. At the time, we thought we were pretty crafty. Probably not, but we sure did have our fun just the same. To the best of my knowledge, none of my friends or acquaintances ever got caught!

Yes, I learned to appreciate the logistical benefits offered by Oolitic, highlighted by "cruising" Ted's Drive-in in search of girls and a drag race. Now that I have come to think about it, there wasn't much of anything else to do in Oolitic unless you were into watching the hands on a clock move. For the local yocals, a good day was driving the three miles into Bedford to watch the trains travel through the middle of downtown (through the square)...a major source of joy that words had difficulty in describing. The English language (or some version of it) was rumored to be heard from time-to-time. But an intellectual bastion it was not. Having their fill of Bedford, these yocals would hurry back to Oolitic in hopes of finding words to describe to their friends the unspoken joys of visiting Bedford.

Which brings me to another "first" in drag racing. I went up against my old band buddy (trumpet, in my case), now deceased, Dennis Potter (he was never a "Denny"), a.k.a. Dennis "The Ford Eater" Potter. Guess whose Ford he was devouring? I know you guessed correctly; it was little old me and anyone else who was driving a car with an automatic transmission. If you were, you were toast! It seems so incongruous to me that Dennis could just chew-up other cars with automatic transmissions while his own ride was a bulky-looking, heavier than it needed to be, 1955 Buick with an automatic transmission! Just another boulevard cruiser? Wrong, that sucker could flat out have flown if it had wings, and all the more so, if you happened to be driving a Ford. I mean, that Buick of his loved to do in Fords....my personal misfortune. I had visions that my petite 272 cubic inch engine could handle that much larger and heavier old Buick. It's a sad commentary to say no. Moral to the story: Don't judge a book by its cover (hope you like mine). The same holds true with a car. Unlike Weight Watchers, the only carbs you should care about are under the hood, especially, if you went up against Potter when Dennis leaned into that old Buick. "Goodbye Hilderbrand, See ya!"

Having survived my 16th year and still physically in one piece (thank you, dear Jesus), I'm ready to see what the 17th has in store for me. At school, I'm being told that I should be giving some thought as what I want to do with my life and that it is time to get some plans put together. After all, high school graduation is just around the corner (or maybe not). I pretty much knew what my plans were going to be.....nothing! My grades sucked, to put it mildly, but I did find a remedy for this sad reality that drastically improved my grades, overnight. Stay tuned for a detailed report as to how this miraculous change all came about. Even if my grades had been average over the course of my four-year stint, I really didn't want any part of another four years of school, or any activity that might get in the way of my automotive pursuits. I had no inkling what that might include other than getting myself behind the wheel of that first new car.

Trying to come to grips with an undecided future and figuring out how I was going to buy that new dream car taxed my little brain nearly into oblivion. I mean, I loved and lusted after cars much of my life up to this point (you probably surmised as much by now,) but I was beginning to realize I needed something else in my life, besides cars and being able to sit back and enjoy them. In other words, cars would continue to be central in my life but, at the same time, not be consumed by them. After all, I was persuaded to believe there was a great big world out there, ripe for discovering.

So I figured, in an effort to minimize my indecision, that I needed to come to grips with my relationship (or was it totally in the past?) with God, reminding myself of a couple of biblical passages that I had repeatedly heard in church; Jeremiah 29:11 and Philippians 4:6. These are scriptures I could get my arms around. They gave me a sense of hope and trust that would be more fully realized when facing concerns for the future. In effect, I was saying in so many words "let God be God" (as if I had power to do so). In other words, just let go...He will make all of this known to me in His perfect timing. God's response? "Get out of the way, Roger Paul, I have work to do for you. Know that I want an enduring relationship with you, now and forever!"

Some of my indecision was born out of lack of direction, that in all fairness, has to be laid at the footsteps of my recently deceased dad, who we lost at age 91 in April, 2015. Unquestionably, Dad could be correctly characterized as a hard-working, loving, gentle, non-confrontational, Christian man who always wanted to the best for his family. And in that enlarged role, he completely succeeded. However, there was another side to Dad that I struggled to understand but, frankly, never came up with an answer for. At the heart of it, Dad never, and I mean never, had any time for us kids, something I just recently learned from my half-sister and two half-brothers. My response to this inattention was to think that Dad didn't care enough to engage himself with me for whatever reason(s). Eventually, I adopted an attitude of not caring what he thought, and how I spent my time detached from what I viewed to be his need to control me.

My reaction? I could best describe myself as "rebellious," (I chose that word very carefully) showing its ugly characteristics in a variety of settings from the way I was treating Dad, the total disregard I was showing to those who were attempting to control me (they failed), and the quality of my school work (or lack of) and the subsequent poor grades that followed.

The only memory I have of Dad having any involvement in my high school activities was his coming to one of my basketball games, arriving late and leaving early. However, he was there long enough to see me score a basket while being fouled, leading to a free throw I made (this is big stuff back in Indiana.) That became the basis for an ever-so-short conversation when I got home that night, telling me that I really had a good game! Really? How would he know? He didn't stay long enough to find out. Even on the day I was born, Dad was AWOL from my mother and the moment of my birth, doing something that, apparently, was more important, having something to do with Uncle Chloral, that required driving over to Illinois to take care of.

Dad was forever trying to control me, but it didn't work. Case in point, he absolutely insisted upon me attending weekly worship services as a part of the family at Bedford's Free Methodist Church. I really didn't have a problem with the "attending" part; it was "where" I attended that became the issue for me as I wanted to attend the Episcopal church located nearly next door to where we lived, a church where several of my friends went. But no, that wasn't going to be! Well, I learned to make the most of this imposed, unwanted reality by finding a way to have a little fun at dad's expense without his being any wiser. Upon arriving at the church for services, Dad had the habit of placing the car's ignition keys in the floorboard under a mat, then not locking the doors, a sure recipe for a little unanticipated fun for yours truly. My love of cars and basic mischievous nature took over with this scenario handing me all the ingredients for a pleasurable experience that I will call, for lack of a better description, a "joy ride."   Dad never knew, to the best of my knowledge that I was out driving his car while he so dutifully sat in a pew taking in the worship service. I always made a special point to get back to the church a few minutes before church let out so Dad wouldn't know that I was a MIA. He presumed (wrongly) that

I was sitting with some friends up in the balcony in the rear of the church, outside his view, which I wasn't...not once! And, of course, I had to return the car with enough gas to approximate the same level that he might remember, usually about 25 cents. And, what fun and better yet, I never got caught...not once and I did this nearly every week for months! Then, there was this little matter of added miles on the odometer that he hadn't noticed or let on about. Had he noticed, my young axx would have stood convicted! Had he, I was prepared to offer up the "big lie." If this had been in a school grade setting, I would have earned an "A" for planning, an "A" for execution, and another "A" for lying, but it never came to that. Surely he knew, but, if he did, he never let on!

Let's get to some fun stuff. During my junior year, our high school continued in its role as a breeding grounds for future teachers by encouraging student teachers from nearby Indiana University to come to our school to polish up on any teaching skills that might be lurching just below the surface, that might be in need of a little nudging to help bring these budding skills to fruition. That nudging would be happily provided by any number of students in my class who valued excellence in education, whether in the classroom or, as in this case, a location for parking a car. As it turns out, we got this new student teacher who was assigned to our Biology class, who was of the habit of parking his little yellow VW Bug at the curb, directly across the street from the main door leading into the school building. Seizing an imagined opportunity for a little clean fun, a few enterprising male students took it upon themselves to lift this little parked VW up off the curb and replant it in a yard adjoined to the curb, leaning it up against this old oak tree. Imagine with me the fun watching that car getting removed from that helpless old tree. That tree belonged to a fellow classmate, David Parker, who was a bit of a prankster himself. So, it's entirely conceivable that Dave played a major role in that noteworthy deed. If he didn't, he certainly was capable of providing some leadership to complete such a dastardly task.

Memories...great to draw from when they are happy or pleasing but a double-edged sword when they are not. I've been told numerous times over the years that I have an excellent memory. This, I don't doubt but it's always nice to hear someone else confirm what you know to be true about yourself. In fact, I have been called part elephant more than once and, yes, I am flattered to hear this, reminding myself of what a blessing to be able to recall something that has positive meaning for you but, at the same time, that same memory carries with it, the ability to remember things you don't want to remember!

Pranks were such fun, especially, when it was being directed at high school events, facilities, and teachers. Community-related pranks were an altogether different matter because of the stronger likelihood of police involvement and, of course, that ran counter to the whole point of playing pranks which was intended to generate fun and laughter...not getting arrested or paying fines for a deviate behavior. Well, with that commented on, I have to tell you there were a couple of instances where some friends and I nearly stepped over that line in our search for some memorable fun. Some could even argue that we definitely stepped over that line. Either view would not have been entirely wrong. And, yes, cars always figured into these devilish shenanigans. Expressed more pragmatically...our mischievous activities were an unquestionable threat to prolonging human life, MINE! These shenanigans would not have been possible without the aid of an automobile for the timely execution of our disgraceful, though thought to be creative by some of my buds, exploits.

One such prank stands out for several reasons, none of which had any lasting value other than the memory that remains. I had this friend in high school, we'll call him Joe (in protection of the aXX that belongs to yours truly), who along with a few other carefully selected friends decided to add a little more joviality to "Prom Night." As it became custom to make every hour count on this special night, staying out until all hours of the night (make that morning), just to keep the fun a comin'. In this particular instance, rather than spending more money on our dates and ourselves for corsages, tuxedo rental, and the like, we unanimously decide a more appropriate expenditure would be the purchase of beer.....and lots of it! Anyhow, Joe and our friends decide to travel down to nearby Spring Mill State Park in hopes of finding a safe haven (from police) to freely drink our beer without getting caught, no small thanks to Dad for lending me his new 1961 Mercury, which made our little escapade possible. Surprisingly enough, in those days, the park remained open without any curfews (that I can recall). In any event, the park gate was open and we helped ourselves to an uninvited entry into the park, looking for that secluded spot where we wouldn't be discovered drinking our golden nectar. Without much trouble, we located a suitable spot to practice our budding libation skills, sitting on top of a wooden picnic table, situated right next to this rapidly flowing creek (pronounced "crick" to those not familiar with the Hoosier language). Well, after enjoying a significant amount of our liquid refreshment, old Joe ups and decides it would be great fun if we were to set fire to this old picnic table that we had been sitting on. Since the table was old and in some degree of disrepair, we decided to put that table out of its misery. At this point, I am beginning to feel a little remorse and thinking, "what if we get caught or somebody snitches on us?" This, I believed, required some vindication while removing any lingering source of remorse. Without any grand announcements, we decide that table deserved to live for an another day; so, we lifted up the burning remains of the table, and tossed it in the creek. Naturally curious, I wanted to know, among other things, if that table could float, it didn't. So, its life was snuffed out right there on the spot. All that was left to do was retrieve its remains out of the water. We left that to others.

Now, with that event behind us, it's time to go in search of a new source of entertainment, because we had fully consumed our supply of beer. We had to, as we believed it was perishable. That would never do and, besides, one should be ready to take care of thirst when that need occurred. Think of us as caregivers or protectors of that nectar! After seemingly having our fill, old Joe ups and decides to decorate the interior of my Dad's new Mercury, 4-door hardtop, with the remains of the evening's refreshments (yes, definitely in the plural). I can tell you first hand, a new car smell (that I love) and the discharged contents of the human stomach through the mouth don't mix. As Joe and my buds worked frantically to return the car to its former, original scent, making liberal use of bathroom deodorant, soap, water, loads of "elbow grease" and an ever unending flow of prayers. Through all of this, I was picturing what it was going to be like to be killed at the hands of my own father! I knew, if caught, there would be no more borrowing his car(s); worse yet, maybe I was looking right into the face of death...neither was acceptable. With non-verbal prayers completed, I didn't have to find this out, as miraculously, we returned the car to its former newness as if nothing had happened. But, I was not going to take any needless chances that the gross smell might freshen somehow; so, I left all the windows of the car down for the balance of the evening (it wasn't long) so that puppy could air out more thoroughly. With dread, morning arrives and Dad gets in the car to drive off to work with me fully expecting a phone call from the garage, asking me what that peculiar smell was. That call never came. God is good, no, God is great!!

Allow me to share, yet, another event that borders on being outrageously funny, challenging me to do justice to it with mere words, as this prank should go down in the local annals of human history as one of the best pranks ever pulled off in this innocent little town of Bedford, Indiana. First of all, I don't personally lay claim to any involvement in this much repeated chronicle. The only thing I will admit to, is being overwhelmed by uncontrollable, gut-wrenching laughter. I mean, if a prank were to be nominated for an Oscar for originality, this would be the one!

Let me set the stage by telling you how inhumane, yet, comedic, this deed was. This story, no doubt, has been embellished a lot over the years as it happened nearly sixty years ago but the essence of this caper will live on forever.

It all started out one night in the wee hours when four very bored, yet, enterprising, senior-class boys took it upon themselves to go in search of a goat...not as in the car version (GTO) but in the animal kingdom that goes "baaaaaah." They found such an animal, totally minding its business while removing clumps of grass for sustenance from some farmers fenced-in pasture. Somehow, some way, these four pranksters managed to ever so artfully abscond this innocent, grass-chewing critter, tying its legs together and muzzling its mouth, making for a hasty exit back into town. They knew, if caught, there would be hell to pay, topped off with an unplanned visit to the local pokey. These perpetrators, apparently, lived by the mantra, "no guts, no glory." They ingeniously executed their plan flawlessly by off-loading their prized capture, thoughtfully depositing the same at the site of our high school's gymnasium, a building some fifty feet high (if it were a foot). With ingenuity that would make a physics teacher proud, these boys concocted some kind of a makeshift apparatus by jury-rigging a pulley and rope for the purpose of hoisting this goat up alongside the building with the eventual goal of elevating this beast to the top of the building and onto the roof. If that weren't feat enough, upon successfully placing the goat onto the roof's surface, these animal-loving, enterprising lads, with fullness of heart, decide to liberate this poor little creature by releasing it leg bindings and mouth muzzle, setting it rapturously free to roam the vastness of that building's rooftop...entirely in the dark. As the story goes and as you might have imagined, all hell broke loose, beginning with this indescribably frightened goat with all of its shrieking and carrying on. If that animal could talk, this one would probably be profaning such that it would make a sailor blush. A cleaned-up version might be, "Before I jump off of this roof, I want to ask you one thing. Did you a##holes get a lot of enjoyment out of goatnapping me? I hope you all roast in hell!"...or something to that effect. Apparently, all of this commotion didn't go unnoticed by some the nearby neighbors as they were so rudely taken from their slumber, reaching for their phones to call the police, demanding the noise coming from atop the gymnasium be removed immediately. As it turns out, the police were a no show, apparently, more inclined toward writing speeding tickets to teenage boys. Instead, the Fire Department dispatched a truck, ladder and mobile lights that could have blinded a wide-eyed eagle! Thus ended the boys fun for that evening, officially.

Let's move on to the matter of money and how I proposed to pay for gas, insurance, tires, brakes, you name it and still have money left over for the occasional date. Having accomplished my vision of buying that first car (not quite "dream" status yet but it was a serious start). I decided on making more money and finding work more to my liking, thus, removing myself from the ranks of would-be career car hops with all of its attending b.s. that got so unmercifully heaped upon me with some regularity. While eagerly seeking out a new career opportunity, I was joyously blessed to learn of and apply for a job with a local cinema operator, in both an indoor as well as outdoor setting. I successfully made a   smooth, seamless transition from a drive-in restaurant to a drive-in theater, where a "passion pit" lifestyle was fully entrenched and movie-watching was a secondary consideration (at best). In my new role, my mission was to identify "passion pitters" in the act and strongly convince them of the need to vacate the premises. As I look back, I have to admit my physical stature had a lot to do with my effectiveness, or lack thereof, in getting someone kicked out of the drive-in. If they were physically bigger than me, more than likely, they would get a pass, as my job didn't offer life or medical insurance as a benefit. In short order, I learned to love my new job as "moral code enforcer" which offered new avenues, leading to new friendships where my high-beam flashlight became a trusty friend and, in times of questionable peril, one of my very best friends.

Actually, this job offered a much more recreationally-centered work environment that was much appreciated. Of course, anything after car-hopping would! To perform my new job to my manager's satisfaction, I developed a skill for moving fleet of foot, as quietly as a mouse in darkened church. With flashlight in hand in making my appointed rounds, I would come upon a vehicle where several oddities might be taking place simultaneously, but, one certainly did stand out. Similar to a bushwhacker, I would approach a car from the rear and gently place my hand on the rear fender in search of seismic activity. Even in Indiana, seismic jolts have been recorded in the heat of a summer's night! When so discovered, you might find me coughing at a higher decibel level than normal. If that didn't diminish the seismic level, Plan B called for accidentally bumping the rear fender with my leg or slapping the trunk lid with an open hand. If that didn't work, Plan C called, no more Mr. Nice Guy, flashing my trusty flashlight onto its high-beam and point it directly into the interior of the passion pit. Trust me, folks, that works! On a rare occasion, I actually arranged the details for getting a particular patron dismissed from actively pursuing his or their evening's planned entertainment. Such power, in the hands of a seventeen year old! In a word...awesome! Yes, a sense of power that was intoxicating, making me a much-feared commodity around show time when the car's occupants were busy getting themselves all settled in for the night.

Another duty I performed was greeting a car's occupants as their car approached the entry ticket gate where I would exchange their cash for a admission ticket to see the show(s). In this ticket-giving role I became aware that some would-be patrons were attempting to sneak into the show by concealing themselves in the trunk of the car. How uncreative and stupid is that? One is willing to suffocate themselves to get into a movie without paying. Besides taking a needless risk, how much fun could it have been, being trapped like a rat in a makeshift casket, enduring a typical southern Indiana, hot, humid night? Some people are set on deception and saving a buck, no matter what. And, at my high school, we seemed to have our fair share of those "no matter what's." It got to be such a regular occurrence that I would jokingly walk up to a car's trunk lid, as if talking to the trunk lid itself, and ask, "Is everybody OK in there? If not, there is plenty of fresh, cooler air out here, all for the taking." Ever so occasionally, someone would respond to my question, politely suggesting where I could go and spend my eternity. How thoughtfully considerate to offer such a suggestion in a spirit of wanting to help me with some advance planning for my future!

Then, there was this minor matter of working with an older lady (in her 30's, I'm guessing) whose job it was to dispense tickets for the cash I collected from each car. She was seated inside a smallish ticket booth while I stood outside in the humid heat, collecting money for the dispensed tickets. As you might imagine, there were lulls and idle times between cars arriving, time enough to socialize a bit with this woman. After getting to know her better by working together as a team, she assertively asked me, in a minimal amount of words, if I would have any interest in broadening my sex education with her acting as my dedicated tutor, with the added benefit of not having to sit in a stuffy old classroom to acquire this newly-found knowledge. Imagine that! I didn't have a clue as to how to react to this offer, being a bit short of courage as to what to say to this. I was fairly sure an offer like this wouldn't come along again anytime soon. But, I have to admit to being flattered with the offer, nevertheless. OK, OK...for the record I graciously declined, not out of any moral conviction (which it should have been), but out of a lack of self-confidence as to what to say or do. And not that it would have mattered, she wasn't going to be winning any beauty pageants, ever! She wasn't any Mrs. Robinson from the movie "The Graduate" nor was I any prize, either.

Working this job nightly as I was rapidly coming up on the

end of my second semester of my senior year, readying myself for a much-hoped for graduation, I made it known (on several occasions) that a particular graduation gift to me would more than fulfill my unending love for my dad. My pronouncements, loud and often, were so bold that the only thing missing was a troupe of trumpeters, brazenly blasting away in support of my hoped-for gift...a brand new, navy blue, 1961 Ford Sunliner convertible. He did get the "navy" and the "blue" properly fixed in his brain, but not quite in the form I was hoping for. For Dad's part, he never once acknowledged any of my boldly-made conspicuous remarks. Absent that, it encouraged me, even more, in believing this "detachment" was a feigned attempt to conceal his plan to buy me this dream car, a supreme act of "unaffected simplicity" (you read it here first) if any such thing ever existed. Believe me, folks, I chose the word "unaffected" with great care much like those two porcupines I referred to earlier.

Well, the big day finally arrives as I proudly sport my tasseled cap and flowing gown in heightened anticipation of the gift that I pray to God will follow. Trying my best to contain feelings of euphoria for this much-hoped for moment of glorious anticipation of what was about to take place and prior to the graduation exercises being on the agenda for later that evening, I took it upon myself to go snooping, checking out our storage garage located back of our house...no car there. OK, that's not the end of the world. Dad could really be creative when he set his mind to it and, just maybe, this is one of those times. So off I go to what I think would be the obvious choice of a hiding place...the garage (as in Ford). I scoured every square foot of that building while, at the same time, trying to manage my leaking sense of joy, that I had misjudged my dad and I had been chasing a pipe dream instead of a dream car. Now with a downtrodden heart, I began preparing myself for the evening's commencement program, resigned to accepting that this dream car was never meant to be. So much for unaffected simplicity!

I did, however, receive a gift, a gift I would have never guessed in a hundred years, nor expected, nor wanted – two (count 'em) pieces of navy blue-colored luggage! So, in one unfathomable swoop, from a car to luggage, to say the least, my gratitude for this gift was not exactly overflowing. I was so underwhelmed. What a colossal letdown! To add to my facetious delight, I was informed that this wasn't just any two pieces of luggage as my step-mom so proudly announced for others to hear, According to her,"this luggage carries the name brand "Skyway" as if that would have helped me get over this monumental disappointment. What difference under the canopy of heaven did this brand name mean to me? Nothing, nada, zippo. My first guess, after getting over the initial shock, was asking myself if there was a not so subliminal message intended, to awake in me possibilities of travel or a permanent change of address from 1311 14th Street, Bedford, Indiana? I mean, who gives luggage to a teenage boy unless there was some declared/undeclared message being conveyed? Maybe, they were helping me out and neither of us realized to what extent and, just maybe, I should be making my own plans for getting out of Dodge! Eventually, which took some doing, I got over this ginormous disappointment by blaming myself for being so freakin' naive!

Wasting no time to getting something going in my life, I learned about a job that was opening up within the month, where the major task would not have taxed the finer details of my high school education, at least, not to any measurable extent. The main attraction of this job was MONEY, as in, for buying a new car. This job paid a whopping $10.00 an hour which made that a big deal back in 1961. Although that would be great pay for the time, it had to compensate, in part, for the likely lack of job satisfaction that went along with the work performed which was digging up graves for transplanting to another location to make room for a huge new lake being planned for the area , later named Monroe Reservoir. Imagine what all that entailed, being sequestered for extended periods of time due to health concerns and a limited amount of time off, not to mention the wear and tear on your psyche. Little inconveniences like these weren't going to get in the way of my dreams of buying a new car, though. No siree...bring on those graves.

So, first things first, I sat through a preliminary interview that, falsely, built up my hopes that I was qualified for this job without a detailed knowledge of how to use a shovel. During the interview, it came out that all job applicants were required to join the union that represented their employees. No problem with that. Then, he dropped this little bomb on me stating that one must be eighteen in order to join the union, something I was not going to be until August, and this was May! Any effort I would have made to apply for this job in August would have been futile as "the train would have left the station" by then and I wasn't going to be onboard.

To validate this age requirement in order to join the union, their Personnel Office's representative told me I had to present my birth certificate, accompanied by a written application; but, the interviewer failed to tell me about one little minor detail that I will get to, momentarily. So, enter center stage, my classmate and dear friend, Kennetha (Hartmann) Miller. With her, I m commiserating my tale of woe about the need to join the union if only I were eighteen. After telling her the bad news associated with the date of my birth, she yelped out, "I've got it" (or words to that effect), telling me there was a way around this dilemma. She, then, proceeds to reveal her masterpiece of an idea – change the year of my birth by physically altering its date on the birth certificate. How splendid, you say? I know I thought so. So, she set herself to the task of changing "1943" to "1942" which she did an outstanding job on, the result appearing to be genuine. You know, if she had chosen a career in counterfeiting, she would have gone to the head of her class. She was a natural. Her end-product looked so convincing you couldn't have chiseled that smile off of my face with a sledgehammer, beaming with confidence that we had pulled this one off and, voila, here I am now a serious candidate for a job that would put me behind the wheel of that new dream car.

Well, folks, that euphoria wore off rather quickly as I was informed, not only must I present my birth certificate, I, also, needed to show a second form of identification. This little inconvenient detail was trivialized or not even mentioned in the earlier interview or, perhaps, I wasn't listening carefully enough. In any event, imagine my shock, probably bordering on cardiac arrest, much too harsh for my little 125 pound body to take, all in one setting. Now what? The interviewer picked-up on my visibly shaken countenance in obvious dismay, asking to see my driver's license as to take care of this minor oversight. So, I forked over my license knowing I had just blown this job opportunity because the age on my driver's license was not going to agree with my birth certificate. I mean, I was sweating bullets by the nanoseconds! As he took his time examining the two documents, he never once let on to me or uttered a word about any disparity, leaving me to ponder whether he caught the discrepancy or not. He politely returned my license, thanked me for my time and application, bid me a good day, saying, with a smile on his face (it was that smile that anchored any hope that I had, that all was well and I was going to get that job, after all), I should expect a call from him within the next few days. How long is a "few days?" I was about to find out. Three weeks had come and gone and still no call or letter...nada, leaving me to reluctantly conclude that I had been had by my own undoing. A post note – so much for digging up graves. I dug my own!

Now, with no serious prospects of a job and my car dreaming still very much alive, along with a strained relationship at home (had nothing to do with the shi##y luggage), with no means of buying that new car, and with absolutely no interest in going to college, but, with a real need to get out of Bedford...NOW. All of a sudden, the Navy started to appeal to me, thanks to a couple of uncles who had served and couldn't say enough great things about this service, training, schooling, traveling, and on and on. Given my choices, the Navy was sounding pretty good about now. To join, I had to be seventeen provided my parents signed an authorization for me to join. If you were eighteen, you could freely join up on the strength of your own signature. You talk about an irony. I go from a counterfeited birth certificate, making me appear to be eighteen and now, I have a situation on my hands where age, again, is rearing its ugly head, once again, becoming a deciding factor in qualifying for a job. Will I ever see my eighteenth birthday? I'm thinking...get these rules and regulations out of my life...they are killing me. So, I, less than enthusiastically, asked Dad to sign for me. Dad had no problem with that and with that response, I was more sure than ever that it was no accident that I got two pieces of luggage as a high school graduation gift!

Here I am, despite not being able to join the Navy without my dad's signature, I am increasingly getting excited about the prospects of departing Dodge "to see the world" as the Navy put it. I talked up the Navy to some friends from my graduating class and found two who said I could count on them for the three of us joining the Navy together. Those two friends turned into culprits overnight as both up and decide to change their minds about joining me. Those culprits went by the names of Fred Cummings and David Mitchell. In the case of Fred, although color-blind, he, apparently, preferred Army "green" to Navy "blue" and, David, just got a case of "cold feet," something he came to specialize in as a mortician. So, off I go to see Uncle Sam, disguised as a Navy Recruiter, who had the simplest of mottos, "I want you." You know "the rest of the story" as the famed newscaster Paul Harvey was accustomed to saying. The recruiter persisted in reminding me that my decision to join up was irrevocable with no "change of mind" card on the table. Why the need to drill me on this point was a mystery to me because I saw the Navy as offering me a one-way ticket out of Bedford and that was worth the price of admission or so I thought at the time. Trying not to second guess Old Sam about his claims, promises (darn few) and slogans (aplenty) made me a little anxious, knowing I would be paying one heck of an ongoing price if I was wrong. Hoping I had rid myself of any lingering child-like naivete, once and for all, I rolled the dice. They came up "Navy."

Now as a fresh, untrained future sailor, I had to come to grips with several changes that needed to take place if the military and I were going to get along. All the toys belonging to a teenage boy had to be put away (as in "permanently"). Those old nearly discarded copies of Playboy Magazines, never used prophylactics (one always needed to be prepared,so went the Boy Scouts' motto "Be Prepared"), drag-racing, grandiose dreams of chick-attracting dream cars, under-developed dancing skills and under-used study habits. These items, worthy of being fought for and won, were relegated to his-to-ry!

On June 12, 1961, exactly two weeks and two days from receiving my high school diploma, I was, officially, a full-time employee of the U.S. Government, masquerading as a sailor on behalf of the United States Navy, which turned my world upside down overnight. I was addressing everybody and everything. If it moved, I saluted it! Even my name went through a metamorphosis of sorts...from Roger Paul to my family, to Roger, Rog, or Hornsby (there's another story behind that name, Larry "The Toad" Webster can fill you in) coming from my classmates, and ultimately to "Hey You" in the Navy. But, on that rarest of occasions when I was being addressed by someone outranking me (as in, nearly everyone), when trying to be a little more civilized at the expense of a little less horsesh## and more like the human being God created me to be, I, eventually, answered to the elevated name of "Seaman Hilderbrand". Has a nice little ring to it, don't you think? So much for human kindness – Rog or Roger would have been so much friendlier and simpler. But, as I was soon to find out, the Navy was not all about being "friendlier!"

My first assignment was reporting to San Diego, California, for twelve weeks of boot camp. Looking back, I am still amazed how I could travel from Bedford to San Diego in a day's time. It's a miracle that only the Navy can provide an answer for. To put a finer point on the subject of travel, prior to the Navy, my worldwide travels included jaunts around Brown, Bartholomew, Jackson, Johnson, Lawrence, and Marion Counties, and a lot of what was located in south/central Indiana that was not particularly representative of the world I didn't volunteer to be a part of.

My introduction to Navy life began by being ordered to stand at attention (a newly acquired posture as in "rigor mortis"), while being duly informed by new Company Commander, First Class Petty Officer Brown (E-6), who had the misfortune of being my surrogate father. He was assigned to the supervision of my young a## while working to convert me into a real, live, functioning sailor. The utterance of his first words directed specifically at me, is a thing nightmares are made of ...words I will never forget. "God may own our soul, but your a## belongs to the United States Navy and you would be wise to remember that. Put that right up there with your birthday." Now, that got my undivided attention. All of a sudden in the blink of an eye, this Uncle Sam who seemed so jovial and likable was pushing me around with unkind words with frightening prospects. And, to think, I wanted sooooo much for him to take a liking to me. The next shock I put my body through was getting used to (if that's even possible) Navy food, something I was persuaded to believe was the best of all the armed services. Whoever perpetrated that lie should have been court martialed and hanged. Without a doubt, the stuff I was being fed would have been rejected by the unpickiest of pigs! I mean the food was soooooo bad that my fellow sailors and me prayed after we ate, which brings into focus the realization that a Furpo's hamburger or a

Alfred's breaded tenderloin sandwich in Bedford would have just beat the snot out of anything the Navy had fed me up to this point.

Drum roll!! I am 18...finally! I now can legally do anything the Navy permits with the exception of voting and drinking beer, one of which I could care less about. Despite still being a teenager, I can be court martialed for disobedience, become a father, and die for my country. What a combination of human possibilities at such a tender age! BTW, I had no intentions of seeing any of those events ever taking place. But, it was becoming clearer by the day that I was assimilating into military life which largely meant accepting a lot of rules and regulations that, a year ago, I would have held to be incorrigibly unacceptable. After all, weren't rules made to be broken? Not unlike golf, many of those rules were worthless as TOAB – female genitalia on a boar. Mine was not to say but to do. If in doubt about complying with a rule or reg, the Navy way would have you erring on the side of just going ahead and doing what you thought "might" be the correct course of action or verbal response. Why chance something that could have been avoidable with a little humility and lot of common sense! Case in point - saluting anything that moved. Somewhere in the annals of naval governance, I'm sure it has been recorded that a small child riding a bicycle got an unwarranted salute because some hapless sailor wasn't sure if he was supposed to salute a moving, possible government-issued, vehicle. As in golf, there are, no doubt, several rules obscured by practicality and expediency. But, the rules are still there on the books for me to decide which ones I would be obeying and which ones might stand in the way of a honorable discharge.

As if turning on the lights, I became aware of how some sailors, where I was stationed, had cars. It seemed that there were several but I was not included in that "several." How can that be? Some had to be making the same $80 per month that I was, and yet, here they are tooling around the base, fashionably situated behind the wheel of a car. This realization was the onslaught of a privately attended "pity party" hosted by yours truly, feeling a bit sorry for myself. I struggled with trying to figure out how others did it, how they could afford something so desirable yet so unattainable for the average "Joe Doe" wearing pins and strips, like me. Sadly drawn, I came to the conclusion that those "Joe's" had savings or resources that I didn't have and I had better get used to the habit of dreaming about that special car that was somewhere out there in my future.

It didn't help any to be constantly bombarded with ads heard or read, sponsored by local car dealers, raving about how afford-able a car could be, if only you bought it from them, today. Yea, right...in your dreams (as in mine). For sure, some naivete was still at work just beneath the surface of my brain, but a stupid, spur of the moment act was not in the cards for this soon-to-be homesick boy, not so much for home as it was for CARS! See-ing those cars for sale was like dangling candy in front of a baby. Eventually, like all things, I got over it. Thank you, Lord. Look-ing back, I can now see this severe degree of torture was a conse-quence for disobeying the Second Commandant (did I get you to look that up?) Little did I know that, before my tour of duty was up, I would be breaking most of the other Nine, at one time or another!

My early Navy experience was filled with "awe", a not too strong word in describing the newness of everything; southern California weather, discovering the lifestyle of an eighteen year old being exposed, for the first time, to palm trees, desert land-scapes, surfing, a new era for Rock & Roll music featuring cars, Disneyland, and fantasies of Annette Funicello. And would any-one forget listening to Wolfman Jack on KRLA? I could go on and on. I had friends I was stationed with who were from south-ern Cal to thank for getting me exposed to all of this. What fun it was to go to their homes with them on an occasional weekend and be a part of that scene. As for my own personal lifestyle, I learned to get by on Lucky Strikes and Lucky Lager, served up down at the local Enlisted Men's Club, where ID's were infre-quently checked. And if they did, didn't this baby-faced teen-ager from southern Indiana look twenty-one? But, get by I sure did, thanks in parts to 10 cents a pack cigarettes and 25 cent beers. At these prices, I finally found something I could afford.

Here I am in the "holy land" of automobiles. If you can dream it, that car existed somewhere in this most populous state in the country, within seeing distance of Seaman Hilderbrand. The car gods (no doubt related to Satan himself) did that on purpose just to tease my young, impressionable a##. I never saw so many '55,'56, '57 Chevy's and, of course, Corvettes (any year). They seemed to be everywhere! You know, you couldn't avoid seeing fantastic cars if you tried, as they were as common as palm trees that lined Colorado Boulevard in Pasadena, the former home of our friends, Gerry and Dianna Sharpe. Seeing so many neat cars spawned some pretty neat fantasies of car grandeur, testing my ability to remain sane. After all, a man can only take so much. One piece of good news is worth reporting, there were no Pontiac Astek's in those days as this model wasn't introduced to the market until 2001. With no Astek's around to spoil the landscape, you rarely saw a car you would call ugly. You certainly would not be describing a Corvette. I mean, have you ever seen an ugly Corvette? I'm sure there are, but, they are so few and far between, that you would have to go out dedicating yourself to finding one.

Until I was discharged nearly four years later, I remained car-less, not to be confused with careless-huge difference. So, this reduced my Navy lifestyle to a catchy little jingle, "no money, no car." You suppose that had anything to do with "no dates?" as well? I could have been hung like a bull with a face like Paul Newman and it wasn't going to make any difference. Cash was king and I didn't have any. In all fairness, my choice of a haircut (what choice?) didn't help matters any, making me look like a "posture boy" for a Buddhist monk. And to be sta- tioned in the "land of cars" where so much "eye candy" could test one's visual strengths just wasn't fair. Closing my eyes and looking the other way took more willpower than I could muster up.

This was 1962, '63, and '64...just picture the great cars that came out of that era. If you can (and care to) picture with me the 1963 split-window Corvette, the first Stingray. How about the 1962 and '63 Studebaker Gran Turismo Hawk, the 1963/1964 Studebaker Avanti? And how about the 1959 Pontiac Catalina, 2-door, 389 cubic inch engine with three carbure- tors sitting atop of the engine block, screaming, "I'm thirsty, I'm thirsty", the 1959 Chevrolet Impala, 2-door hardtop which, from a rear view, looked like a big bird in flight with its wings spread, the 1959 Cadillac Coupe de Ville and convertible with it ginormous (that's no typo) tail fins, the1963 (and a half) Ford, Galaxie 500 XL, R Code, 2-door hardtop with a 406 engine and a floor-mounted, four speed tranny, the first Pontiac Tri-Power GTO's in 1964, and the pony of futurely defined "muscle cars" the Ford Mustang, introduced as a 1964 and a half model. And, who, if anybody with a modicum of good taste could ever forget one of the most beautiful cars this country (or any country, for that matter) has ever produced? I am, of course, referring to the 1963-1965 Buick Riviera, arguably, the best designed car to ever come out of Detroit. Others, apparently, feel this accolade is appropriately bestowed on this car, as well. Hagerty, the noted experts on car collecting and pricing of collectible cars, has chosen (10/16) these Rivi's as the #1 car "to collect", not to be confused with another category (found elsewhere?), "for collecting" which identifies future car candidates, deemed to have collector appeal. That list includes the 2005 Ford Thunderbird, 2009 Cadillac XLR, Platinum Edition hard-shell, roadster, and the 1970-1972 Chevrolet Monte Carlo. You would be justified in shooting me if I didn't mention the highly desirable, "Baby Birds" a.k.a. 1955-1957, 2-seater, Ford Thunderbirds. How grievous Ford's decision was in dropping this model in favor of a larger, 4-seater version, which, as it turns out, heavily outsold the 2-seaters and enjoyed a run at sales records for model years 1958 through 1976. There were a few dogs in there, but not many. I'll be commenting on the dogs a bit later in this discourse. Of all the cars I am drawing your attention to (assuming you are still awake!), I have to tell you, hands down, the 1957 Ford Thunderbird was my all-time favorite dream car, going back to my sophomore year in high school.

Another drum roll, if you please. On my 71st birthday, I finally found and bought a '57 Bird – right condition, color, equipment, and price (that's a lot to ask out for from one car). Holding onto my dream, I never stopped dreaming for 57 years. That's right, it took me 57 years to buy a '57 Bird! So, I am living testimony that dreams can and do come true. The trick is never stop dreaming, because, if you do, you are guaranteeing that dream is going to die! You can't keep it alive if you aren't dreaming it! So, get with it, DREAM!! After all, it belongs exclusively to you.

Prior to leaving for Japan and a two year tour of duty aboard a ship permanently deployed to several garden spots in Southeast Asia, including Viet Nam, qualified me for some much

46

needed "leave" or furlough. Instead of basking in the California sun and sporting a Southern Cal "wannabe" lifestyle, I decided it was high time to go back to Bedford for a few days and get myself reacquainted with things I had to give up to keep old Sam happy with my compliance to Navy life. The town I couldn't wait to leave is now beckoning me back, saying "all's forgiven, come on home!" So I did. Looking up old high school class-mates that most assuredly included girls, eating the local junk food i.e. Furpo's Hamburgers, Alfred's deep-fried tenderloin sandwiches, and pizza from Grecco's reminds me how much I was missing and didn't know it. And, not to be forgotten, there were the illegal purchases of beer from a local, unnamed liquor store (rhymes with "lobby's) and all things familiar and taken for granted, i.e. sleeping in your own bed, cruising, and, of course, anything that had to do with CARS! With the exception of go-ing back to Bedford on leave, I did not have a single date, not one, for about eighteen months (went with my birthday, right?). Even if that special girl had existed in California, it would have been tough sleddin' around San Diego on $80 a month. I mean, what can you do, more than once, on 80 bucks? At this rate, I was never going to learn how to use a prophylactic. Things got to looking so bleak for me that I found myself getting aroused by gawking at naked mannequins...sadly so, but in all fairness, they were looking pretty good.

While home on leave, I got an unexpected phone call from a buddy who wanted to know if I would be interested in selling my former dream car, the 1956 Ford, 2-door sedan, thinking that, if he was lucky enough, that car might have a little more "cruising" life left in it but not much. That car had long lost its lustre and dream car status; so, it was no great loss. It would only have had value if I could have had it in California, which clearly, I couldn't afford. Anyhow, I had the good sense to tell him that everything I owned, including a dog (which I didn't even own) was for sale, if the price were right. Well, apparently, the price was right because I found myself forking over a set of keys to him, the very set that Dad had given me two years previously. Knowing that I was back in town, prompted by Uncle Chloral to lend me his new 1963, red Galaxie 500, 2-door hardtop, forever cementing his place in my heart as one of my favorite uncles...I had six oth-ers to choose from. If that kind gesture couldn't help solidify his #1 ranking in my books, nothing could!

The Navy holds a lot of memories for me, mostly pleasant and enjoyable to recall such as my travels through Southeast Asia with the possible exception of Viet Nam, where my ship was entrusted to provide a glorified taxi service for Army and Marine Corps personnel, transporting their Jeeps, tanks, helicopters and weapons deemed "weapons du jour" in our fight against North Viet Nam, Also, gratifying was my qualifying (through tests) for some classroom language training in conversational Japanese.

My take-away for the nearly four years I spent on active duty in the Navy were many; but, I could reduce them down to two objectives I wanted to aggressively pursue once I was released from active duty: Get my a## into a college classroom, faster than a speeding bullet (this coming from a guy who nearly didn't graduate from high school) and becoming a commissioned officer in the Naval Reserves). Those became my burning goals that NOTHING was going to stand in the way of my achieving...NOTHING!! And, my rewards for successfully completely these goals? Buying myself my own college graduation gift...a 1967 Ford Thunderbird and getting myself groomed for a career chucked full of cars. After suffering through the disappointment I experienced with my high school graduation gift, I thought it only fitting to buy myself something special in the way of a car. What else?

With Dad and Uncle Chloral out of the car business, my continued loyalty to Ford was subsiding somewhat, although if one dug deep enough into my being, you would have found little blue ovals (Ford's logo) buried in there somewhere. Somewhat of a response to the disappointment of the garage being sold, growing tired of getting my a## wiped by Chevrolets and, to help get me through college, I accepted a salaried position with General Motors at their Chevrolet stamping plant located in Indianapolis. They made truck parts for the Chevy, GMC, and Corvair models (bet you didn't remember Corvair made a van, did you?) For the time spent at GM, I enjoyed excellent pay, cost-of-living allowances, and great benefits that included buying a new Chevy product with an employee discount which was a benefit I fully made liberal use of. So, in consecutive years, I bought a 1965, 1966, and 1967 Chevrolet, all three were Super Sports, two of

48

which were convertibles, with these years corresponding to the three years I was employed by GM. Now, I am really cashing in on some of those dormant dreams stored away while in the Navy; but, these cars soon became a thing of the past as it became necessary to sell the '67 Chevy to help free-up some much needed cash for tuition and living expense money for my wife and me, if I expected to graduate in 1969 (I did). Enter center stage...a 1960 Chevrolet Corvair followed by a 1962 Mercury Meteor...two, force-fed doses of humility in gigantic proportions. You gotta do what you've gotta do. Was it worth all that for a college education? That question doesn't need answering...end of sentence!

With two major goals realized and behind me, I felt I was ready to get serious about the career I always wanted that as a franchised Ford dealer, where I could proudly hang out my shingle that I had seen a hundred times (so it seemed) in my mind's eye that read "Hilderbrand Ford." I would have settled for "Hilderbrand Chevrolet" if that would have helped me reach my dream of becoming a new car dealer.

Plans shape our lives and as I learned, life changes plans. Case in point, my dream of owning a new car dealership, sadly, never came to fruition.

CARS & SCHOOL

They say drinking and driving don't mix. This, I don't doubt for a minute. BTW, neither does cars and school. I am living proof to the validity of that statement. Now, as an adult , I want to go back and discuss the riveting dichotomy that tortured me endlessly as a teenager, constantly, in a conflicting relationship where school attempted to sway my allegiance away from what REALLY mattered in life-cars and music-both of which I held sacrosanct. School just got in the way, period. For this teen-age gearhead, cars and school positively didn't mix. As you have read, my poor judgment and lack of willpower nearly did me in.

As a car luster extraordinaire, my prized possession was constantly getting in the way of my learning as evidenced by the grades I was making or not making. The inside of a classroom was no substitute for the interior of a car. Attending classes was deemed more of an inconvenience than an opportunity to learn. After a grueling day in the classroom, I needed to hop into my car, any car, just to chill out, forgetting the cares of the day and the less than enthusiastically acquired knowledge of the day, which was minimal at best.

One reason why this was so difficult to accept by the car luster, along with teenage boys in general, was cars were viewed to be the epicenter of one's social life. If one were bored, you cruised, provided one had the means to do it. If you were look-ing for that special someone or something, you cruised. As a practical matter, much of the time, cruising was a waste of time and money...something teenagers have precious little of, pro-viding they were studying as they were supposed to be doing. As for time, heck, I had plenty of that, since I wasn't wasting any of it on homework. And, then, there's Joe, the stereotype of a seasoned cruiser, always in hot pursuit of something that might or might not happen, but, he's prepared to make the investment in time and money to find out, usually, becoming a little poorer by night's fall. It's kind of an expensive and inefficient lesson that, generally, doesn't get learned, easily, because old Joe will be out on the street, again, tomorrow night in his endless search for that special something or somebody...that may or may not even exist!

You didn't need a reason to cruise, you just did it, provided you had at least 25 cents of gasoline left in your car's tank. I was always out there cruisin', trying to draw attention to myself, showing-off, or whatever. So, if I was unlucky looking for that special gal who could harden my eyeballs, at least, I had a fighting chance of impressing some of the guys with my precious little Ford as I was continually spending money on "souping" that puppy up. Besides my dust covered Bible, I always had my trusty J. C. Whitney catalog, ever ready by my side, enabling me to keep my car dreams alive. Some guys had fresh copies of Playboy and Mad Magazines. Not me...I had the much heralded J. C. Whitney catalog with its endless pages to feast on, selling everything imaginable for a car, especially, when it came to parts that produced more power (translation - more speed.) It carried high-lift cams, multiple carburetors, glass-packed mufflers, chromed side pipes, spinner wheel covers, racing tires, you name it. If it wasn't in J. C. Whitney's catalog, you didn't need it. But chances are, if it was in their catalog, you, probably, still didn't need it (that was a little of dad's rhetoric coming out there).

My cruising and less than arduous study habits were about to catch up with me. Actually, poor to non-existent study habits only offer a minuscule glimpse into what was going on in my school life. My total lack of discipline, just doing what I wanted to do rather than doing what needed doing, made me my own worst enemy. This staying out until all hours of the night, hob-knobbing with the local big boys with their big bad speed machines, smoking cigarettes, drinking coffee (a big no-no with Dad), and on and on, always doing something that pleased me, was surfacing in a multitude of ugly ways. My lack of self-discipline was eating away at my weakening self-image, haunting me nearly daily, such that I came not to like myself a lot. I needed a swift kick in the a## to retrieve my much underused, misplaced moral compass. As you might imagine, my dormant relationship with God and family were suffering from inattention, thanks to my narcissistic ways.

Simply put, I had pretty much given up on school and the feeling was becoming mutual. To put a finer point on that, I had given up on me in terms of how I was living my life and realizing that things had to change and quicker than you can say "now". If I didn't, my life was going to imitate a dropped, uncooked egg, too late to save. This precipitous fall didn't just happen. For months, I was either sleeping in class (mimicking our football coach,) cutting class, tossing homework assignments aside like dried boogers and, in general, being confrontational over just about anything with anybody. Make no mistake, this was a tough, spiritless period in my life. What in the world had to happen to get me back on track? Well, little did I know there were events and things about to be set in motion, totally unbeknownst to me that would change me in ways that I could never have imagined. Please read on.

Near the end of the final grading period in the second semester of my senior year, Dad got a phone call from Bob Baugh, my Indiana State History teacher. Bob told Dad, in no uncertain terms, that I was failing his class and that I needed to get a passing grade for the semester. Otherwise, I would not be graduating with my class as that course was a state-stipulated graduation requirement. Not only had I dug myself into a hole deeper than the bottom of sh## creek, without a step ladder in sight, Mr. Baugh explained to Dad that the only way I could pass this course was to get an "A" on the final exam. You talk about pressure? It was like I had made a fifty cent bet with only a quarter in my pocket; meanwhile, the clock was ticking away like there was no tomorrow. Dad was dumb-founded by this revelation and asked Mr. Baugh how could this possibly be because he distinctly remembered signing my most recent six-week Report Card that showed I had "earned" a "B." Mr. Baugh, with a bit of grace, proceeded to gently tell Dad that it was not possible that I got a "B" in his class, that, in fact, I had the dubious honor of receiving a big fat "F!"

Getting an "A" on the final exam? That was right up there with selling air-conditioners to Eskimos! Are you kidding? This news of having to make an "A" on the final, left me feeling hopelessly lost. I saw my high school experience passing before my eyes, realizing how broken it had irreparably become, or so it seemed at the time. It was over. I had run out of excuses and, more importantly, I had run out of time. No "do-over's" for me! And yet, here's Bob Baugh talking to my dad under no compunction to do so except for his genuine concern (you can be sure of that) for my situation. Clearly, he didn't want me to fail and felt the best way to shake me out of my lethargy was to go to the boss man himself. I saw that as an impassioned attempt to help me when, if it were any other teacher, they would have cared less. So, with my toes in the fire, so to speak, I set myself to the task of breaking my a## for the next five weeks in the vaguest of hopes that I might ace his final. As Elvis once sang, "It's Now Or Never" time.

Back to my dad remembering that I got a "B" in Mr. Baugh's class, there's a little background information that I need to share with you in order to clear up that mystery. What Dad didn't know was, on an earlier occasion, I paid a visit to Mr. Charlie Hartmann, Dean of Boys, down in the school's office, where I eyed a stack of fresh, never issued...Report Cards. What good fortune would drop right into my hands if only I could help myself to one of those cards without getting caught! Always taking a degree of immeasurable risk (I still do), I decided right then and there that my biggest goal in life was to find a new home for one of those cards. And, you might have guessed it. I made off with, not only one card, I stole four of those suckers, keeping two for myself and selling the other two to some trusted friends for $10 apiece. So, with a blank Report Card in hand, I proceeded to give myself grades that would shocked a priest out of celibacy! All my grades were either"Λ"s or "B"s, befitting a would-be scholar on this fanciful, make believe Report Card and, it was one of those very "B"s that dad recalled seeing and signing off on. Dad never let on what was going on in his mind but, as it turned out, he had a plan and was determined to get to the bottom of all this fishy business. (I have to give him credit for involvement in my school life here!!).

Dad ups and decides to pay an unannounced visit to the School Office with me in tow and asked to see my filed Report Card which Mr. Hartmann promptly gave Dad to examine. Sure enough, there's that big fat "F" that Mr. Baugh had alluded to. I was about to get caught up in my own "doo doo" as if I had

54

been attacked by a squadron of vultures whose droppings were raining down on me like torpedoes! Dad led me out of Charlie's office as if leading a sheep to slaughter. I remember thinking no more bullsh##, time to 'fess up and get this whole ugly scenario behind me and, at the same time, gain a better appreciation of life because mine was about to come to a screeching halt! I just knew there was going to be hell to pay for my colossal misdeed and was suffering at the thought of what dear old dad had in mind by way of exacting some form of personalized, capital punishment like removing the gas tank from my car. That ought to do it! Equally painful was a vision of my car being held hostage for lack of keys as dad was going to assume possession of my car until he learned that I had somehow, miraculously, aced Mr. Baugh's final exam. And, if it turned out otherwise, I would be kissing those beloved car keys good-bye. As hard as it is to believe, Dad didn't utter as much as one word to me for days, my anxiety grew by the waking hour. Then one day, Dad, without ever lifting his voice, asked me if I truly wanted to graduate with my class and was I willing to break my a## studying in preparation for taking that dreaded test. I think Dad was trying to scare me into a realization that failing that test was more than a possibility and nothing but a total surrender to the task of studying was my only option, like it or not.

NEWS FLASH...after studying, days on end (a totally alien experience), luxuriating in the liberal use of burning up a ton of that "midnight oil" (you have to be 60 years old or older to know that idiom), some days later as I wait with baited breath to get the results of that test, Mr. Baugh informed me, that to the best of his knowledge, I was going to be a high school graduate in 1961, graduating with my class! I had, in fact, made an "A" on that test and that "A" is still resting in the archives of my little-used brain. By George, I got 'er done with no endless thanks to God and the all-consuming fear of losing my cars keys forever. Strangely enough, Dad wasn't overcome with euphoria, as I had hoped, which would have been vindication enough for my disastrous misdeed and, surprisingly, he seemed fairly casual about the whole thing...at the time. But, over the years, Dad never ceased reminding me how close I came to failing Mr. Baugh's course, taking some credit for making me understand the gravity of my situation.

That single event made a lasting impression on me and the subsequent impact it had on my self-esteem, knowing I could pretty much do anything, if only I set myself to the task at hand. I was becoming more serious about what needed to become important in my life and what needed to be re-thought, getting myself up onto that narrow road that could lead to a more Christ-centered, productive life.

Well, folks, here it comes...something you would never have thought possible. I was in the embryonic stage of realizing how imbecilic my love of cars had become, cars that ate up my limited resources; money, time, school and relationships. Were cars really worth all that? What an ongoing price to pay for what in time, would become a heap of depreciating metal! And, even if I loved a particular car for a period of time, I was sure to tire of it eventually. To this day, I have a notable history of buying cars and reveling in it. I would no more than buy a particular car, a car that I might bestow with knighthood status, a "dream car" if you will, and as quickly as I decided to buy, I would trip this magical switch that called for me to immediately start planning my next car purchase as there was no shortage of car dreams; hence, this book's title, "Sooooooo Many Cars, Sooo Little Time." If I were asked what my favorite car was, my stock answer was "the next one."

What was about to be revealed to me was a need to get all this car "stuff" out of the way and work on developing a fresh assessment on the importance of figuring out what I wanted to do with my life. In short order (surprising even myself), I was developing a paradigm unlike anything I had ever experienced or thought. Clearly, I was thinking outside the "box," the only one I knew, the one that allowed me to do and say whatever pleased me. Although a car qualifies as a material blessing, in the final analysis, it is still only a car and remains that until something dies, preferably, the car. Looking back, I could see how stupid, yes, stupid, I had become in my reckless, over-powering pursuit of automobiles...a poster boy to idiocy!

Now, as a fully functioning adult (Sandi might care to differ with that view), my love affair of cars remains firmly entrenched, without a doubt. But, here's the difference. I have enjoyed and embraced God's blessings in discovering and acting on a much needed vision for myself in the real world, where cars are merely cogs on a bigger wheel. God, as my guide, has ushered me into circumstances where I have enjoyed indescribable blessings in my life that had absolutely nothing to do with cars, having full rein over my hopes, dreams, ambitions, and, most importantly, my faith in the Almighty that I have since zealously put into motion in my opportunities to glorify Him.

Another drum roll, please.   I now have our roles all figured out...GOD BLESSES...I glorify.

CARS COME

CARS GO

CARS & MUSIC

Gearheads and music go together like butter on bread. Little wonder so many songs have been written about cars. The fun and joys it expressed were timeless and euphoric. Who could ever forget: "Little Old Lady From Pasadena," 409," "GTO," Little Deuce Coupe," "Until Her Daddy Took Her T-Bird Away," "Pink Cadillac," "Little Red Corvette," and even earlier, "Maybelline," "Hot Rod Lincoln," and "The Little Nash Rambler That Went Beep, Beep?" Those songs sure beat the mucus out of some, what you would think would be forgettable songs, that had absolutely nothing to do with cars, but somehow, they didn't – songs that hung around like "Don't Let Your Chewing Gum Lose Its Flavor On The Bedpost Overnight," "It Was A Itsy, Bitsy, Teeny Weeny, Yellow Poke-A-Dot Bikini," " A One-Eyed, One-Horn, Flying Purple People Eater," and the very forgettable, unsingable lyrics made famous by The Chipmunks. Oh, by the way, have you ever noticed there haven't been any songs written about Volvos or Fiats? I've got the answer for that one...there's nothing to write about!

So, here I am in cruising mode with a full tank of gas, telling myself to crank up the radio, so I can better hear the "hot" song of the day. In joyous response to the music, I get a little buzz going that needs addressing. I, dutifully, attend by mashing the gas petal to the floor of my much-prized beast (seldomly referred to as such, by my very small legion of fellow gearheads, countable on one hand), unleashing a needless surge of power, knowing I had awakened the "speed demons" from their slumber. That little foot mashing exercise probably cost me in the vicinity of a dime for every twenty-five cent gallon of gasoline I bought. You think that got my carburetor's attention? If carburetors could talk, this one might be saying, "Here he goes again, one day closer to a speeding ticket!" Fun, you ask? Oh, heck yes, and, then some. If this little escapade comes to the attention of Yogi (as in "The Bear", named for the style of hat worn by Indiana's finest), it instantly becomes a whole different matter. That surge of power just turned into sh## faster than you can shift out of first gear. Was it worth it? I think that all depended upon whether you got caught and faced a hefty fine or luxuriated in some after-glow knowing you got away with it.

OK, I'm turning that buzz into some goose bumps at the moment as I go radio dial surfing, looking for the strongest signal I can find and end up settling on WAKY out of Louisville, KY. Some nights, I would get a better reception out of KOMA, Oklahoma City or WLS – Chicago. As I zero in on the song that is playing, old Elvis is putting the hit on some young thing with "Are You Lonesome Tonight." And, if that didn't work, watch out because here comes "It's Now Or Never" and, then, not to be outdone, there's old goody, goody, two-shoes, Pat Boone, with some bimbo poking fun at him for singing ever so prayfully, "Writing Love Letters In The Sand." "What's the matter, Pat, can't afford paper?" And, who could ever forget Chubby Checkers (named by his less than skinny mother). It turns out that name was not a wasted choice, after all. He could have just as easily been named "Chunky Checkers," who taught a generation of teenagers how to "twist." Sadly that music eventually faded away much like its artists, although two major exceptions comes to mind - The Rolling Stones and The Beach Boys with Brian Wilson, in particular. To this day, they continue to tour the U.S. with their special brand of Rock & Roll music, deeply vested in choreographed dance movements that would send a seventy year old to a chiropractor, and rich, multiple harmonies, hanging around like a 1957 Chevrolet, Bel-Air, 2-door hardtop. Those guys are working their collective buns off, trying to keep me young. I've got news for Messrs. Wilson and Jagger...it isn't working! Bottom line through all this-music to a teenager is like gasoline is to a car. As Doris Day once sang, "You Can't Have One Without The Other."

Between the years 1955 and 1965, that era produced some fabulous music and, equally so, some very finely-styled automobiles. What a decade that generation lived through with Detroit pulling out all the stops, bombarding the market with high horsepower V-8 engines; two/three-color paint schemes; 4-speed, floor-mounted, manual trannys: high-lift cams; less restrictive exhaust systems that growled like a NASCAR racer, air conditioning, and, what we now refer to as "muscle" cars with soooo many ponies under the hood. It must have given Europeans a good laugh pointing their fingers at those crazy Yanks over there who must have got their brains frozen from all that air-conditioning. How else can one explain why Americans were gobbling up those cars as fast as Detroit could produce them with upwards of 500 horsepower when the maximum posted speed limit almost anywhere in the U.S. wasn't more than 70 miles per hour! Yea, they might have mocked us a bit on that but we got the final laugh, that's the only one that counted and that was at the gas pump! Our gasoline prices at the time hovered somewhere between 25-30 cent per gallon. So there, Euro's...take that!

Let's take a little break from all of this triviality and get down to some serious business for a moment. If you're old enough to remember, there were songs during that era that produced anything but a buzz and if you were a female, what was being produced was more commonly referred to as "tears." I am referring to songs about lost loves and lost lives, resulting from broken relationships and fatal car accidents. As I look back, there seemed to be more fatalities getting reported in the news than today. Or, does the answer have anything to do with people, in general, driving less miles today in safer automobiles. It's plausible, don't you think? Some of those tear-jerkers still resonate in my memory like it was yesterday, remembering, "Tell Laura I Love Her," Jan & Dean's "Dead Man's Curve," "Leader Of The Pack," "Teen Angel," or "Life In The Fast Lane?" On reflection, I wonder if any of those songs saved any lives.

Rock & Roll music was the perfect medium for a teenager's social development. They could interface with their friends while their car radios were blasting away with the song du jour, that unlike today, was danceable and singable, provided you were a girl (boys wouldn't be caught dead singing in a car unless there was no one within listening distance.) Anyhow, compare that with one of today's so-called forms of music...rap (rhymes with "cra#"). Try dancing to that!

I read or heard somewhere that there are experts out there who had researched and confirmed how listening to loud, high-tempo'd music has a definite, correlatable relationship with an impulsive need to speed...excessively. The faster and louder the music, the faster one drove in excess of the posted speed limit. When repeated with regularity , low and behold, we now have a habitual speeding teenager on our hands. Its been reported that speeding is the Number #1 killer of teenagers. Now, add alcohol to that scenario and you have a potentially lethal person and situation just waiting to happen.

If the experts' findings are, indeed, factual, I would suggest one way to get around speeding is having more female drivers (they just don't have the testosterone as the boys do) and have the teens refrain from cranking up the volume so high on those fast-tempo'd songs. And, turn to other forms of music – classical, jazz, country, whatever. Beware of an ever present danger associated with classical music-it might put the driver to sleep. And there is the gas savings derived from driving at slower speeds, where that "pedal" ain't meeting that "metal" nowhere nearly as often.

My dad never quite understood why I liked classical music so much. He just couldn't imagine a son of his going for all that "long hair" music (his term) and, frankly, I was a bit put out by his less than enlightened opinion of my music. Well, I decided to fix that opinion and educate him right there on the spot and let him know that there was a whole big world of music out there that included more artists than Minnie Pearl, Earnest Tubb, Hank Williams, and Tennessee Ernie Ford. I further made my point by informing him that a fiddle miraculously transforms into a violin once one gets educated. I think Dad actually understood that difference as I noticed his facial expression abruptly changed from what I perceived to be one of astonishment that vanished in a spit second, to one that had all of the makings of a smirk. Gosh, it felt good, knowing I had made my point!

Unfortunately, not all cars back in the 50's and 60's had factory-installed radios and that was, indeed, a tragedy for the unlucky few who didn't have the good fortune of having radio in their car. A teenager can do without a lot of things but a car radio is not one of them. I mean, a car without a radio ranks right up there with listening to a castrated bull wheeze! Actually, that might be superior to no radio at all. On the other hand, music heard coming from a car radio had several positive takeaways/ benefits for many a teen. Consider the:

- Pure enjoyment while listening to the radio and being able to recall a particular memory that matches up with the song being played. For me that memory, more times than not, includes cars, girls, or some special event. Songs like, "Runaway" by Del Shannon and The Beach Boys "409" races fondly through my brain as I associate those songs with graduating high school (5/61).
- Music's influence on one's moral, social, and yes, folks, sexual mores and fantasies. Of course, this assumes one has some to begin with.
- Enhancement to one's social development, bringing budding relationships together through their collective experiences relating to their perception of love or something that passed for love.
- Music eased the dreariness of traveling with one's parents to boring destinations.
- Use of music to neutralize those awkward moments when parked. You know what I mean!
- The most important benefit of having a car radio was listening and keeping "abreast" (a questionable word to use around a teenage boy) of the latest hits utilizing the car's superior acoustics, more intimate and alive than any music you might listen to at home. If you were fortunate enough to have a reverberator (something like a muted echo chamber, a device mounted in the trunk) you had it all. Bring on that music!

CARS & PEOPLE; Overview

This chapter brings me to the all-important topic of cars as it relates to the people behind the scenes who helped produce them and, in some noteworthy cases, nearly destroyed the very industry that spawned them. I'll be introducing you to some of the industry's "movers and shakers," past and mostly present, along with an assortment of its most notable or notorious, characters who I prefer to refer to as "losers whose egos and actions nearly killed the "golden egg"...more than once."

To many of you, no introduction is needed in my written portrayal of John Delorean, who heads my list as Detroit's biggest loser, all this neatly wrapped into one person (one would be enough). I follow this up with an exposé on auto executives who were either "in over their heads," maxing out their flare for incompetence and/or their overgrown egos that decimated careers, marriages and, in some cases, lives. There were others who, though competent and well-meaning, nearly killed their companies in terms of lost revenues, profits, and market share. After carefully considering my use of the word "kill" I've decided that it isn't too strongly put, and fairly describes the impact some of these bozos had on the industry.

No written presentation on the bad guys and losers would be complete and judged fair without an equal number of "good guys" that I truly feel were monumentally astute in their professional achievements. Their respective companies would not be where they are today without the legacies they left for others to build upon (if possible.) In this category, I put Bob Lutz at the top of my list, and he gets my most enthusiastic nod for being an insightful, hard-charging, talented auto executive who had the seemingly innate ability to draw key people to his side and meld them into a team, largely redefining the art (yes, art) of cost-effective, desirably styled, product development projects that made it to market as highly successfully launched products numerous times! He and his team brought us the C-7 Corvette; Cadillac SRX and CTS/V coupe and sedan; Chevrolet Malibu, Buick LaCrosse, Pontiac G-8, to name a few. Prior to GM during his tenure at Chrysler, he worked his magic on the development and launch of the "LH" platformed cars i.e. Dodge Intrepid; Chrysler Concorde and 300 M-lettered models; the Eagle (formerly owned by AMC that was bought from Renault;) and brought Dodge trucks out of mothballs and transformed them into serious competitors of Ford's F-150's; Chevy's Silverados; and GMC's Sierra models. Arguably, his crowning achievement was bringing the Jeep Grand Cherokee to market that, according to Lee Iacocca (not one of Lutz's buddies), was the best known automotive product in the world! Bob Lutz, the product wunderkind, enjoyed similar successes at BMW, where he tactically destroyed the "good old boy" distribution system for U.S.-bound product and envisioned and helped create, perhaps, the best sports sedan ever made, the BMW, 3 Series. Later in his early career, he joined Ford Motor where he brought his considerable talents to bear, resulting in the highly successful design and launch of the Ford Explorer. What a marketing genius Lutz was, who's talents we may never see the likes of again. And as all good things must eventually come to an end, Bob's situation was no exception...he retired. Retired from GM, yes, but hardly retired. He has since founded a communications company, finding the time to write best-selling books when he gets a little bored, does consulting, sits on several boards, has launched a line of luxury watches, and, in concert with Henrik Fisker, is relaunching what hitherto was known as the Karma, a four-door luxury, sports sedan that was battery-powered, to give Tesla a little run for their money. This project has since been renamed the "Destino", with the powertrain converted from electric to gasoline, now powered by a Corvette engine, finely tuned to the performance spec's that were formulated to make this car a "rocket in car's clothing" (my wording, maybe I should rush out there and copyright it before Lutz gets ahold if it).

As a reader, I hope my chronicle that follows on Bob Lutz is living proof that it is NEVER too late to work on becoming the person you want to be. Heck, he didn't even finish high school until he was 22 years old; but, don't let that fool you. He earned a bachelor's and master's degree; was selected to receive an honorary doctor's degree, all from Cal, Berkeley, earned a commission and became a pilot in the Marine Corps; owns and flies his own jet today at age 85, and recently remarried, and is a serious collector of wristwatches, motorcycles (you can go to the bank that one or more of them are BMWs), and a corral of sensibly-priced vintage automobiles, whose names I can't recall but one of them is a very famous French make that belonged at one time to his Swiss-born father. Oh, I nearly forgot...Bob speaks French, German, Italian, and if the occasion calls for it, English.

Cars & People; Up & Comers

Beyond the "movers and shakers" and "losers", there is a whole host of seriously talented executives on their way to the top, if not there already. One such person is Mary Barra, GM's Chief Executive Officer and recently named Chairman (I don't care for this politically correct stuff – I'll stick with Chairman). In her mid-fifties, she has spent 30 plus years at GM in a variety of management roles, one of which was heading up Human Resources. She holds an Electrical Engineering degree from Kettering (formerly General Motors Institute) and an MBA from Stanford.

And there is Reid Biglund, who wears three (count 'em) different hats at FCA (Fiat Chrysler Automobiles) where he heads up Alfa Romeo and Maserati; as CEO of FCA, Canada, and heads up sales of all Chrysler products sold in the U.S. He is enjoying huge amounts of success for the record-breaking sales of the Jeep and Ram makes, which is the new heart of Chrysler's product line.

Another exec who easily stands out is Joe Hinrichs as Ford's President of the Americas, and a corporate Executive Vice President of FoMoCo. As head of Ford/Americas, Ford's most profitable region, this profit-producing dynamo helped Ford to earn $45 billion in pretax profits...all this since 2011. According to Automotive News (4/16), while Ford lost $1.8 billion for the rest of the world, Joe achieved an unprecedented operating margin of 12.9%, this in the First Quarter, 2016. In time, I look for Joe to replace Mark Fields as CEO. Joe knows what is in his toolbox and he isn't afraid to use them, one tool at a time!

GM has a rising star in the person of Mike Simcoe, recently appointed as only the seventh design chief in General Motors history. Two of their former design chiefs, Harley Earl and Bill Mitchell, were widely acclaimed in this industry and, also, to its impassioned historians, a field I lay some claim to (more as a student than as a bona fide historian). Australian-born, Simcoe is an engineer by training, which puts him in rarefied company at this automotive behemoth.

Over at BMW, a 49 year old, former design chief, Harald Kruger, having joined the company 9 years ago, is running the show as CEO and holds a degree in Engineering. His first executive position was heading up Human Resources. What a gargantuan leap he has made in a very short period of time. Have you noticed how he shares a similar career path as Mary Barra, CEO/Chairman of GM?

On the engineering front, GM has a winner in Pamela Fletcher, who is the executive chief engineer for EV's. She is a driving force behind the development of the Chevrolet Bolt, recently selected as 2017's "Car Of The Year" by Motor Trend Magazine (01/2017), beating Tesla to market with their new Model 3, no small achievement.

Mercedes-Benz is blessed to have the considerable design talents of Gorden Wagener, Chief Design Officer, creating a renaissance of sorts in re-emphasizing the importance of design that shows up in several new models...the S, E, and GLC classes and the sub-brand EQ that will debut in 2020.

Thomas Doll, CEO of Subaru, can rightly be regarded as an "up and comer," growing sales at twice the industry's rate, building cars that are not just safe for the college professor-types and snow-belters, but reliable, stylish, capable of being self-driven, thus, making their owners look brainy for having bought these high quality vehicles in the first place.

And, then, there's Johan de Nyschen, President of Cadillac, who is re-inventing the brand for both styling and performance with the goal of displacing Audi and Acura, his nearest competition. He has been hugely successful in a past life as head of Audi and Infiniti. That skillset should transfer seamlessly into Cadillac, working to re-establish the Cadillac brand as the "Standard of the World." Good luck with that!!

Cars & People; On Their Way Down ?

On the top of my list would be Joel Ewanik, the one-time Chief Marketing Officer of GM, who, as it turns out, was unceremoniously fired by entering into a contractual agreement with a European soccer team in a seven-year commitment, amounting to $600 million for, now get this...an attempt to gain Chevrolet increased brand exposure with soccer fans in Europe. The only thing he got exposed to was a view of the other side of the door, the one he saw as he left his office for the last time! To say that Ewanik was a "job-hopper" is an understatement of gigantic proportions, and would easily get my vote for the number of jobs held in the shortest period of time. Beat this if you can. Prior to General Motors, Ewanik had brief layovers at Porsche; Hyundai; Nissan; Fisker; True Car; Global Auto Systems, and, presently, heads up First Element, a California-based company involved with promoting hydrogen as an viable alternate power source for EV's. The prospects of that happening are akin to Indiana University beating Kentucky in basketball, 109 to 54, in Lexington! BTW, most of those jobs were for the top marketing position for each of those companies and, all were held in less than twelve years!

John Krafcik, also, an alumnus of Hyundai and True Car, is now all settled in as head of Google's autonomously-driven vehicle program. Krafcik is another Stanford grad who has done well as a marketing innovator but now finds himself in the role of replacing key people who have "jumped ship" at Alpabet (parent company to Google); trying to find a partner in Detroit (or elsewhere) to shoulder the development costs of getting Google's AD product to market; and deciding whether that product will be a car itself or as a supplier to makers of autonomously-driven vehicles. If those weren't challenges enough, there's fellow Silicon Valley aspirant, Apple, owners of all the cash in the world, feverishly working to beat Google to market with their internally-developed version of an AD car. It appears that Silicon Valley is on to something not commonly known...Even Intel is getting in on the action as they just announced the forming of an automotive group.

LOSERS

JOHN ZACKERY DELOREAN

Allow me to begin with a brief overview of this fascinating character as I boldly work to describe my selection of Delorean as the all-time #1 a##hole in modern day automotive history, having solidly established himself as a the loser, numero uno. I don't believe it would be an overstatement to call him a "scoundrel extraordinaire," richly earning this disreputable distinction. Even the spelling of his surname was a fabrication from Delorean to DeLorean. I wonder how his brothers felt about that?

Not only was he a despicable character, he pi##ed away any possibility of going down in automotive history that would recognize his exceptional engineering prowess. Personally, I am disappointed that his considerable talents didn't find a way to serve others in some praiseworthy endeavors, leaving a legacy that rightly reflected his questionable status, as some regarded him a genius. A genius of what...a master manipulator? Delorean habitually and avariciously attacked anyone whom he perceived as adversarial, that would get in his way of accumulating fame, wealth, and power. If one found themselves in Delorean's crosshairs, knowingly or not, their future had no future!

Delorean raised $200 million to build a state-of-the-art automobile manufacturing factory in Northern Ireland, funds provided courtesy of Margaret Thatcher's British government, in an attempt to create lasting jobs and plenty of them. It's a shame things worked out the way they did, as many an Irish dream went the way of a toilet flush, to say nothing about the UK's inability to recover funds lent to Delorean. It was widely speculated that some of the funds found their way into John's pocket in support of his lavish lifestyle. No amount of accounting could ever confirm the exact amount of this monumental embezzlement or fraud. Whatever it was, he pulled it off, pure and simple.

I have carefully placed my use of the word "sh##" into a contextual setting, intending to make a point of Delorean's lack of integrity. Pick any one of the ignoble descriptions below; in fact, pick them all if you like-they all richly apply to John Delorean!

John was reported to be all of the following:
* One of Detroit's biggest losers in its 100 year history, both as a businessman and as a person
* Delorean defined the meaning of a scoundrel
* A master manipulator without peer
* Slippery when truth was of paramount importance
* Deceitful and misleading in words and actions
* An overgrown ego that held no bounds
* Knew how to use other people's money (OPM), taking it to an elevated art form

Did I miss anything? I apologize if I did. To be sure, JZD knew how to use other people's money which passed for pre-sumed wealth in the eyes of others. What it did achieve was the appearance of a significant amount of wealth, when in reality, he was so highly leveraged financially to the point that it nearly landed him in prison. Accused in his role of master-minding a $24 million sale of cocaine into the U.S., he was later acquitted on the grounds of entrapment. This acquittal came in no small thanks to his crack, heavy-hitting legal team, the same one that successfully defended O. J. Simpson.

Please keep in mind that it is not my intent to judge this man. I am merely reporting what has already been chronicled, although admittedly, I am relishing my role in bringing this into an unvarnished, corrected light, in support of what has already been written about this deceitful man. Sorry, I left "pretentious" off of my earlier referenced list. What a grievous oversight on my part-my apologies. Rather, they are observations made by a close associate and officer in Delorean Motors Corporation and a couple of well-respected financial journalists who knew the intricate political maneuverings of the British government. William Haddad, former V.P., Planning and Communications of DMC has written a book, entitled "Hard Driving...My Years With John Delorean" which is an excellent depiction of the character, or lack thereof, of JZD. This book necessitated reading another book on his life, entitled "Dream Maker –The Rise and Fall of John Z. Delorean," penned by Ivan Fallon and James Srodes, noted financial journalists with assignments to cover Delorean's financing agreement with Margaret Thatcher's government. No small potatoes in this scenario! Again, any and all character-altering impressions or printed words were originated by others.

I am merely your personal carrier pigeon in zealous pursuit of exposing this man for what he was.

Another revealing, negative trait surfaced when John would tell members of his staff that someone needed to metaphorically "put some sh##" on some particular person's shoes, indicating how he intended to smear or demean an individual who was viewed as adversarial; thus, setting that person up for a "hit" that would pay Delorean dividends down the road. Haddad even devoted a chapter in his book, "Getting A Little Sh## On His Shoes" to Delorean's antics, an interesting read! John, without fail, enjoyed a vast repertoire of bullsh## that he called upon in times of need. No one, I mean, no one ever accused Delorean of being overly veracious. Far from it, as the truth never seemed to fit the script.

My character study of John Delorean all started by reading Patrick Wright's book, "On A Clear Day You Can See General Motors." Wright, being a highly regarded financial journalist, learned the car business inside and out as a Detroit-based writer, with writing assignments exclusive to the auto industry. After Wright finished writing the book, Delorean was reported as wanting his contractual agreement with Wright nullified, for fear of reprisal from GM, where Delorean enjoyed enormous success in his roles of General Manager of Pontiac and Chevrolet. He was credited with creating the GTO, Grand Prix, and Monte Carlo, Chevrolet's answer for an more affordable personal luxury car. He did, however, successfully do battle with Ford's Torino Elite and the re-positioned Ford Thunderbird. Clearly, this man was on a roll. Some people in the know began speculating that this young (at the time) turk was pre-destined to become head of GM in no time. Well, things didn't quite work out that way. For reasons only John knew, he resigned to have more time to work on some of his personal interests, many of which were located in California. Out West was where he enjoyed the glitzy fanfare that Hollywood had to offer, with a major emphasis on escorting younger ladies around town. He took time out of his busy schedule to get a divorce, eventually, marrying a young Hollywood starlet, Kelly Harmon (sister to Mark Harmon of t.v.'s NCIS). At the same time he began aggressively putting together plans to build an American sports car that would give Corvette a run for its money. By now, it was becoming obvious that John had lost his way by the likes of the company he was keeping which brings to mind a few choice words he never heard, "If you step into a pig's pen, you're sure to get some pigsh## on your shoes and the answer is not to take your shoes off!"

Patrick Wright would not let Delorean out of their agreement to write and publish this book about John and his life at General Motors, fearing GM might come down on him with both feet and kill any hopes of obtaining any future financial support for the dream car he was planning. After all, covering his a## might be a prudent plan if his ambitions didn't take hold and he found himself looking for a job. If you've read Wright's book, you know it is just chuck full of derogatory narrative about senior people and policy at GM. Little wonder Delorean was a bit frightful about possible repercussions coming his way, courtesy of his old employer! Too bad Delorean was no Bob Lutz, who would have the skills to pull this off, pi##ing a few people off, maybe, but survivable and gaining respect for telling it as it is/was. But unlike Lutz, this was not Delorean's skillset.

Wright was so confident of the book's impending success that he went out and mortgaged his house to raise the necessary funds to get it published. Meanwhile, Delorean was trying to distance himself from Wright with threats of suing and whatever it would take to keep that book from getting published. The good news is, there was no stopping Wright and that book went on to achieve meteoric success with multiple printings in several languages, two of which I have some familiarity with, Japanese and Spanish. Another glimpse into JZD's character would have shown his callous disregard for the contributions of others for his own fleeting success in how he refused to pay Wright the $35,000 fee for writing the book! As things turned out, this non-payment was of little or no consequence other than revealing just how shallow Delorean's integrity was and would continue to be. Justice was served, thank God, as that book went golden, earning Patrick Wright beaucoup bucks, richly deserved!!

Just for kicks and giggles, I have an idea for another book that Patrick Wright could pen, the vulgaries and hypocrisies of being employed by GM (the GM at that point in time, since massively changed), entitled "On An Unclear Day, You Can't See

Sh## at General Motors" and while at it, sprinkle in a chapter or two on Delorean's supposed moral uprightness and who was it, really, that stole his moral compass if, in fact, he ever had one?

Delorean's "dream" car can best be described as a pregnant Camaro...at best! It did, however, turn a few heads in Hollywood with some unique features that would appeal to a certain market segment but, at the end of the day, one was left to conclude this car just didn't have it and would never be any more than a modest competitor to a Corvette, a car that sold in the thousands annually. This dog, known as the "DMC-12", with its gullwing doors (similar to the 1954 Mercedes SL roadster), in its stainless-steeled body, did enjoy some fleeting fanfare when it was featured in the movie, "Back To The Future," starring Michael J. Fox. All of the supposed fanfare, while achieving some free publicity and exposure, thanks, in part, to the movie, helped Delorean find financial sources for obtaining the necessary funds to get this car project off of paper and onto the road. With Delorean hob-nobbing with the Hollywood set, he persuaded Johnny Carson to invest a reported $500,000 followed by a sizable amount of money coming from Sammy Davis Jr., that eventually lead to JZD's $200 million loan from the British government.

Unfortunately, that marks the end of my superlatives for John's sales and sourcing abilities because the limited number of DMC-12's manufactured, primarily, for the U.S. marketplace, were shodily built and, when I write "shodily built," I am being generously kind. Some would suggest the car wasn't even a complete portion of cr##...end of sentence. Just to name a few issues and defects, how about broken suspensions (from date of manufacture); missing mechanical components; door misalignments; some power components that did not function... you name it. Plus, Delorean was having great difficulty taking delivery on several key components, none the least of these, were engines supplied by Volvo in Sweden. All of this added up to cost overruns and disappointing, slower than projected, sales. This car, like the man behind it, was doomed but Delorean did not know it, expecting to recover from this temporary setback that turned out to become permanent. To help remove the sting of this mammoth failure, its been speculated that John had the short-lived comfort of having salted away a significant portion of the $200 million he borrowed for his own personal, financial enrichment.

JZD monstrously befits the word "ignominious." Trust me on that one as I carefully chose that adjective among many and ignominious won out, hands down. Even that word doesn't do justice to describe the depths of disgust and shame that so characterized this man's life. In all fairness (although undeserving), this has not been an intended character assassination as much as it might appear to be so. But the sad fact remains, JZD did not measure up to his considerable ambitions and potential for success as he self-destructed along life's way, ignoring the Bible's oft repeated message.....live for yourself, lose your soul... and all things in between. Undeniably, Delorean died a bitterly, disappointed, broken man, forced to live off of a monthly Social Security check and an ever so occasional consulting fee that a friend or former associate might send his way. Death found him at age 82 with burial in a public cemetery in Troy, Michigan, decked out in a pair of blue jeans and a half-waisted, Harley-Davidson leather jacket...a tragic end to a talented man.

Well, John's story doesn't quite end there. I trust what I am about to share is as believable as I want it to be. It was reported that John Zackery Delorean died a "born-again" Christian.

JACQUES ALBERT NASSER

Jac "The Knife" Nasser - Lebanese born, held dual citizenship in Australia and the U.S., spent 33 years at Ford Motor Company, the last 3 (1999-2002) as President, CEO, and Chairman. This Aussie- Yankee came by his nickname by way of being a ruthless cost-cutter. As such, that necessarily includes his own professional version of the 4 P's – people, product quality, programs, and, profits. According to The Economist Magazine (6/2010), Ford lost $1.4 billion in the last six months of his tenure before getting fired by "The Deuce" (Henry Ford II) with the full backing of the board of which Nasser chaired.

On the subject of "firing," I see a definite trend in play here that would strongly suggest that working at Ford under the dominion of "The Duece", could be hazardous to one's economic health. The names Bunkie Knudsen, Lee Iacocca, Hal Sperlich, and Jacques Nasser, readily come to mind. I'm sure there were others.

This "bean-counter" acquired his nickname making liberal use of a tidy, little lethal weapon of his choosing...a metaphorical knife. It allowed him to cut through whatever got in the way of his operating objectives, which, mainly, was changing the focus of Ford from an auto maker into a consumer goods company, specializing in automotive products and services, not cars, per se. It was reported that "The Knife" fancied himself as a modern-day Jack Welsh, former CEO of General Electric where product and service diversification was the order of his regime. In Ford Motor Company's case, "The Knife" conceived, launched, or acquired a bundle of unrelated products and services totally alien to a car manufacturer; i.e. purchase of junkyards, a car dealer certification program that didn't set well with their dealership network, and a national car rental company to name a few. Another report I read in Automotive News (5/2000) had Jac infatuated with e-Commerce and other Internet-based businesses. Junkyards, e-Commerce...you've got to be kidding me! Yes sir/madam, that's the vision he had for Ford, entirely at the expense of its core business, producing automobiles at a profit. And on the topic of profits, it's interesting to note that Ford was turning in record profits when Jac was named CEO, only to deteriorate dramatically like a high-speed bullet train without a conductor!

His supposed business genius didn't just stop there. Jac was not about to abandon auto manufacturing, although it would no longer be Ford's core business. He envisioned Ford as the world's largest manufacturer of luxury, boutique automobiles. Up to this point, Ford Motor Company's lone luxury car, hardly a boutique auto, was (and continues to be) Lincoln. To his view, that would never do, especially, when there were a number of European auto makers struggling to stay in business, companies that he attempted to buy at fire-sale prices. In a year's time, he formed the Premier Group, charged with overseeing the manufacture and sale of Ford's newly acquired collection of luxury, boutique brands e.g. Jaguar, Land Rover, Aston-Martin as well as the purchase of Volvo, all stagnated by huge operating losses. But, he did correctly determine their collective need for fresh styling and the capital it would require. However, he incorrectly projected these makes as a major source of future profits. He probably got the capital issue right but he totally erred on the side of acquiring so many new brands in such a short period of time and with the prices Ford paid, it would take years to recover their investment (if ever), much less make a profit. On Nasser's watch, for instance, Ford bought Volvo in 1999 (Jac's first year as CEO) for $6.5 billion only to sell it to the Chinese in 2010 for $1.8 billion!!

Although it didn't make the news, Ford tried unsuccessfully to buy Alfa-Romeo and Saab. Saab was eventually sold to GM but, as a result of their bankruptcy filing, they were forced to sell. Like Volvo, Saab found itself owned by, yet, another Chinese company.

Another program "The Knife" put in place was a performance rating evaluation system that management personnel had to submit to, a method of weeding out senior personnel who were replaceable with younger managers with lower incomes. This was taken right out of GE's playbook. This evaluation procedure was eliminated, rather quickly, due to lawsuits brought on by discharged employees who filed age discrimination complaints against the company. Way to go Jac! Where was your legal council through all of that?

So, here we have a company losing money, getting into businesses they knew little of, measuring performance levels that only succeed in pi##-ing off valued employees who are now motivated to sue the company. For all of his cost-cutting endeavors, he turns around and gives much of it away by paying what turns out to be a premium price for luxury brands that doesn't fit their business model. Go figure! In short order, The Premier Group was viewed to be about as worthless as a degree from Trump University; so, upon Nasser's dismissal (officially reported as an retirement), Ford sold off each of these luxury brands, all of which are doing well today, especially, Jaguar, Land Rover, and Volvo.

For reasons of Jac's colossal mismanagement of Ford's considerable assets, the cash dividend had to be cut in half in order to conserve cash. That didn't earn him any points with the

Ford family who control 40% of the voting shares, thus, creating a serious loss of immediate income. The reduced dividend didn't escape the attention of Wall Street, either, where shares of FoMoCo stock plummeted from $31 to $17 per share.

In a nutshell, it would take Ford 10 years to undo the damages "The Knife" inflicted on this storied, American car company. According to Fortune Magazine (4/2013), Jacques Nasser will go down in history as one of the 10 worst auto CEO's of all time!

ROGER BONHAM SMITH

If anyone ever personified the word "incompetence" while, at the same time, adding a whole new dimension of meaning to the management theory, "The Peter Principle," it would be Roger Smith while serving General Motors as CEO and Chairman between the years of 1981 and 1990. His track record (or lack thereof) gives this assertion an indisputable validity at an executive management level never experienced before or since. Lightly regarded, television network CNBC (2/1991) labeled Smith as one of the "worst CEO's of all time." If that is factual, how did this squeaky-voiced, hard-charging, conservative, bureaucratic bean-counter ever get to be CEO and Chairman, of the once largest manufacturing company in the world?

During Smith's 9 year tenure as CEO, GM's market share dropped like a brick from 46% to 35%! On his watch, he is credited with wasting $5 billion on the development and launch of a miserable "wannabe" competitor to Toyota...the Saturn. In the nearly 20 year history that followed, Saturn never as much as generated that first dime of profit for GM. In 2008 when GM went into bankruptcy, they were forced to sell off several car divisions out of economic necessity. Sadly, there was little or no interest shown by any of Saturn's competitors in possibly buying this terminally sick, under-appreciated piece of cr##. Even the Chinese took a pass; they weren't stupid. As a result, GM closed down this division after all the billions invested in that brand. In due course, Pontiac, Saab, and Hummer suffered the same fate.

And, who can forget the disastrous outcome of GM's redesign of the highly successful Monte Carlo, Pontiac Grand Prix,

Oldsmobile Cutlass Supreme, and Buick Regal, the so-called GM-10 internally designated models? This, apparently, was a redesign that represented their best response to government-mandated regulations (CAFE), covering fuel consumption rates – a redesign that just tore the heart out of these much beloved, beautiful automobiles. This little foray cost GM a mere $7 billion.

In my view, GM, even to this day, is feverishly working to recover much of the lost ground that came by way of Mr. Smith's occupying that corner office...some 30 years after the fact. His damage was so complete as to set the stage for the inevitable bankruptcy filing that followed, ever so conveniently, allowing him to blame others for setting into motion this cataclysmic eventuality...years in the making.

FERDINAND PIECH

Mr. Piech is the renowned, former Chairman of Volkswagen's Supervisory Board (comparable to a U.S. company's Chairman of the Board). He was not only renowned for his accomplishments but equally accomplished in his notorious dealings with people. Put it this way, he could never be accused of being a "people" person, especially, when there were automobiles around. Piech's career left a sea of cadavers in its wake. As such, "ruthless" probably isn't too strong a word to describe this very talented engineer who rose to the top of VW for a season.

Piech is largely credited with putting Audi on the map and assembling a group or brand of automobiles through acquisition that became market leaders that, in addition to Audi, included Porsche, Bugatti, Seat, Skoda, Bentley, Lamborghini, and, of course, Volkswagen. This successful endeavor allowed VW to grow to become the world's largest car manufacturer. But this success came at a huge price in the form of destroying the careers of several, established beyond doubt, executives or anyone who would care or dare to disagree or confront his decision making capabilities (largely done behind his back). It seemed he dismissed key managers (becoming ex-managers overnight) at the drop of a hat. Just ask former Porsche CEO Wendelin Wiedeking, and Piech's hand-picked CEO to run VW, Bernd Pischetsrieder.

For all of that success, he failed miserably in building market share for VW's in the U.S., the world's second largest new car market. Nothing seemed to gain traction for all of his planning and personnel changing with a historical market share hovering around 2%.

Ferdinand, no doubt, suffered greatly from the terminal disease known as "a##holitis. See the Glossary for a description of this dreaded disease for which there is no known cure.

JOSE IGNACIO LOPEZ

Here's another despicable character that you might enjoy reading about as he is unique to automotive history and, in particular, General Motors.

John "Jack" Smith, residing President and COO of GM/Europe took Jose Lopez under his wings as his imprimatur, the one person whom he could truly trust to make a difference for GM in his role as purchasing chief of GM's European operations. Jose made a not-to-be-believed contribution to profits by saving the company billions in purchasing costs, while paralleling his efforts at streamlining production. In doing so, he acquired the moniker, "Grand Inquisitor." While Smith and Lopez were working at GM's European headquarters together in late 1991, Jack became CEO of General Motors, which necessitated a geographic move to Detroit, and he convinced Jose to make the move as well with an accompanying promotion. Jose, in his new role as worldwide head of procurement, picked up where he left off in Europe, by saving the corporation untold billions in purchasing costs, something you wouldn't find examples of in a Harvard MBA case study. I mean, this guy did everything but walk on water...in a class all his own. Interestingly enough, his employment at GM in Detroit lasted all of one year. Detroit can do that to you!

Which begs the question, how did he accomplish such a monumental feat in such a short period of time? The cost savings he was achieving came, largely, out of the hides of some key vendors, where he gave them ultimatums about reducing prices or losing their business with GM. We are not talking about a percent or two, here and there...he was forcing re-negotiation of existing contracts (Trumpian-style) in terms of "take it" or "leave it." Many chose to keep supplying GM, even if it was only marginally profitable. So, he repeated this purchasing tactic countless times, all the while building his stature within the company. How he could continue to pull this off without the aggrieved suppliers openly, though verboten, complaining to his boss, Jack, or its Board is a mystery to me as an armchair car historian. Perhaps management went along in support of Jose because it was all about MONEY; for every dollar he saved the company, it flowed directly to the "bottom line" as one more dollar of pre-tax profit! Another possible alternative was being quietly speculated upon. In addition to severe cost-cutting, Jose just might have been getting his pockets lined a bit. If true, he more than likely was working both sides of the street, simultaneously. Corrupt? Yes. A dummy? No. Keep reading.

If you haven't guessed it by now, ole Jose was in the throes of orchestrating his master plan to a "T," wherein he would be viewed as indispensable and positioned to ask for and receive certain concessions in achieving his personal goals, one of which was to persuade GM's board to build a manufacturing plant in the Basque region of Spain, Jose's home turf. Well that never happened, although Jose insisted he was promised that it would. When it didn't, he promptly announced that GM had betrayed him and it was time to move on. He tendered his resignation just to have it not accepted by Jack and the boys. GM, desperate to keep this man on the payroll, offered him a $1.6 million salary + bonus, in a futile attempt to dissuade him from leaving. After a supposed brief period of time (a day or two) of gut-wrenching indecision, he then decides not to leave GM after all, accepting the money. And oh, I nearly forgot, he would, also, be named President, North American Operations, in effect, the #1 operating manager in the most profitable region in the company. So Jack Smith, essentially, hands Jose the keys to the front door, while announcing to the press Jose's newly elevated role, only to have Jose change his mind and announce his "re-resignation." With that portion of his master plan completed, Jose bolts, totally unexpectedly, for Volkswagen, taking with him two million pages of top-secret documents that contained GM's product and production operating plans, including ten year product plans for German-built Opels, a clear case of industrial espionage and thievery, heretofore, never imagined in the annals of automo-

tive history! This act marks the beginning and makes it official...
Mr. Lopez is corrupt!! And with that affirmation concluded,
Jose has firmly established his character, or lack thereof. As
someone once said, " if it walks like a duck, quacks like a duck,
cr##s on golf courses like a duck, by golly, I think we have got
ourselves a duck!" He is as he appears to be...a crook!

Now Jose finds himself in the employ of VW, fully ensnarled
in a viper's den that is controlled by Ferdinand "take no prison-
ers" Piech, himself, no stranger to discord or ruthlessness. How
and why did this happen? It turns out that VW was suffering
from the same woes as GM in terms of overpriced, badly built
product and the word on the street was that Senior Lopez could
tidy up those two little problems with bravado and dispatch.
Piech needed both and was willing to pay for those two million
pages of stolen documents by offering Jose compensation just
south of $2 million annually in exchange for those 70 boxes con-
taining GM's top secret product plans, competitive intelligence,
and Jose's ongoing cost-cutting expertise.

As you might imagine, GM didn't take too kindly to Jose's
dastardly act and sued VW to get those 70 boxes returned. Piech
said "No way, I'm sticking with Jose." Some sparring took place
for a time, then finally, VW recanted to GM's threats to take this
case of thievery and industrial espionage to a courtroom, settling
out of court for a the tidy little sum of $100 million along with
being contractually forced into buying $1 billion of automobile
components from GM over a seven year time frame. What a
small price to pay when you consider the economic impact on
lost careers, sales, profits, and never-to-be-recovered competi-
tion-based intelligence, and vendor relationships that took years
to build.

The damage was done and it was high time to move on.
And so, Jose did, which GM had insisted upon as a condition
in resolving their legal dispute with VW. During his brief time
at VW, Jose and three other associates were indicted for em-
bezzlement and theft of documents considered top secret. The
Germans, with more than a little "egg on their faces" decided to
join the fray and leveled their own legal response to Mr. Lopez's
misdeeds. Eventually, all charges against Lopez were dropped
in exchange for a $320,000 fine, made payable to local charities.

But, as so often, the case with biggie bucks on the line, Senior Lopez remains a free man where he is a living testament to the expected revelation... it's all about money. And, from what I read, no one has heard from this villain in professional circles for years (another Bob Eaton impersonator). But if you should bump into a panhandler who speaks with a decided Spanish accent, with a sign hanging from his neck that reads, "GM Sucks," begging for dollars (yours), ignore him and go on. This man is a conniving scoundrel who would kidnap his own mother-in-law and is about as believable as an IRS agent who says he wants to be your friend!

ROBERT JAMES EATON

You talk about lucky? More on that shortly. For the moment, keep reading.

Bob Eaton was CEO of Chrysler for a relatively short time, hired by Lee Iacocca as his hand-picked successor. While retired in Bel Air, California, Iacocca said he truly regretted hiring this man who would later sell out Chrysler to the Germans, i.e. Daimler-Benz, in an acquisition both sides claimed to be a merger "of equals". In truth, it was anything but. Daimler bought Chrysler on the cheap for $38 billion, at a time when Chrysler was on top of its game plan...making money, not something it was accustomed to doing for any extended period of time.

It's ironic that Iacocca chose Eaton over Bob Lutz, Chrysler's #2 go-to guy (President and COO), to become CEO (over Lutz,) thanks to unsettled disputes that managed to wedge themselves into their relationship. Reportedly, they clashed with regularity. This disagreement disappeared when Iacocca selected Eaton over of Lutz. Despite this setback for Lutz, he strongly supported Eaton as CEO in his well-established role as President/COO. The only thing that they had in common was their first names. That's where any possible comparison ends. Actually, Lutz's stature must have improved immensely with Iacocca as he was quoted as saying, "Lutz could chew up Eaton and spit him out." Not a bad accolade coming from a former boss, especially, coming from Lee Iacocca, whose ego was larger than life which he was accustomed to exercising often!

Sometime after Iacoca's remark that he truly regretted hiring Eaton, he went on to say that placing Eaton at the helm was "the biggest mistake of my life." Apparently, bigger than his short-lived marriage to an airline flight attendant. At least, he got the chance to meet her while flying first class, something Bob Darnelli (Chrysler's CEO when bankruptcy was declared) and General Motors CEO Rick Wagoner couldn't lay claim to. They were too busy luxuriating in their corporate jets, foolishly appearing self-important as they flew into Washington looking for a federal government handout. All they accomplished with this little faux pas was raising the ire of the American public. Well, the press was all over that in a New York minute, making sure GM and Chrysler richly got their "come uppin's." Got to sell more newspapers, right?

The criticism and damage to Eaton's legacy was the widely-held view that he sold Chrysler for $38 billion, not exactly chump change, but a diminutive figure nonetheless. He turned over those proverbial keys to the front door with nothing more than his board's support and Daimler's offer in hand, which included rich rewards for him if he were to go along with the merger being proposed. He did, of course, resulting in a payday that would be counted in the tens of millions of dollars, some speculate north of $30 million, in stocks and options; thus, guaranteeing Eaton's happy compliance with the deal. Upon leaving the keys to the door behind, Eaton left the building, not to be seen, hide nor hair, in any of the usual haunts frequented by auto exec retirees; apparently thoroughly enjoying his reclusive lifestyle in Florida. Could you become reclusive in exchange for 30 big ones?

The mere mention of Eaton's name was enough to set off a sh##storm with many institutional investors, people in the "know" and, no doubt, those employees who had sacrificed themselves to work their way through past disasters that nearly put them out of business. All this compounded by a man perceived to be a lightweight without the tenure of an employee, much less that as a CEO to justify such a huge payday. $38 billion for this much venerated American stalwart of a company truly made many trips to hell and lived to see another day. And, when that "another day" came, they were again viable and making money for their investors, stockholders, and employees...a company with a continuing history of "boom or bust."

84

Frankly, Chrysler has had more lives than an alley cat. Somehow, someway, Chrysler has managed to not only survive, but thrive in their much-colored past. Iacocca, while CEO, rescued them when they were nearly broke; but, thanks to a gargantuan effort to save this venerable company, Iacocca and his management team successfully persuaded the U.S. government to lend Chrysler beaucoup bucks and pronounced them to be worthy of a bailout. That bailout amounted to a loan in the billions...billions rapidly repaid, way ahead of schedule...no small feat!

So, Iacocca handed over the keys to a company that had survived hell, only to have Eaton help orchestrate its near death as an American automobile manufacturer by selling it to the Germans!

Fortunately, Chrysler survived the near carnage that resulted from this change of ownership but continued to weaken in its slide from America's #3 car producer, allowing Toyota to displace them.

Suffice it to say, Bob Eaton was considered by some to be "MIA" while getting his "On-The-Job Training" as CEO, no conceivable comparison to Bob Lutz....none! Eaton was to "dufus" what Lutz is to "genius"...end of sentence. But he did uncover a recipe for his personal aggrandizement – jump ship, find another ship, then sell that ship!

One final note that I find interesting is Chrysler's resiliency to changes in ownership. Even after the Eaton/Daimler debacle, Chrysler has survived, yet, another two owners, Cerberus, who knew nothing about the automobile business and its present-day owner, FCA (Fiat Chrysler Automobiles). Is there anymore juice left in that lemon? Speculation has it that China has been buying up unsqueezed lemons of late...on the cheap!

Who benefited from this so-called merger "of equals?" Three little words says it all...Robert James Eaton.

ROBERT LOUIS NARDELLI

More than likely, you haven't heard of this man, right? That's because he is/was a born loser and losers aren't, particularly, memorable. Well, countless automotive workers aren't about to forget how this man, single handedly, nearly destroyed Chrysler (2007-2009) through senseless policy changes and dictatorial practices, that he couldn't back up with performance, leaving the impression that he cared less and knew little about Chrysler and knew, even less, about how to manage an executive staff. This man had a history as a loser long before he landed at Chrysler. He was forced out of General Electric as the 4th highest ranking executive, where during his 29 years of employment, he became known as "Little Jack" for his tenacious loyalty to Jack Welsh, who, ironically, forced Nardelli into looking for another job. So much for loyalty! Then, he lands at Home Depot in Atlanta, a place where he had no retail work experience and, somehow, a bit later down the road, he gets himself dismissed, yet, again, leaving the building with a severance package reported to be $210 million! How's that for being repugnantly obscene? Somehow, as if by magic he gets himself hired by Cerberus Capital, known to be corporate turnaround specialists, recommending to their Board they acquire Chrysler, where the smell of death was in the air, compatible with his vulture-like character. No doubt, Nardelli was thinking he could buy this struggling company for a song and get himself positioned as their new leader, who would bring them back from the fringes of extinction. That was about as likely to happen as pleasuring a bull in search of milk! Why Cerberus' owners hired and installed Nardelli as CEO and Chairman of Chrysler was viewed to be beyond the comprehension level of Detroit's keenest observers.

During Nardelli's short two year tenure, he not only failed to turn Chrysler around, he turned them upside down, diving rapidly into a cash-burning furnace that, once again, found the company at the watering trough of the U. S. government. Who will ever forget Nardelli's infamous trip into Washington, D.C., via a Chrysler corporate jet (same scenario as GM's Rick Wagoner, begging for a government-supported bailout.) The story came out later that the fed's were prepared to endorse a $750 million bailout to help keep Chrysler alive, but as a condition for getting this loan or guarantee of a loan, Chrysler was required to cap the compensation of its executives. Nardelli, in his typical rapacious self, turned down this offer because it would have meant taking a huge hit to his own income. So, what did he do to get access to $750 million? He entered into some expensive loan agreements with private banks so as to avoid having his own compensation capped. Aren't you just enamored with this spineless shill that Cerberus planted inside Chrysler Corporation, all in an attempt to make a quick buck and the presumed glory that would follow, for once again saving Chrysler?

To sum up this man's legacy, he was a clueless, self-serving, corporate klutz, whose only interests were his own, leaving it to others to jettison the train wreck he left behind. Conde Nast Portfolio (12/2007) named Nardelli as one of the "worst American CEO's of all time."

G. RICHARD WAGONER

Let me start by way of writing that Rick, his popular name within his inner circle, served as CEO of General Motors from 2000 to 2009 and was yet another example of a less than stellar career as a bean-counter. That begs the question, when does this assiduous tradition of selecting financial types ever end? Not quite yet, because Wagoner was relieved as CEO by what you might have guessed, another bean-counter, Fritz Henderson, a 30 year GM veteran who lasted all of 9 months on the job as Chief Executive. For me, it is interesting to note that, out of 14 CEO's in the 100 year history of GM, only 5 were not bean-counters, and interestingly enough, all 5 were college-trained engineers, beginning with Alfred Sloan (1923-1946), one gifted engineer and marketing visionary; Bob Stempel (1990-1992), forced to resign, in part, due to Roger Smith; Ed Whitacre (2009-2010), a production engineer who relieved Fritz Henderson; Dan Ackerson (2010-2014,) a Naval Academy graduate engineer with a Master's in Eonomics; and the current CEO, Many Barra (2014-   ). Apart from Sloan and his 23 years as CEO, the number of years that CEO's with non-finance backgrounds held that job totals 15 out of the 100 year history of the company.

At the core of Rick's demise was his inability to make fuller use of the time needed to get to the essence of a problem/issue identified and get a possible solution initiated. He just wasn't decisive enough when he had no choice but to be so. In a nutshell, he took too much time to work himself through this problem-solving process...taking time that he didn't realize he didn't have! There, seemingly, was no timely closure to major problems, none the least was the amount of cash GM was burning through on a daily basis. This shortage of cash came as part of the perfect storm that was brewing, precisely at the time the market for new cars was turning southbound. On reflection, I think you would have to agree that we all have the same 24 hours in a day for what needs doing; some people are more adept at squeezing more out of their 24 hours than others. In Rick's case, he needed to make every one of those hours count for something corrective if GM were to survive, much less make a profit. Regrettably, he didn't judiciously use the time available to him. So, allow me a bit of pontification by pointing out, whether you are a Rick Wagoner or a panhandler, looking for your next handout, make every day count for something. After all, you are exchanging a day out of your life for it, aren't you?

Some would further suggest (count me in) that Wagoner was a country bumpkin, amazingly naive with a thinly disguised "quiet" arrogance about him, who, nonetheless, projected warmth and sincerity as a "good old boy" persona when charm was required. He was darn likable, no matter the setting. He, more than likely, was all of those things, but one thing was certain and it mattered greatly to him. He was a "devil" (as in Blue Devil,) through and through, loving that alma mater of his where he played collegiate basketball (5 years prior to Coach Krzyzewski's arrival.) I guess he could be forgiven for that, unless, one hails from Chapel Hill, home to the University of North Carolina's Tar Heels. As a side thought not particularly germane, one might think the Tar Heels name would have been a natural for a basketball team located in Los Angeles, as in reference to the La Brea Tar Pits.

Clearly, the Rickster, sans fait accompli and being naive to boot, created a disaster of his own making when he so triumphantly arrived in Washington via corporate jet in search of a cash bailout from Uncle Sam. What's a little fanfare worth? Not much if you consider the aftermath and fallout of that ill-advised, monumental blunder. As I wrote earlier, the press was all over this as if it was Super Bowl Sunday. If you will, think about this – what is the cost of operating one corporate jet in comparison to the countless millions it was going to take to get GM financially healthy again? One caveat remains firmly cemented in reality – perception is everything, all the more so if you don't have all the facts at hand and that's precisely what the

88

public didn't have. Thankfully, Congress wrote the big check anyhow and thank God they did because tens of thousands of jobs were saved and now, 10 years later, GM is turning in record profits with zero debt. Way to go, GM, screw the naysaying public! Reflecting on this positive, factual reality, I don't think things would have turned out the way they did if Mr. Wagoner had remained as CEO.

Did he fail more than once in that 10 year career as Chief Executive? As a church friend of mine from North Dakota is fond of saying, "you betcha," starting with:

- 47,000 employees lost their jobs despite the thousands that were saved
- He was late getting CUV's (crossover utility vehicles) to market
- Cars produced on his watch were booooooring and poorly conceived
- He, like Roger Smith before him, knew precious little about the car business....too busy counting beans
- Bought and sold a sizable portion of Italy's largest auto maker, Fiat, with disastrous results
- Allowed Delphi, wholly owned by GM, to fall into bankruptcy
- GM's much anticipated bankruptcy filing took place on his watch
- He actually beat Roger Smith's record for losing market share, falling under 18%
- Lost billions of operating dollars...too painful to count

Now that I have beaten this guy to a pulp, I think it is only fair to point out some of the successes he brought to his job... unlike Roger Smith, his predecessor, who's only repertoire was losing money and pi##ing people off.

- He hired "Maximum Bob" Lutz, arguably his greatest single act as CEO
- Recognized the strategic importance of the Chinese marketplace, the largest in the world
- Developed a Brazil-based subsidiary that became viable for GM's ongoing role in the South American marketplace, the #8 ranked, largest new car market in the world
- Offered the U.S. buying public 0% financing in the after-

math of 9/11 that might have kept the U.S. from sliding into a recession.

Takeaways? Once again, the phrase, "you betcha" comes to mind.

- His management team allowed Toyota and VW to overtake GM as the world's largest auto maker
- Losses in his last 4 years, alone, topped $18 billion. There were other sizable losses reported during his previous 6 years as CEO
- Got himself fired by the U.S. sitting president
- GM was no better off, but, decidedly worse off upon Wagoner's departure, this coming from one of the "good guys," who couldn't deliver when he had to, as if missing a winning free throw at the buzzer.

But, here comes the real personal bottom line for Richard Wagoner. He walked out the door with a $10 million severance package (peanuts to Bob Nardelli). Now, just maybe the Rickster can afford to go out and buy himself a decent wristwatch that keeps good time, ever reminding him that time waits on no one, even a G. Richard Wagoner, Jr.

BTW, the "G" is for George.

WINNERS

J. PAUL BERGMOSER

J. Paul, an uncle by marriage, was difficult to warm up to as his attitude toward lesser souls (I would be one of those) left little room for cordiality and harmonic co-existence. Since he shared little of his professional life and was a man of few words (unless he wanted something from you). I didn't get to know him to any serious degree. In all fairness, I really don't feel like I knew him. And for that matter, who did? He gave the impression that he was too busy being into himself with little to no room for anybody who wanted admission into his elevated mancave.

For the record, allow me to begin by stating J. Paul Bergmoser was the master of secrecy as evidenced by a career at "Fords" (in the plural as Ford Motor Company is referred to by

90

many of its employees) that spanned nearly forty years beginning in 1946, staged by a Detroit-based employment agency, where he hid the fact that he was not a college graduate. In my estimation, that would not have been a popular thing to do if ever discovered by his peers or superiors going up the corporate ladder in competition with each other. Those superiors included Lee Iacocca, who would later become President, and Henry "The Deuce" Ford, grandson of the company's founder. In fact, he regularly hob-nobbed with The Deuce, accompanying him on trips to Europe which, many times, included London, one of The Deuce's favorite watering holes. Even in his seemingly extroverted ways (which he was not), J. Paul and wife Yvonne would regularly entertain or be entertained by some of Detroit's most notable auto exec's, making them instantly recognizable in the Bloomfield Township social scene such as my old buddy, John Delorean and wife Christina Ferrare. That entertainment, many times, took the form of playing golf at one of the many prestigious country clubs such as Forest Lake in nearby Orchid Lake (where I was invited by J. Paul to join him in a round of golf on one occasion) and Bloomfield Hills Country Club. This socializing included frequent dining at popular restaurants like the Chop House in downtown Detroit and the Fox & Hounds (now "Bill's) along Woodward Avenue in Bloomfield Hills. And, there was a perceived need to impress others with one's parent-worthiness by sending their kids off to private schools i.e. Cranbrook Academy in Bloomfield Hills, being transported around the prestigious enclaves of Birmingham, Troy, and Bloomfield Hills in style...driving that company-furnished luxury automobile that got regularly exercised getting noticed at the posh boutiques in those areas. And, lest I forget to report, that luxury car got replaced as frequently as four times a year depending on one's executive ranking within the company. That freebie was not only for the indentured slave (a.k.a. the auto exec), but also for his/her spouse, as well or, at least, that was the case with J. Paul.

J. Paul never had the benefit of an influential relationship that could have ushered him into employment at Fords. As you just read, he got his entry level job by way of an employment agency (remember those dinosaurs?), preparing him for the political realities so prevalent at Fords in the 1940's (some would argue that it is equally true today) that were part and parcel of working for Ford Motor Company (FoMoCo). Apparently, he got real good at getting himself recognized by the right people, enjoyed numerous promotions as he worked himself up Mount Ford's summit. As a senior executive, he became known as a hard-charging bargainer in his role as Vice-President of World-wide Procurement, a position he held for five years as a direct report to Lee Iacocca. He, later, went on to become Executive Vice-President, perceived to be somewhat of a reward for being a loyalist to The Deuce. He traveled around corporate America as a directive coming from the Deuce himself, in search of funds to complete the construction of a new world headquarters for FoMoCo. This was The Deuce's brain-child that became known as the Renaissance Center or RenCen, for short, located near downtown Detroit on the banks of the Detroit River. In order to construct this massive building, it became necessary for J. Paul to raise $40 million, which he did, from the likes of Firestone Rubber, General Tire, U.S. Steel, Budd Company and several other major vendors to Ford, as reported in a book written about Henry Ford II by Victor Lansky in 1981. I wonder how J. Paul went about deciding who he was going to put a hit on in order to raise such a sum of money? Interestingly enough, and at a much later point in time, RenCen was sold off and is now the corporate home to General Motors.

His illustrious career came to an end as a result of Ford's mandatory retirement policy. But his retirement didn't last long as Mr. Iacocca had his sights on J. Paul, bringing him out of retirement into an executive position at Chrysler (without jeopardizing his monthly retirement check from FoMoCo) that he couldn't say no to, that would be as President and Chief Operating Officer. Not that J. Paul was sufficiently presidential in term of qualifications and experience at such a lofty corporate position, but, Iacocca needed Bergmoser's considerable purchasing expertise, which was exactly what Chrysler needed at that critical point in time, where every dollar saved at the purchasing level, flowed directly to the "bottom line," this, at a time, when Chrysler was in another one of its recovery modes. As you read earlier about his superb fund-raising skills, J. Paul tenaciously attacked any assignment zealously, particularly, when ordered to do so by his old boss, Lido Anthony Iacocca. His monumental, never to be forgotten, task was to raise the necessary funds and supervise the refurbishment of the Grand Old Lady...the Statute of Liberty, and to accomplish this without asking for that first penny of taxpayer money. Quite a feat! I wonder what vendors of Chrysler felt about the appropriateness of making what one would have to assume was a major cash contribution to giving the Lady a bath and freshening up her image? The project was completed with fanfare and it was interesting to note that Iacocca accepted the credit (so freely bestowed by the press) for the project's successful completion and, to the best of my knowledge, J. Paul's name never went to ink, allowing Iacocca to fully bask in the enormity of the freshly reawakened patriotism this project created with an admiring public.

ZORA ARKUS-DUNTOV

For those of you who don't recognize the name Zora Arkus-Duntov, I bet you know of the Chevrolet Corvette. The names "Corvette" and "Arkus-Duntov" are synonymously lumped together, as Zora was known as the "father" of the Corvette. Although the "Vette" was designed and developed by the famous GM designer, Harley Earl, it was left to Zora to perfect Earl's design, building it into a world-class sport car. This perfection was derived from his ingenuity as an engineer and love of racing, which were put to profitable use in a GM career that began in 1953 while rising to become Chief Engineer, Corvette Engineering, a title he held until retirement in 1975. Zora made the most of his 89 years on this earth pursuing his love of high-performance automobiles. Born a Russian-Jew and migrating to Belgium as a child, he, eventually, made his way to New York and followed his nose to Detroit, where he was hired on the strength of his engineering credentials by Ed Cole, who would later become President of General Motors. To commemorate his legacy, GM plans on placing the name "Zora" into the name-plate of the upcoming C-8 Corvette, rumored to be a mid-engine design, something that Duntov fought hard and long for, now to be possibly realized, posthumously.

The Corvette was launched into the U.S. marketplace in 1953 as a 1953/1954 convertible model. You could order a Vette from the factory in any color you wished, provided it was white with a red interior. All models were equipped with a Powerlide 2-speed automatic transmission, a feature that found its way into other Chevrolet badged products. Beginning in the model year 1955, Powerglide transmissions grew to become a popular option on Chevrolet's Bel-Air model.

Even today, most teenage boys and young male adults, who are "car crazy," (like you know who) fall in love with the Corvette, on the spot!! Nearly an overnight sensation, unquestionably, embraced by the market, this sports car became an icon for power, styling, fun driving, and its immense social possibilities associated with the opposite sex, or at least that's what guys thought. OK, gals, is that a true statement? If you could afford a Corvette, you were "king of the hill" and a "stud muffin," par excellence. Sadly enough, the Corvette's pricing was a bit over the top for the average young person to afford, resulting in many would-be Corvette owners settling for Chevy Camaros and Ford Mustangs. That was a sure recipe for disappointment down the road, knowing the joys of driving a Vette had passed them by (literally and figuratively). No way was a Mustang or Camaro in the same league with the Corvette. But, one could always dream that one day, that fantastic car would be parked in their garage. I hold that, if you dream hard and long enough, somehow, someway, that dream takes on a life of its own and has the power to direct one through actions that have the potential to pave the way for those dreams to be realized ...owning that Vette. It wouldn't matter what equipment or color it was because there isn't any such thing as an ugly Corvette. The one that comes on the market for sale and, finally, agrees with one's budget may force some concessions as to personal preferences; but, in the scheme of things, it matters not. If that person is you, you are now telling the world you live in, that your Corvette is a celebration of the American dream that you have personalized and made come true. If, on the other hand, you feel no financial constraints in keeping you from owning a Corvette, you should get on your knees and thank the Lord for being so blessed because you, clearly, are. So get out there, buy one, and stop missing out on the fun. Even though the Corvette is priced as an upscale, upmarket vehicle, it actually is quite affordable when compared with Europe's sports car offerings. You can own four Corvettes for the same price as one Ferrari and, better yet, Corvettes can run all day long on regular, unleaded gas with those Italian stallions. Dollar for dollar, you can't beat a Corvette when comparing it with the likes of Ferraris, Lambos, Maseratis, and Alfas. Sure, they're hot and fantastic looking but, at what price? You want value, power, looks, prestige, extended styling cycles and a price that wouldn't embarrass a thrifty-minded, penny pincher? Check out the C-7 model Corvette, beginning in model year 2014 that continues as today's current model. Better yet, buy one!

Mr. Ghosn has a well-earned reputation as a winner beyond description using mere words. Give this man a task, like running three companies as CEO, (Nissan, Renault, and Mitsubishi) at the same time, and you will get a glimpse into this visionary's considerable talents. The profitability of all three companies is a living testament to this man's abilities.

Possibly, his greatest claim to fame is his saving Japan's third largest auto manufacturer – Nissan – from bankruptcy. In Japan, for a large corporation to declare bankruptcy is a rare occurrence and companies go to great lengths to avoid this, as it is viewed to be the most shameful form of corporate death. Nissan was within the length of a cigar of going "belly up" when Ghosn assumed the reins in 2001. Today, 17 years later, Nissan is the fourth largest auto maker, globally (as measured by brands), according to Focus2Move blog (11/2016). In terms of sales revenues, Nissan is ranked sixth with Toyota as #1 followed by VW, General Motors, Ford, and Chrysler. It's interesting to note that Honda is #2 in Japan's domestic marketplace but can't hold on to that position on a global basis, much like Mercedes-Benz sales in the U.S. makes it the luxury car leader, but globally that's not true, as BMW holds that crown as of this writing.

One source has pegged Nissan as the second most profitable auto maker (just behind BMW) as well as the fastest growing. Those results don't just show up at your doorstep one day because they are a hoped-for aspiration; they are attained through the unquestionable abilities, work ethic, dedication to task, and leadership traits of one Mr. Carlos Ghosn, and his management team, who would get my vote as the #1 executive in the business... today. To a millennial, he is the closest thing to a rock star. He's even become a hero to Japan's youth as a comic book star. In the U.S., he turned down the opportunity to run GM and Ford, for reasons he chose not to divulge (smart man).

As a college-educated engineer from France, this Brazilian-Lebanese acquired the reputation as "Mr. Fix-It," in effect, a man with a solution in search of a problem. Fortune Magazine (10/2013) reported, "nobody works harder than Carlos Ghosn"; others saying he has to be "crazy" to fill these three CEO roles concurrently. But, you know what, crazy never takes a day off! Motor Trend Magazine (01/17) related that Ghosn is the "most watched" executive in the business and has a habit of popping up in headlines with, heretofore, unexpected announcements, taking the market by surprise, like the recent acquisition of a 34% equity interest in Mitsubishi that no one saw coming. His magnificent flair for operating results is unparalleled. If the word "profits" has had a role in Ghosn's prayers, then, his prayers have been abundantly answered.

This speaker of five languages - Portuguese, Japanese, English, Arabic, and French is an effective communicator in establishing goals. To him, identifying and achieving goals gives purpose to the life of a company. Those goals are, often, born out of crisis as he feels that the occasional crisis can bring out the best in people, coupled with his belief that, "the role of leadership is to transform the complex situation into small pieces and prioritize them."

As for my takeaways, two negative ones stand out. Ghosn highly over-estimated the size of the EV market as part of the development of the Leaf, a car that has not lived up to his expectations and a marketplace not quite ready for this alternate-fueled vehicle in volume numbers. But, that's all going to change, and soon, in my estimation. I go back to Bob Lutz's comment about EV's being inevitable...it's just a question of time. Who knows, Ghosn might have that forecast right, yet, just not in the time frame he envisioned. The other bug-a-boo is he is rapidly approaching retirement age and, to the best of my reading, hasn't indicated who his possible successor might be. As usual, he's just full of surprises...that has turned out to be a good thing for this man with the Midas touch.

On the positive side of the ledger, Carlos will leave one whale of a legacy, most noteworthy the profits generated on his watch; increased market share; correctly identified emerging markets (India, Indonesia and much of Central and South America) as a growth opportunity overlooked by much of his competition; and getting a zero-emissions type car built to substantiate the claim that "the Leaf is the world's most affordable EV." He can thank God for his enormous talents, energy and work ethic in support of his shrewd business acumen, and, most importantly, his ability to correctly identify the sources of a problem, develop a solution that attacks the problem, and judiciously exercise a plan of attack. His talent for spotting and promoting management talent, has allowed him to sit back and watch his management team do their thing. Without peer, Carlos Ghosn is a "one of a kind, profit-making machine!"

BRUCE HALLE

Can you name me one company that is privately owned, the largest company of its type in the entire country where every one of its 18,000 employees has an active, daily part in managing this profit-producing dynamo? If one works for this company, whether a novice or a seasoned veteran in the tire business, you will have a career with this company from day 1. If you show a serious interest in the business through work ethic or desire to succeed, this market leader offers its employees ready access to planned advancement. You've probably driven by one of their business locations and, no doubt, many of you have bought their products and services but, somehow that kind of business didn't strike you as the behemoth that it is in its industry.

I would be describing none other than the Discount Tire Company, founded by Bruce Halle in Ann Arbor, Michigan, in 1960, and corporately headquartered in Scottsdale, Arizona, the market leader in replacement tires, wheels and installation services.

Bruce Halle is Discount Tire Company's sole stockholder and has been roundly reported that his net worth is north of 6 billion big ones. Can you count that far? I can barely type it! How many tires, wheels and services would one have to sell or serve to amass that kind of wealth...in one lifetime?

Although Halle is reported to be Arizona's wealthiest man, making the Forbes 400 list, you would never know it if you knew the man and how he lives. He's no one to step into a limelight, leaving that to others, especially, his employees (that he revels in supporting their efforts to continually grow with the business).

Halle never lost sight of his humble beginnings and strongly identifies with the ambitions and aspirations of his " people." Did you notice how "employees" became his "people," just like that? The man doesn't see anything magical or mysterious about how he and his people continue to build a profitable business. It's as simplistically put as

- Give the customer a level of service that exceeds their expectations.

- Price the service or product as if buying it for yourself.
- Never lose sight of who taught you how to dance and kept you on the dance floor...your valued customers and his dedicated people.
- Guarantees to match or beat any bona fide price from the competition.

What an impact Discount Tires has had on the tire replacement marketplace. Tires may not be as glamorous as cars but are, nonetheless, a key market component in the automotive industry. Try driving a car without tires! That market isn't going to go away anytime soon. Even autonomously-driven cars will have tires that, in time, will need replacing.

ROBERT ANTHONY LUTZ

Robert Anthony "Maximum Bob" Lutz – retired from General Motors in 2010 as Vice Chairman. He championed the highly successful launch of the Cadillac CTS coupe and sedan; Cadillac SRX, Chevrolet Equinox, Malibu, Camaro, and Corvette; Buick Enclave and LaCrosse, the GMC Terrain and Acadia Denali, the Pontiac G8, the best performing Pontiac ever, only to have GM decide to sell or spin off this car division as a part of their bankruptcy restructuring. He was also overseeing the re-launch of the Pontiac GTO that was limitedly successful, having been manufactured and assembled in Australia, badged in Aussieland as the Holden Monaro.

Bob's life is full of achievements from the get-go. Earning an advanced degree in marketing from the University of California at Berkeley, where he sold vacuum cleaners, door-to-door in support of his burgeoning family. If that wouldn't humble and motivate you, nothing would but in Bob's case, it probably strengthened his resolve, not to allow anything to stand in the way of achieving his goals. And, brother, did he have ambitions to back up those goals, whatever they were! I would be curious to know how many of those goals involved the car business or did things just work out that way? Personally, I would be all over an opportunity to sit down and talk with him about some of the things we share in common...entrepreneurship, linguistics, military life, timepieces, cigars, and, just maybe, we could find some time to talk about CARS.

His automotive career began in September, 1963, with GM/

98

Europe, where he had senior management responsibilities for the Opel brand. From there, Bob moved to BMW, serving as Executive Vice President, where he keyed the very successful launch of the highly regarded 3 Series, arguably, the world's best sports coupe (for the past 40 + years). It was Maximum Bob who took responsibility for creating the slogan, "The Ultimate Driving Machine." Upon leaving BMW, Bob landed at Ford/Europe, where he served as Chairman/Europe and had a leading role in the market introduction of the much-heralded Ford Sierra model in Europe and, after relocating to the U.S., the original Ford Explorer, both resounding successes. Building on those accomplishments (how is that possible?), Bob moved over to Chrysler, working for one Mr. Lee Iacocca in a tenuous relationship, doomed from the get-go. As a result, Bob Lutz would never be Chairman and CEO of Chrysler, thanks to a relationship between the two that never developed. Lutz did, however, become President and Chief Operating Officer for worldwide car and truck operations as well as a corporate Executive Vice President. In this role, he was instrumental in conceptualizing and, ultimately, bringing to market the LH-designed Dodge Intrepid, Chrysler Concorde and the Eagle, along with repositioning the role of Dodge truck products, now since renamed "Ram." At Dodge, he helped develop the styling theme, resembling the "beefy" look resembling heavy-truck manufacturer, Kenworth. Another crown proudly worn was the conception and successful launch of the Dodge Viper, a car that he all but built himself, a car that became America's second true sports car, after the Corvette, a car he would some years later have the pleasure of having product development responsibility for. When first built, the Dodge Viper became the most expensive car built in the U.S. with a base price north of $85,000 PLUS options!

Although there have been a few hiccups along the road that Bob traveled to get where he is today, few people who know Bob would disagree with the significance of his successes and the impact he had on "product." Some would argue that Bob is the greatest marketing guru in Detroit's history; but, no one in their right mind would say that he was not a seriously talented executive who made a lot of money for his employers, stockholders, suppliers, bankers…and himself! I freely admit Bob would have been my first choice of a mentor if I were younger and in the market for one. This much I do know. I am a huge fan and if I could scratch him off of my "bucket list" for having sat down and shared a Cubano, life would continue to be grand or, should

I write, more grandiose. In any event, I am truly blessed for the life I am living BUT my old cake could use a little more icing!

The common fibers that run through Bob's successes are his boldness, his response to challenge, his making the most of what was handed to him and his eagerness to embrace risk, calculated risks. And, anyone who regularly communicated with him would tell you that he had quite a flair for writing witty, scathingly direct emails and memoirs that would make your eyeballs burn! The depth of his wit is mind-boggling and to be able to translate that into written or verbal words and do it with panache speaks volumes about this man's talents and intellect. A couple of oft-quoted collection of words, passionately offered were "Being able to think outside the box presupposes you were able to think in it." Or how about, "Forcing auto makers to sell smaller cars with the objective in mind of improving the gas mileage is like fighting the nation's obesity problem by forcing clothing manufacturers to sell garments in only small sizes." A personal favorite, when asked about Ford's presumed copying of Bentley designs for the 2017 Lincoln Continental, he prophetically stated, "If you're gonna steal, make sure it is from a bank, not a grocery store."

My take away...Bob Lutz can be rightly perceived as a free spirit, a maverick who knew few bounds when it came to speaking his mind. His attendant outspokenness, his crippling candor, kept the seat of his pants plenty hot for prolonged periods of time. His genius, seemingly, swamped any serious possibility of ever being fired for speaking his version of the English language. On the contrary, his direct reports showed unwavering loyalty and respect for him, personally, and for his immeasurable talents while fully embracing the leadership he provided.

Yes sir, Bob's acquired language skills doubtlessly helped him build a vocabulary that might stump an English professor, a repertoire of words that he put to aggressive use and, sometimes, a bit too boldly for his readers. No one would ever accuse Bob of not telling it like it is or was. As such, Bob Lutz is a much sought after speaker and writer (three books that I know of). Being able to communicate in five languages doesn't hurt any, either. His down-to-earth, witty writing style leaves no room for embellishment, something you kind of expect coming from a non-traditionalist who attacks the ideas and theories of others and their long-held perceptions...a pure iconoclast, with no subject sacrosanct.

If he chose to, Bob could write yet another book, an auto-biography this time, borrowing from the title he penned for an earlier book, entitled "Guts And The Eight Laws Of Business." With that title put to rest, he could name the book, "No Guts, No Glory" because that's the way he lives his life. Ever the entre-preneur, he subscribes to the pragmatic notion, and correctly so, that if one is going to enter a farting contest with the expectation of winning, one had better be prepared to clean out their pants from time-to-time.

No doubt, risk-taking is a part of the business landscape, whether rewarded or not. If rewarded, it provides an incen-tive to reinvest in our capitalistic-based economy, encourag-ing others to share in this risk-taking role that rewards those who correctly calculate them. Nothing magical about that little economic tidbit...the greater the risk, the greater the reward but know that that sword cuts both ways...the greater the loss if the risks were calculated incorrectly. This is where Bob Lutz enters center stage. He knew precisely the nature and degree of risk he was exposing himself to, teamed with a keen intellect and, with the latest, verifiable information available, he was able to ha-bitually manage risks such that they were merely a disguise for reward. For most of us, getting out of bed in the morning can be a risky proposition...you can't calculate what you can't foresee even if your name is Bob Lutz!

Worth noting, Bob found his ship adrift in some choppy waters on occasion despite his long and illustrious career but... darn few. He spent a few years as CEO of Exide Battery which I find a bit incongruous given his thoroughbred, singular focus on automobiles. What was he trying to do...market a line of digital, battery-charged dildos? While he was there, it would have been nice if he could have directed his engineering group to come up with a gauge that could show the remaining life of a car bat-tery. Had he, conceivably, he could have sold it as a patented product to all of the car manufacturers, the rightful domain for such a product, and reaped millions in the process. This much I know for sure...he could have sold a sh##pot full of them here in Arizona. You see, excessive heat and batteries don't get along. In our daily inferno that lasts a minimum of five months with temperatures averaging 100+ degrees EVERY DAY, batteries don't last more than two years as a rule and when they die, they don't warn you of their impending death...they just die!

And, then, there was his active involvement in the Cunningham Motor Company where Bob founded a partnership (partners sink ships), where he eventually found himself being sued for security violations associated with his role as a major stockholder. I haven't read any account as to how this all turned out; all I know is he didn't go to jail, presumably, the complainants had bigger and easier fish to fry!

It's worth further noting that Mr. Lutz, regularly, found himself at odds with his bosses who he routinely interfaced with, whether it was any of the 4 "P"s – product; price; promotion; or place (distribution channels) or the price of a good cigar from Havana. There was ALWAYS a battle to be fought or so it seemed. It was a well-known fact that Bob didn't see eye-to-eye with Red Poling, CEO of Ford (few did!), who nearly wrecked Ford single handedly, and Bob's old buddy, Lee Iacocca (only kidding!). As for his relationship with Iacocca, Lutz, with his ever-ready, sharpened mental sword was prepared for the battles that would surely follow. You didn't have to count past one to know who won the majority of those battles. As I alluded to earlier, Iacocca did not take a "shine" to Lutz with Lee thinking that Lutz was something of a smart a## which, of course, he was. But, the sad reality was, there wasn't room enough for the two of them in the same room at the same time! With Lutz' habit of telling things like it was and Iacocca's combative management style (more on that later) that became an unending source of strain on their would-be relationship. So, they never became the "Lee and Lutz Show" The relationship convinced Iacocca that Bob Lutz was not going to succeed him as CEO and, as a result, he went to great lengths to find what he believed and hoped would become the new "Little Lee" in an attempt to protect his legacy. He found his man in Robert Eaton, who I described, elsewhere, as one of the true "Losers" in the car industry. Well, it didn't take long for Iacocca to figure out that he had selected the wrong horse for the right race but stuck by him, nonetheless. As reported earlier, Iacocca went so far as to get himself quoted as saying, "selecting Bob Eaton to replace me as CEO was the single worst decision I ever made in my life." He was so upset with himself that he found himself being mildly supportive of Lutz when he said he (Lutz) was a vastly stronger manager than Eaton and went on to say, "Lutz could chew up and spit out Bob Eaton." Taking names and faces out of the complaint about trying to manage Lutz (if at all), Bob found himself at odds with the so-called "bean-counters" (not an affectionately bestowed description), who, by their very own tendentious nature, were charged with the responsibility of establishing operating costs that, ultimately, help define profit projections. In Bob's marketing role, he found himself doing battle with these bean-counters frequently, faced with the need to defend a particular product proposal at a cost point significantly higher than what the "b-c's" wanted. Bob's take on that was, they were too busy "counting" rather than "accounting"...big difference! One thing was absolutely clear...Bob was fully battle-tested. That's a good thing 'cause battles had a way of finding him!

Bob, also, was grounded in pragmatism when confronted with an inescapable reality. For instance, he has been roundly quoted for saying, "Electrification of the automobile is inevitable" (thank you, Mr. Thomas Edison). No wittiness needed there! In his view, it's no longer an "if" or "when" proposition. The only remaining question is, how long is it going to take to get electric-powered, safe, reliable, economical, and affordable vehicles in American driveways? Certainly, Tesla, Nissan, and Volvo are doing their part.

Present day, Bob is anything but retired as he operates a consultancy, writes books, engages in professional speaking, and get this, ever the entrepreneur, Bob helped found and is an active partner in VLF Automotive (guess who the "L" belongs to), where he is the resident marketing guru. He is readying an evolutionary car for its U.S. debut, the FIRST four-door Grand Touring (GT) class (always convertibles or two-doors in the past), Corvette-powered (ZR1), luxury sports automobile that is as much "sports" as it is a "sedan" and, as you might suspect, drop dead gorgeous. Its designer is none other than Henrik Fisker. You may remember his name as he was, at one time, the chief designer of several BMW and Aston-Martin models and, more recently, the Fisker Karma, now owned by the Chinese. This new beast is named "Destino" and will be coming soon to an exclusively selected luxury car dealership, near you. It is being promoted as the world's fastest 4-door sedan, developing 638 horses under that beautiful $229,000 hood. He never said the car was inexpensive! So, there you have it, your dream car is just waiting to be built, begging you to get your wallet out with enough ink in your pen to write that check. But before you do, you might want to check in with your cardiologist to make sure your heart is strong enough to handle that task!

Yes, "Maximum Bob" got things done with panache where his considerable talents were always in play. No doubt, automotive historians will recognize him as a "one of a kind," the likes of which we probably won't ever see again.

LIDO ANTHONY IACOCCA

About the only thing "Lee" Iacocca and Bob Lutz had in common, besides their love of cars, was a shared middle name and the not so occasional cigar. What a duo they were, if only a long-term, positive relationship could have developed out of what little they did have in common, if only they could have liked each other just a little bit... Lee the salesman, Bob the marketer! But that wasn't about to happen, something akin to mixing water with oil. From the get-go, it was one ego-clash after another and it was on one such occasion that Lutz got quoted as saying, "good leaders have to be able to criticize constructively." The key word here is "constructively;" but that is of limited value when your boss has an opinion on everything, fully utilizing his bear trap mind, honed over a 40 + year career. This was one of the serious challenges Bob Lutz constantly had to face in his, rocky relationship with "The Lido." Heaven knows,they had ample time to "bury the hatchet" given their simultaneous employments at both Ford and Chrysler. And then there was the word "no." There was nothing about this word Iacocca understood. As a result, he heard a lot of "yes's" from fervently dedicated, direct reports, who, apparently, were serious about their job security. Yet, if Iacocca heard nothing but "yes's" coming from the same reports (a.k.a. indentured slaves), he grew weary while suspecting he wasn't getting the whole story but rather the one they thought he wanted to hear. Either way, they could find themselves polishing up their resumes unless they were blessed with thick skin at birth, could handle criticism regularly and, of course, it helped if you were one of his "hand-selected boys" who routinely performed above and beyond his demanding expectations, holding to the Lee's mantra, "actions speak louder than words. Don't tell me...show me!"

Hailing from Allentown, Pennsylvania, Iacocca entered the automotive field with a graduate degree from Princeton. Right out of school, he joined Ford in their Sales Department for a region based out of Philadelphia in the role of Assistant Sales

104

Manager. Lee came up with an idea that helped propel his soon-to-be realized rocket to stardom – "buy a 56 for 56" which got further explained as, buy a 1956 Ford for $56.00 per month, and in the fine print, "for 36 months with a down payment of 20%." Don't you think..."buy a 56 for 56" sounds a whole lot better than telling folks about the down payment requirement and re-payment obligation? This hugely successful promotion got him promoted and, coupled with several other successful, planned undertakings, Iacocca went on to become President of Ford Motor Company, reporting to the irascible, ostentatiously arrogant, Henry Ford II (a.k.a. "The Deuce"), grandson of the company's founder, the original Henry.

Eight short years later, his most noteworthy success was spearheading the development and launch of the prodigiously successful Ford Mustang and, to a much lesser extent, the Ford Pinto, Mercury Bobcat, Ford Maverick and its running mate, the Mercury Comet. To this day, the Ford Mustang enjoys collector car status right up there with some notable exotics from Europe i.e. the Lotus, Alfa-Romero, Porsche, Ferrari, Maserati and Japan's early model Datsun Z's (formerly named "Fair Lady") and the Toyota Supra (which will soon be returning to the U.S. after a 30+ year hiatus). Early on between 1969 through the early 1980's, Mustang was serious competition for Pontiac TransAm (remember "Smoky & The Bandit) and is still duking it out with Chevrolet's Camaro.

Not all came up roses, though. Iacocca had to take the ultimate responsibility for the ignominiously designed Ford Mustang II, a car that "The Deuce" wanted to name the "Mini-Bird." Thank God he got outvoted, something that rarely happened. This car and its name was so hideously conceived, that no amount of prayer was going to save it. Even with HFII's stepping out of the picture, Lido still got this parcel of cr## to market only to see it die of natural causes as it would inevitably do.

And, then, there was the Lincoln Versailles, a hoped-for answer from Ford to compete with the Cadillac Seville and Mercedes-Benz that was just beginning to develop a foothold in the U.S. marketplace. Even with Iacocca throwing his considerable weight behind his friend, Frank Sinatra, who was featured in their TV advertising, the car went on to become a total, dismal dud. The car was no more than a re-badged Ford Granada and Mercury Monarch. So, "it goes to show ya" or "shows to go ya" (either works), you can fool some of the people some of the time, but, not with this so-called Lincoln, with its controversial styling (with its Continental spare tire grafted to the trunk lid), coupled with its lack of pedigree, spelling doom from day 1.

Nearly as successful but not totally known as such was Iacocca's role in bringing the "minivan" (heretofore an unknown word) to market, a vehicle conceived by one of Lee's direct reports while at Ford, Hal Sperlich, who like Lee, got himself fired by the "Deuce" and, also, as Lee did, went over to Chrysler where Lee threw his massive support behind the development of this new type of vehicle.   The popularity of this smaller van soared as it rapidly became a mainstay with soccer moms, even to this day. And as they say, the rest is history. Hal went on to become President of Chrysler, and in time, he retired with his legacy secured, correctly known as "Mr. Minivan." I guess we should have a back-handed debt of gratitude to the Deuce for firing Hal and, while I am at it, kudos to Iacocca for throwing his influence and support behind Sperlich. The minivan made a lot of money for Chrysler in a market segment totally missed by Ford and General Motors. Rightly recognized as the "father" of the minivan, Sperlich went on to become President of Chrysler where, in the span of 12 years, Chrysler had 7 Presidents, one of whom served that role twice...Lee Iacocca. The other six were Lutz, Bergmoser, Sperlich, Eaton, Dieter Zetsche, and Nardelli. In today's minivan market, Chrysler Town & Country and Dodge Grand Caravan own this market segment as much as Toyota wish it wasn't so. Toyota keeps building a better Sienna every year but it isn't enough to catch up with Chrysler's two entries. As an aside statement, when it comes to minivans and pick-up trucks, there ain't no catching American manufacturers. And, it doesn't hurt any that more money can be made building trucks than cars , hence, Detroit's concentrating on trucks. If fact, a case can be made for treating cars as a plus in terms of added, incremental profits. The Big 3 love their truck offerings of which the Ford F-150 pick-up is the best-selling truck, year in and year out, since the 1950's. In today's marketplace, Ford's F-150 out-sells any vehicle, whether its a truck or a car.

Arguably, Iacocca saved one of his biggest snafus at Chrysler for the introduction of the Chrysler-Maserati TC, a lightly veiled Chrysler Le Baron convertible, with an optional hard-shell, removable top, that featured a side port hole, reminiscent of the 1956/57 Ford Thunderbirds. You suppose old Lee had a hand in that design? This car, like the Ford Mustang II, was dead on arrival. Remember the riddle, "three little piggies went to market, three little piggies went crying "wee, wee, wee" all the way home? Well, substitute the three little piggies for the Mustang II, Lincoln Versailles, and Chrysler-Maserati TC in this little ditty and you pretty much have identified the markets' response to three of Iacocca's sorriest car products.

No amount of success achieved by his staff mattered long-term to The Deuce, particularly, if it involved disagreement on product development projects such as put forth by Iacocca and Sperlich. Long term, he knew his judgment was correct and (silly him) suffered the opinions of others just to keep a semblance of peace in the office for the key people he knew he had to passify. The occasional firing or resignation was a given, but, the possibility of a mass exodus was an entirely different matter, something that could reduce the "Glass House" (name given to Ford's corporate headquarters in Dearborn) to a sea of shards. Despite those fears, he was totally intolerant of anyone or anything that went on behind his back and therein became what is believed to be the real reason why The Duece handed Iacocca his a##. Although Henry didn't put up much of a fuss when Iacocca put a thumbs down on naming the Mustang II the "Mini Bird, he, nevertheless, could and did kill product development projects at will and could do so with the simple snap of a finger. But success sometimes breeds independent thinking and requires getting on a crash diet to get those britches properly refitted. Iacocca, a strong personality, a personality much like the Deuce's could be easily threatened by another strong personality. So, Iacocca, thinking he was as secure as the Queen of England, overstepped his bounds as president of the company in an attempt to get Henry fired by his own board on the grounds that The Deuce...was senile. As a side note, this has been widely disputed by Iacocca and others. But, while ole Henry was out of the country, he learned that Lee had been quietly talking to more than one board member, or so he was persuaded to believe, about Henry's crippling senility. All said while The Deuce was in England on business. On first hearing, as reported elsewhere, old Henry went ballistic on that bit of news and, upon returning to Detroit he wasted no time in informing Mr. Iacocca that he was officially relieved of his duties as President of Ford Motor Company, this, after 32 years of service, and posting a $2 billion profit in the year of his dismissal. You suppose, just for a moment, that Iacocca forgot whose name was on the building?

Upon hearing he was fired, Iacocca asked The Deuce, "What did I do wrong?" The Deuce wasted no time in replying, "I just don't like you," ...this after working most of his adult life for Ford and his company (in the Deuce's eyes) and creating billions of dollars of profits, some of which trickled right down into The Deuce's pockets.

Despite Iacocca's history of ineffectual management of difficult personalities, his inability to handle constructive criticism, individuals with huge egos (which he refused to feed, having to leave some room for himself) and the way he ruled the roost by power rather than by consensus, Iacocca, nonetheless, got himself hired by Chrysler as President and Chief Operating Officer. That tenure lasted a very brief time and with the board's support, he was duly installed as Chief Executive Officer in short order (a matter of months), leaving the door open to selecting his replacement as President. The winner was J. Paul Bergmoser due to Paul's astute skills in purchasing as Ford's procurement department head for many years. And, due to Chrysler's economic health at that time, largely non-existent or sickly, at best, Chrysler needed someone who could minimize dollars going out the door while leaving it to others to maximize dollars coming in the door. On paper, Paul looked like a good fit, although I have no reported knowledge of how effective he was or was not in that role. As an aside, Iacocca was asked by government officials to spearhead a much overdue project in restoring the Statue of Liberty's appearance to her former glorious self, which Lee delegated to Paul (J. Paul must have had a lot of spare time on his hands to handle that assignment and be the President at the same time), both the fund-raising as well as overseeing the actual restoration to completion. As reported earlier, this assignment went per plan with Iacocca recciving rave reviews for the completed project, a project that did not cost the taxpayers a dime! That statue, today, thanks to Paul and Lee, stands tall and proud with a clean halo, welcoming others to our shores.

Lee Iacocca's successes were timely and numerous. His most famous moment, probably, was receiving a federal government "bailout" in order to save Chrysler. Without it, Chrysler was doomed to failure, putting thousands upon thousands of employees out of work. Lee persuasively convinced a congressional committee that Chrysler was good for the money. He (Chrysler) was good for the money, alright. In fact, he orchestrated the repayment of those bailout funds in record time...years ahead of schedule!

108

How could this, possibly, happen? Well, Iacocca, ever the salesman, got himself featured in television ads, hawking the virtues of Chrysler's internally designated "K" cars. Iacocca, while poking his forefinger into the TV camera, emphatically pronounced that "if you can find a better car than these three makes of the "K" car, buy it!" His pitch was so compelling that people thought it was their patriotic duty to go out and buy one of these Chrysler's K cars, trusting that the car was as good as Iacocca said it was, while helping save the company from going out of business and preserving beaucoup jobs. Apparently, it mattered not that these cars were, in fact, tinny little overpriced, econo-boxes because people were all but waiting in line to buy them! To state that this was a successful campaign to sell a lot of cars and do so quickly...would be an gross understatement. But, in all fairness, the car's styling wasn't going to embarrass its owner; in post-truth, though, it was not a very well-built car but it served its purpose when time was of the essence in order to save this company and its employees from extinction.

Lee Iacocca's persona at Chrysler grew larger than life thanks to his dogged determination to show The Deuce a thing or two, saving a competing company with its thousands of jobs, repaying a loan years ahead of schedule and, of course, the profits he made for the corporation. He was so benevolently liked and respected, larger than life for some folks, that an serious effort was mounted in an attempt to get him to run for the presidency of the United States. That did not materialize but what did was the legacy he left to others at Ford and Chrysler, the industry at large, and an adoring public who scripted the expression, "Chrysler's Savior."

For a season, Lee enjoyed writing books (had a couple of best sellers), his philanthropic activities, golf, and had a pioneering role in launching a line of "power bicycles" or "E-Bikes" as they became known as. The fate of these bikes was sealed by battery-related issues (should have conferred with Lutz over at Exide), lackluster styling, and insufficient power. Other than that, the product might have had a future. Actually, it still has one, as it spends its days resting in various junkyards with more rest in store!

Seriously retired in his 90's, Lido lives in Bel Air, California, where a primo golf course or a cigar store can't be far away! No doubt, Lee Iacocca will go down as one of the greatest chief executives in automotive history. As for his overbearing personality and intimidating ways, I think historians will be kind to this man's legacy, preferring to applaud him for his considerable abilities and accomplishments...a man for the times.

HAKAN SAMUELSSON

Samuelsson, a Swede on the fast track and CEO of Volvo, has committed his company, through a public pledge, that no one should be seriously injured as the driver or occupant in a Volvo automobile by the year 2020. In fact, Samuelsson guarantees that Volvo will assume the liability for any accident caused by its self-driving cars. That's how confident he is in their technology and probably explains how it is that Volvo appears to be the first auto company to introduce their version of a self-driven car. Their model XC90 has already launched a partnership with Uber in December, 2016. Volvo's self-driving capabilities are reported to be class-leading, this according to Car & Driver Magazine (5/16), which helps explain how they expect to beat their competition to market. On his watch, Volvo tripled its operating income to $780 million, pre-tax in 2015, on sales of $20 billion. Do the math...that's a return on sales of 39%, all the more spectacular when you consider that a significant percentage of their auto production was done in Sweden with its higher labor costs associated with European-based (union) labor rates. If that wasn't achievement enough, Volvo sold 550,000 vehicles worldwide, 80,000 of which were manufactured and sold in China's domestic marketplace, no surprise as Volvo is owned by Geely of China, setting an all-time sales record for this much storied 90 year old company. Automotive News, a weekly tabloid read by car dealers, reports that Volvo is on track to build 800,000 vehicles by year 2020. Break that figure down and you come up concluding they are going to grow sales by nearly 50% in the next 4 years. If they accomplish this, it will be viewed by industry followers as a feat not easily attained, putting them squarely in the category of an industry leader.

Samuelsson is the catalyst behind this growth (which he denies), offering rave accolades instead that recognizes his staff and hard-working employees in Sweden and China. He has been hugely successful for three, noteworthy reasons. First, he recognized that Volvo had created a misconception in the marketplace as to what they do. In his market research, he uncovered the likely explanation for this fallacy... people were of the

110

mindset that Volvo stopped making "cool" cars long ago in exchange for producing "safe" cars that were no longer stylistically-inspired. Samuelsson has successfully buried that falsehood by bringing products to market that are not only safe, but cool. In a nutshell...superior results flowing from Volvo's product development group. Second, Volvo has spent huge bucks on R & D leading to the technological edge that they enjoy today. Third are the products themselves, offering looks, safety, and features, all appropriately-priced to the market.

Ford Motor Company owned Volvo for a number of years, feeling they needed a car to compete with Sweden's Saab, owned by cross town rival, General Motors. Give Ford credit for hanging around for several years in their futile attempt to grow this company. Apparently, it wasn't meant to be. But, in 2010 along comes Geely Holdings, China's largest manufacturer of automobiles, that buys Volvo for $1.8 billion (a fire sale price) and, in short order, turns this boutique auto company into a profit-producing machine. It begs the question, what did Samuelsson, or the Chinese for that matter, know that Ford didn't? Do you suppose those Chinese fortune cookies were packing away little secrets that Volvo acted on? According to Forbes Magazine (11/15) Ford bought Volvo back in 1999 for $6.5 billion, taking a loss of 72% (sold it to Geely in 2010 for $1.8 billion). A similar situation existed for Ford when they ended up selling Jaguar/Land Rover to Tata Industries of India that like Volvo, is now turning in records sales and profits. Aston-Martin was sold to some private UK-based investors who have struck a joint partnership arrangement with Daimler (Mercedes-Benz) to build SUV/crossovers. Although I have no sales or profit data to back this up, I believe A-M is doing reasonably well for themselves.

They may not write songs about Volvo but they surely heap praises on Hakan Samuelsson, who is living proof that any door can be unlocked. Personally, I believe that to be profoundly true. In Hakan's case, he found the right key to that door and relished using it.

ALAN ROGER MULALLY

Anyone who has "Roger" for a second name can't be all bad. The one you've got to watch out for is "Roger" as a first name. Big difference! Alan Roger Mulally, with his God-given gifts of FORESIGHT and COURAGE, unquestionably, saved Ford

Motor Company in his timely role as Chief Executive Officer (2006 -2014). Those two words pretty much sum up the man, and to think he came to Ford without having spent one day in the automotive industry. Uniquely enough, he came to Ford by way of Boeing where he spent nearly forty years, coming out of the engineering ranks to become an Executive Vice President, who is largely regarded as the leader behind Boeing's resurgence against Europe's AirBus. At Boeing, he correctly perceived that they were no longer in the airplane business but in the "mobili- ty" business (notice how he leapfrogged right over the "transpor- tation" business?). He brought that same mindset to Ford, repo- sitioning them from an auto maker with a focus on the future to become a key player in mobility products and services.

Alan grew up in the Christian faith as a youngster back in Kansas, where he went on to receive engineering and business degrees (graduate level). Through his life experiences, he devel- oped a personal Mission Statement of sorts...to "give" takes care of the "getting" and, whatever you do, don't try to keep score on those points. He gave with a gracious heart, if you will. Isn't that straight out of the Bible, just another version of "you reap what you sow?"

In his first year at Ford, Mulally mortgaged Ford's much- cherished "Blue Oval" badge along with collateralizing all of their plants and facilities worldwide, to raise cash in support of daily operations. These actions allowed Ford to buy the nec- essary time and resources to put in place the plans and assets to retool or reinvent the company, all at the same time that GM and Chrysler were preoccupied with working themselves through bankruptcy. That is to say that Ford "was making hay while the sun shined."

You talk about big kajoles? To pledge the considerable as- sets of this 110 year old company, yes, all of them, was unheard of; most companies would never even consider taking on such a huge potential level of risk, being about as common as see- ing a stripeless zebra! Flush with cash, he and his team loaded up their guns and went "General Motors and Toyota hunting," confident of their weapons...vision, people, plans, products, all reinforced by CASH, and lots of it... billions, in fact. Meanwhile, GM and Chrysler were waffling through bankruptcy, trying their best to keep from running out of cash just to keep their doors open, all the while their operating losses kept piling up with no end in sight, burning through cash like there was no tomorrow. In truth, there weren't too many tomorrows left! Lest I forget to draw your attention to this major fact, you have to give a lot of credit to the Ford family in supporting Alan, who was putting their own personal fortunes at risk as well.

Clearly, Alan was anything but risk-adverse. This degree of risk-taking ultimately screams "reward me." He was like a river's never-ending flow, with its currents ever carrying increased profits, market share, better asset utilization, and higher transaction prices, into a sea of corporate and personal wealth... for many. Today, Ford is within two percentage points of catching General Motors as the leading U. S. automobile manufacturer. Interestingly enough, Chrysler is only three percentage points behind Ford, thanks largely to their sales of Jeeps and Ram trucks.

These successes gave Mulally an almost God-like status among Ford's thousands of employees. Now, nearly a decade later, not only is Ford producing record profits, they have recently declared a "special" dividend with bonus' and cash bumps to all that actively participated in making these successes real and repeatable. Sadly, Wall Street, apparently, hasn't jumped onto the Ford bandwagon just yet for reasons that defy economic reasoning...Ford's stock is going nowhere! Who says the market correctly reflects reality at any given time? For Ford's sake, I trust this is not so because Ford has become one of America's premier companies. What does that say about Wall Street? Through all these market machinations and speculation about future profits, Ford continues stockpiling profits like squirrels hoarding nuts, ruing the day that surely would come when Alan would announce his retirement plans.

His daily mantra, "Fix Ford" reflected the care he felt for people, ever remembering that it is people that precede plans. Mulally's methodology began by fully understanding "the" problem and learning how it came about and here comes the dicey part, deciding what to do about it (puts a premium on knowledge, foresight, and judgment); developing a plan that attacks the problem AFTER putting a team together, keeping them together on the same page and aggressively going after the problem or issue, confident of the outcome. He would routinely follow a plan's progress with weekly meetings, every Thursday morning at 7:00 in the Thunderbird Room at Ford's corporate headquarters in Dearborn, Michigan.

Alan's persona became larger than life when a movement came afoot to get him convicted to make a run for the Presidency of the U.S. As with Iacocca, nothing, actually, came of this as it went on to die a natural death, but it sure does make one ponder the "what if's." To my way of thinking, Alan's legacy has for its foundation, performance. Why risk tarnishing this for a job in politics that does not judge performance objectively unless expressed by members of the same political party? He had nothing to prove to anybody, his track record was robust enough to be rightly compared to some of the true visionaries of our decade i.e. Steve Jobs (Apple), Elon Musk (Tesla), Jeff Bezos (Amazon), Howard Schultz (Starbucks), Tim Cook (Apple), Bill Gates (Microsoft), Warren Buffett (entrepreneur), and Mark Zuckerberg (Facebook), to name a few.

In July, 2016, Alan was inducted into the Automotive Hall of Fame, where in his prepared comments, he lauded Executive Chairman Bill (once known as "Billy") Ford as his daily motivation to save Ford from financial collapse, recognizing him as an extraordinary leader and treasured friend. They both had a lot to gain or lose, depending on its outcome. Alan walked away from nearly forty years at Boeing where he was an accomplished leader and a likely candidate to be named CEO at some future point in time in exchange for joining a floundering company stuck in reverse. Clearly, Alan never doubted his own abilities and the support he was going to get from Ford's board and family. Now fully retired, Alan presently is serving on the Board of Directors of Google, where they are feverishly trying to beat Apple to market with their version of an autonomously-driven car.

In a nutshell, Mulally's successes were many but the ones that stand out most for me are:

- He saved Ford...end of sentence
- He was an extremely effective leader without being a bean-counter or a car guy
- Others enthusiastically followed his leadership
- Successfully re-launched the Ford Fusion, Ford's answer to the Cambry, the "heart" of Toyota's product line in the U.S.
- Turned in record profits...repeatedly!

- Took market share away from General Motors and increased its overall market share

Any failures – not worth the ink to describe

Take Aways? - Plenty

- Problem Solver...extraordinaire!
- Born leader
- Envisioned Ford as a "one-brand" auto maker who was not in favor of keeping Lincoln in the company's product corral. The jury is out on that one despite Matthew McConaughey's ads on TV which are reported to be successful in developing awareness for the brand.
- Envisioned Ford as a "mobility" company rather than the singular focus of being a car manufacturer and with plans to back up this premise.
- Without question, Alan Roger Mulally was one of the greatest auto industry executives of this generation. He has been favorably compared to Alfred Sloan who was at GM's helm for twenty-three years and gave us a car for every wallet, Chevrolet through Cadillac, depending on one's income and desired social status.

In some ways, Mulally was to Ford what Iacocca was to Chrysler, a couple of decades removed. That is to state that both companies needed rescuing to stay alive. In the post-Iacocca era, Ford avoided bankruptcy and prospered, Chrysler claimed bankruptcy.

CARROLL HALL SHELBY

A former Texas chicken farmer (they do farm chickens, don't they?) went on to become one of the world's premier automobile designers, builders, and race car drivers...all in the same timeframe. Shelby, also, was a investor and helped put the Chili's Restaurant chain into business along with selling his car creations to auto makers, to Ford and Chrysler, in particular.

Carroll lived to be 89 years old, thanks in part to the transplanted heart he received at the ripe young age of age 67. At the time of his passing in 2012, he held the record for the number of years living with an organ he wasn't born with. Couple that with a kidney that he, also, became a transplant recipient of in

1996 and you begin to get the picture of what this man endured, healthwise. Lest I forget, his first hospital stay was at age 7 for a leaky heart valve.

The health-related issues, no doubt, slowed him down but in no way did it ever stop him until the end, when pneumonia finally did him in. Its been reported that he lived every day as if he were in a car race. Things like heart and kidney transplant operations were akin to making pit stops for gas and tires. He wasn't about to let something as trivial as a major surgery get in the way of his purpose for living. To Shelby, auto racing mirrored life itself. The more he raced, the more precious life became.

As for designing cars, Carroll redesigned factory-built Ford and Dodge cars into racing dynamos that are fetching millions of dollars in today's market. It all started with his design and production of the Shelby Cobra in 1965, that today, brings upward of $2 million on the open market. Other huge product successes include the 1965/66 Ford Mustang GT 350, the Ford GT 40 (now known as the Ford GT). And, then, there was the Cobra SuperSnake built in 1966/67 that, routinely brings $1.3 to $1.5 million in today's market. In 2012 he brought out the Shelby 1000 with its 950 horses trapped under its hood, just biting at the bit to get unleashed. More recently, he offered the market a Ford Shelby GT 500 in 2013 with 650 ponies, ready to race. Shelby, also, redesigned and built certain Dodge products that his touch transformed into serious competitors, whether street or track. One such car was the Dodge Shelby Charger, produced between the years of 1985 and 1987, followed by the Dodge Viper sports car for model years 1992-1998. It was incredible to learn that Shelby raced his own creations nearly up to the time of his death; and, that his passing had nothing to do with dangerous living associated with auto racing.

Shelby was characterized by the press as being fiercely competitive by nature, something he didn't acquire being a chicken farmer. He was just built that way. What's more, he never did anything, to borrow his own words, half-a##ed. His love of racing cars he designed and built provided all the thrills he needed to help him lead the successful life he enjoyed, where boldness and courage were his best friends. Carroll Shelby stands as an American icon whose uniqueness found expression in objects that could, and did, fly...without wings!

116

Elon Musk is a 46 year old Stanford grad who with regularity shows he has clairvoyantly and correctly identified several developable technologies relating to energy, to power automobiles, and the greater use of solar power as an alternate source to electricity, oil, and natural gas. Equally important to him is the future need for cost-effective outer-space travel and present-day refinement of rocket science-related technologies. In my view, the advances made on all of these fronts justifies the rightful claim that, today, Elon Musk is America's premier investor, inventor, and explorer, all rolled into one package. Much of the developable advancement he has pioneered has found itself into the embodiment of an electric-powered car...the Tesla, wildly successful to their pleased buyers as well as their major supplier of lithium-ion batteries, Panasonic of Japan. (Look for Tesla to manufacture their own lithium-ion batteries in a new mega-factory coming on stream in late 2016). All that talent is rewarding him as the 83rd wealthiest man in the world, according to Forbes Magazine (4/2016). And to think, he built his incredible net worth in less than 16 years...not too shabby!

Tersely put, Elon Musk is an engaging, accomplished visionary often compared to Steve Jobs, former CEO of Apple. But there is so much more to this man than a risk-taking businessman. His stars brightly illuminate a future, widely anticipated to reflect successes he'll enjoy in space and land travel, solar heating, and rocket propulsion products.

Elon founded his first company, X.com, in 1999, which morphed into what is now known as PayPal in October, 2002. According to The Economist Magazine (11/2003), PayPal went on to get gobbled up by eBay for $1.5 billion in stock. It just so happened Musk held a tidy little stash of that stock...to the tune of 11%! I guess that entitles him to sing his song of success in any key he wants!

Through his Space X company, he is working to convert America from an earth-based transportation system into its space-based equivalent, thus, creating a dichotomy where this enterprise is mutually exclusive from his very much earth-bound car business, working to get America off its addiction to fossil fuels. According to Forbes Magazine (5/2016) Musk will reach Mars before Tesla develops a foothold in China unless

Beijing changes their rules for doing business. Sales of Tesla cars in China, today, are miniscule in comparison to Cadillac, BMW, Mercedes-Benz, and Audi. This weak market penetration is somewhat offset by sales of Tesla's in Norway, the largest present-day marketplace for Tesla outside the U.S. Norwegians love their Teslas as they hunker down in snow like no other car, without fear of becoming immobile. Simply put, the Tesla S Model, much like Bob Seeger's hit song, handles "like a rock."

What is it about the man that has made all of this entrepreneurship possible? And why? At the heart of it, it would be simple to say he is doing it because he can financially do it. But that misses the mark in getting at the essence of the man. First and foremost, Elon has the talent and skills, backed by his wealth, to do pretty much anything he wants. He has an inquisitive, brilliant mind, coupled with his abundant God-given talents and, yes, courage to pursue a particular technology and deliver it to the marketplace with an eye on creating sufficient critical mass to drive down costs while constantly expanding volumes which allows for maintaining or enhancing profit margins and lowering the price to the customer or combinations of the two. For this to happen, he has to have VOLUME and lots of it.

Bob Lutz said it best, "electrification of the automobile is inevitable". No longer an "if" and "when" proposition ...it's just a question of time. Enter center stage, Elon Reeve Musk. His car company's very survival depends on the strength of Lutz' statement. To gain broader acceptance in the marketplace and spread around much of the technology he developed, Musk did the unthinkable. He freely gave away the technology to his would-be competitors. That's like welcoming a sex offender into a nudist camp for the day! To give away the "heart" of the automobile, i.e. its technology, says something about how confident Musk must be that there is a whole lot more to this manufacturer than the depth of his plans, its products and underlying technology.

Musk knows he will never get to the volumes he needs if he puts all of his resources in one model, the current "S" which sells for north of $100,000. After all, how many people can afford or are willing to buy a car with that kind of price tag hanging on it? Purely from an economic perspective, he needs a lower priced car to drive up volumes and to do so...profitably! To partially answer that need, Musk and his team are developing a new car priced in the mid-$30K's, a product that will clearly decide if Tesla Motors has a future…the future they want! You may have heard of this car because of some of its features i.e. greater distances between charges, and at a price a third of the model "S." Early indications are this vehicle, dubbed the Model 3, is going to be a huge success or, at the least, an early, huge success. The very day Tesla announced this new product offering, they accepted advanced orders for 425,000 cars, totaling nearly $15 billion, backed by a refundable $1,000 deposit! How's that for huge? And, get this – It's now 2018 and this model is being produced in limited quantities, suffering from manufacturing-related issues.

In support of the critical mass needed to produce such volumes, Tesla is building a $5 billion factory in Nevada to build battery packs that will power these vehicles and have plans to build cars at this location, as well. According to Automotive News (6/2015), Tesla will build 50,000 cars in 2016. By 2018, they aspire to build 10X's that many and early signs are indicating those numbers are going to be met.

At the moment, one of Elon's greatest challenges is to get various states' franchise laws struck down so he can more aggressively sell Teslas' in stand-alone showrooms on a direct basis, from Tesla to the buyer, without the need of going through a middleman i.e. car dealer. Good luck with that!! He has had some success in getting his unique distribution plan accepted in some isolated instances where a state was catering a favor in exchange for building a factory in their particular state. At this time, few states have relaxed their franchise laws that would allow Tesla to go to market without the involvement of a dealer. Clearly, dealers are threatened by Teslas approach because, if successful, other car manufacturers will follow and they can say "good bye" to the business model that's been around for the past 100+ years. So, you can readily see, Musk isn't satisfied in just bringing revolutionary products to market that, in time, will reach the average household, he wants to control how and where they are purchased. Again, good luck with that! Another challenge that is looming out there just waiting to be awakened by some politician is the current situation where no gas taxes are being collected from Tesla owners because…they don't use gasoline! So how do Tesla owners pay their fair share in taxes intended to support driving needs and road repairs? Obviously, that scenario has got to change and no doubt, will. It will happen when electric-powered automobiles are so prevalent that their lack of gas or road use tax revenues decline to the point that changes, by necessity, will follow. You can take that to the bank! One possible answer might be a requirement to have all Tesla and Tesla-like vehicles prepay a road tax at the time of purchase based on some estimated amount of miles, anticipated to be driven in a specific period of time. Another unfair advantage enjoyed by electric-powered car owners in Arizona is the ability to buy a special-issued license plate that identifies its owner as a user of non-gasoline based fuel and, as such, is entitled to buy this special-issued plate for less than $50.00. You can bet the politicians are going to get in on that one, as well.

Despite these challenges, I wouldn't bet against Musk. Anyone whose mantra could be "there is no tomorrow," has got to be taken seriously. His track record speaks for itself as he has repeatedly brought concepts to finished products in the market, heretofore, yet to be conceived...by anyone. In fact, he continues to define what constitutes the meaning of "state-of-the-art", beyond the imagination and vision of nearly everyone except... Elon Reeve Musk.

WHEN IT'S ALL SAID & DONE

As a student of automotive history, I can see the recurring themes behind the actions taken by many of this industry's leaders, with the same result - just another cast of characters playing out of the same sandbox, driven largely by ego and greed. Less often, cars have been produced, born out of well-conceived and executed plans that, truly, met the needs in the marketplace. Rarer yet, are the cars that were brought to market when no need existed, leaving it to the marketers to create that need, i.e. the Ford Mustang in 1964 and the present-day Dodge Challenger Hellcat with its 707 horsepower engine. Who needs a 707 horsepower monster like that? Apparently, there is a sizable enough market to justify the investment to bring this behemoth to market; otherwise, it is just another marketing blunder that Chrysler can ill-afford.

Detroit appears to be committed to advancing plans that will successfully lead them into a new automotive era big time, with the technological advances being developed in propulsion, connectivity, and usage, (all explained in the upcoming CARS Chapter). This will give rise to a whole new crop of leaders who, unlike in the past, are entrepreneurs, product innovators, and engineers who will adapt to the new norms as to how cars will be utilized in the future. Gone are the days that Detroit could be managed and controlled by so-called bean-counters (accountants and finance types).

The real question to be posed for the industry is whether Detroit can experience a phoenix-like revival from the ashes of pre-21st century technology or will Silicon Valley displace Detroit and become the "new" Detroit and, more importantly, will the U.S. re-establish itself with its previous crown as the world's leading manufacturer of automobiles?

CAR DEALERS

They are either dream "keepers", or dream "killers", depending on how your deal turns out. One day, the dealer can't do anything wrong; the next day, he's a bum. And through either scenario, the would-be buyer is fickle and can change his or her mind like shifting sand. A car dealership is a place where you entrust your dreams with the expectation that those dreams are alive and kicking until such time as you drive the car away. To make this moment a memorable, happy one, the one you anticipated and hoped for, you need to select a dealer with care. In this chapter we will look at what makes a particular dealer a good or a poor choice and what he has to do to earn your business.

The dealer with whom you have had no previous experience, needs to measure up to your expectations in terms of reputation, competitiveness, location, likeability, credibility...someone you are comfortable with. There are plenty of dealers out there meeting those expectations on paper, but, dealing with them on a one-to-one basis is an entirely different and time consuming matter.

Before you step into a dealership, ask family members and friends for recommendations. Check the Internet and the Better Business Bureau in order to judge how effective, informative and credible their print, radio and television advertising is. Just because a dealer makes use of extensive advertising doesn't, necessarily, mean that he is trustworthy, good for his word, and someone you think you can work with. Yet, at the same time, know that advertising doesn't come cheap and, chances are, that dealer is doing a few things right. He has got to sell some cars to pay for that advertising! My point is, don't overly rely on a dealer's advertising, but certainly put it into your mix of things to consider.

You should understand how car dealerships operate in order

to make a good choice. What is the dealer's larger role, besides getting you to commit to buying a car today? Do you feel he is prepared to service your vehicle in a timely manner? In what ways is the dealership's personnel showing an interest in doing business with you and, as importantly, taking care of your ongoing service needs? Are they making you feel special? Know that there are a few bad apples out there but the vast majority of dealers are trying to make a difference in their efforts to earn your business. Beyond simply having a physical presence, many dealers have an involvement in the communities they serve such as hiring people, paying taxes, participating or sponsoring local sporting teams and events, making charitable contributions and sometimes, if they do enough of these things well, you and the marketplace reward them with something referred to as "making a profit."

Why would anyone want to be in the car business where franchising is the norm? Here, the dealer must return a portion of his revenues to the manufacturer (franchisor) just for the privilege of representing let's say, Ford or Chevrolet, in their marketing area. There are credit lines that must be rigorously maintained just to remain in business. This is called "floor planning," and every day an inventoried car goes unsold, there is interest to be paid. FYI- not all dealers "floor plan", thus avoiding the interest expense of buying and carrying inventory. Penske Automotive is an example of a mega dealer who does not floor plan anything. They pay cash for all vehicles they buy for resale. With zero interest to pay, it frees up valuable cash that can and does get used to buy up more dealerships. Presently, Roger Penske's empire stands at nearly 300 dealerships worldwide, while ever in search of more stores to buy, as thcy recently did in Italy, making Penske Automotive the largest retail dealer in Europe and the second largest in the U.S.

What's a dealer got to do to stay in business? After meeting the above challenges, the retail car business, in my view, is a decent venue for developing wealth, thanks to its ability to generate cash in a hurry as a "cash flow cow." I would even venture out to state that a new car dealership is one of the fastest routes to becoming a millionaire. A "newbie" salesman can work in a dealership for twenty years (or less), get himself promoted to a sales manager's position and, in time, become a general manager, all of which provide entreprenurial opportunity for ownership, seldom found in other fields of work. That advancement progression, from a sales rep to a dealership owner, is unheard of in other franchise type businesses in such a relatively short period of time. Equally important, there is a reasonable rate of return (ROI) on the dealers principal investment coupled with the potential for multiple inventory "turns", accomplished by selling more cars as quickly as possible in order to minimize inventory costs. These are the keys to making money off their sales operations. Besides the cash generated from new car sales, the dealership enjoys several other income streams, many of which come into play to offset poor new car sales. Those include: pre-owned car sales, parts, service and collision departments. Then there is financing, extended warranty contracts and other post-sale products and services offered by the finance department that you will learn about before you get out of the dealer's door. So you can readily see there are many avenues available to a dealer to pursue that lead to making some serious money.

A dealer is to service what quality of product is to the car manufacturer. When you strip away all the perceptions and tasks that fall on the dealer, one thing remains.....SERVICE. After all, a dealer is in the service business...period, end of sentence. A dealer's competitors are selling the same products (make and model of cars); but, the one thing a dealer can do to differentiate himself from his competition is to provide a level of SERVICE, second to none!! Every dealer, it seems, talks about their excellent service (who's doing the judging?) Don't you believe that for a New York minute. Darn few, truly, commit their organizations to excellence in service and, interestingly enough, the few that do, stand out like hapless camels meandering down Bell Road (Phoenix).

A dealer can't (and doesn't) always have the lowest price to offer; but, what he can give you is a level of service you won't soon forget. A consistent level of quality-based service is the key to admission for a would-be dealer to get into the business; and it had better be designed for continual improvement because there are more than a few competitors striving to do the same! When the relationship is working efficiently, dealers are to car buyers what a pipe-wrench is to a plumber...inseparably intertwined. Dealers justify their existence by serving the collective car buyers or "you's" out there in the marketplace.

Now, let's take a look at how a service & parts department

operates. S & P have to compensate for lost sales during down markets. It, also, serves as a magnet to draw people back into the dealership when economic times improve. Conversely, a poor S & P Department can hurt new car sales as an unhappy service customer isn't likely to buy a car at a dealership with a poor service department. He wants to protect his "good" deal that came with much effort, with a service department that he can depend on!

The Sales Department is referred to as the "front end" of the dealership while S & P Departments are called the "rear end". In dealer-ese, the front end "gets" the business and the S & P "keeps" the biz. A strong "rear end" promotes and protects the "front end" without the costly expense of advertising, associated with sales.

Have you ever wondered why companies refer to their sales departments as the "sales department," when, in fact, that department functions more like the "buyers department?" Why not rename, as such? The perspective behind the term "sales department" is all wrong, as the would-be customer could and should care less about a company's sales department. They came to buy, not sell.

The heart of the dealership is the so-called sales department and, in particular, pre-owned sales. You would have thought it was new cars, wouldn't you? I know I would, if I didn't know the difference. That is because there is such a small mark-up between what the dealer pays the manufacturer and the manufacturer's suggested retail price (MSRP) which, many times, is negotiated downward, creating even more pressure on maintaining a reasonable level of mark-up. That isn't quite as severe as it might seem, as the dealer can get a more desirable mark-up or profit margin on the resale of your trade-in. So, if you don't have a trade-in and you pay cash, you just robbed the dealer of two possible income streams, forcing him to make a profit out of the mark-up on the MSRP, set by the factory. That profit margin is, typically, less than 5%, a third of what it was twenty years ago. So, if you buy a car with a MSRP (sticker price) of $32,000 (the norm today), the dealer stands to generate a gross profit no greater than $1,600 (if that), an amount that gets further reduced by operating expenses, a sales commission to the salesperson who did the deal, interest expense, taxes, and overhead, which has to be paid whether a car is sold or not. That example however, doesn't tell the entire story because of something the car manufacturer offers the dealer called "holdback", an amount of money earned by the dealer for meeting certain sales goals during a specific period of time. The holdback can range anywhere between 1% and 3%, with the lower percent assigned to higher-priced products such as a Mercedes.

Who are some examples of reputable dealers who, truly, work to earn your business and where can you go to get specific recommendations for a particular make and model in your area? OK, stay tuned.

The dealer identities I am about to present to you have one common denominator that runs through their dealerships which they hold to be sacrosanct and that would be.....customer service. They deserve to be recognized for the superior service they have been offering their customers for years, finding a way to offer a repeatable service that other dealers can't or don't care to replicate. At the top of my list is YARK SABARU of Toledo, Ohio. They're good because they train their people to be good... simple as that. Their personnel turnover rate is 1%, spread over a period of 3 years! That is unheard of in an industry famous for churning sales people and service advisors to the tune of 70% over the same 3 year time period. Any dealer with that kind of turnover rate has got to be doing something right, a something recognizable to their customers in terms of a quality, repeatable service. Yark was recently selected by Automotive News (10/2016) as their "Dealer of the Year" in competition with all franchised dealers across the country, regardless of nameplate. Yark attributes their success to in-house training emphasizing customer service and cross-communications between departments, and management's acknowledgement that perks work.

Next on my short list of customer-oriented dealerships is DAVE SMITH, Kellogg, Idaho, a mega-dealer who sells numerous makes and models. He is, reportedly, the largest volume dealer in the Pacific Northwest, based near Spokane, Washington. His mantra, "success is in the details" works to keep his people focused on the customer and off of themselves. No detail is too small and when the details are meticulously attacked, the deal will take care of itself. Forget so-called salesmanship..... concentrate on identifying the prospect's needs and connect all the dots presented in the details. How difficult can that be? Product knowledge and a dedication to a repeatable model for customer service are givens. With that out of the way, it's easier to get focused on the details. This attention to detail shows up in the form of increased customer satisfaction with the customer knowing nothing is going to be left incomplete or in doubt.

RAY SKILLMAN, Indianapolis (multiple car makes/models), enjoys success by hiring, in his view, the right people and, then, holding onto them. Uniquely, 15% of recent hires are college graduates, many of whom are women. He offers them salaries and sales achievement bonuses to stave-off discouragement associated with slow or low sales results, which is a regrettable part of the business, all this to minimize the daily pressures associated with job security...which doesn't exist in the car business any more than any other business for that matter. So, their customers benefit in knowing the salesperson they are working with, is giving them either an honest "yes" or "no;" thus, making for a higher degree of integrity and respect for both the buyer and the seller. This minimizes any perceived need to stretch the truth in order to get a deal done.

And, then, there is SANDERSON AUTOMOTIVE, who operate one Ford store in Glendale, Arizona, and a Lincoln store in Phoenix. According to Automotive News (1/2017) these two dealerships combined produced something north of $350 million in new vehicle sales, making them the #1 dealer in the U.S. for the average revenue per dealership as well as ranking them #2 nationally for the most new vehicles sold per dealership, estimated to be around 5200 per year. Top that! Those kind of sales statistics don't rain down from heaven or sitting on one's thumbs. Their business model is very simple...give the customer what he/she wants and make the customer believe they deserve what they want. And, here comes the trick...make a profit doing it!

I will conclude with my personal experience dealing with SCHUMACHER EUROPEAN, recently acquired by Penske Automotive, a Scottsdale, Arizona, based Mercedes-Benz dealer, a dealer who is roundly recognized in an annual report as the "best" dealer in the Phoenix area, whether it be for a Mercedes or a Chevrolet. This organization is wired for customer service, personified in each of their salespeople. Typically, they have your service order written up and hand you the keys for your loaner within minutes of driving into the service bay. Their sales people know what they are selling...an excellent example and form of customer service. As if there were a contest to see what salesperson can come off as the most laid back, seemingly without a care in the world except getting you behind the wheel of a new Mercedes, there would be numerous contestants for that honor. One major litmus test that Schumacher passes with flying colors is that there is next to no personnel turnover in new car sales. How can anybody be that happy? As you might suspect, Schumacher isn't the cheapest guy in town, but, many feel they are the best. I only wish that they had other stores with more mainstream, down market products so that more people could be exposed to their terrific customer service!

One source of information on who is considered the best car dealership(s) in your geographic area can be found on www. DealerRater.com. Just punch in the name of the model you are interested in buying, followed by the zip code you reside in, and up pops the names of the top dealers in your area. Although I do not know what is involved in determining who and how a particular dealer gets selected by DealerRater, I do know and agree with their choices most of the time and use this tool to locate a car or dealer in a geographic area I am not familiar with.

There are alternatives to using a dealership when purchasing a car. One viable alternative that you should consider, is using a car buying service (I happen to know a good one), where there are no fees charged until the deal is completed, a deal you must approve before entering into it. Furthermore, a buying service does all the groundwork for you once you have chosen the car that you want to buy. The price is negotiated, while you maintain total control of the buying process, saving you precious time, much of which would have been wasted, time you could have spent on things of your own choosing. The fee you pay for their locating the car and putting the deal together is easilyoffset by the savings the buying service brings. In effect, their service costs you nothing! At Automobile Buyer Services, my company GUARANTEES those savings or we will gladly return your fee. FYI- since 2002 when I started ABS, we have not refunded a single fee...not once! But, bottom line, if you are not happy for whatever reason, we aren't either.

Another approach to buying or leasing a car is buying the vehicle online, minimizing the "dealership experience." Online shopping, which is no more than "catalog buying" with the use of a computer, such as offered by Amazon and eBay, are paving the way to removing the car dealerhip from the buying equation, all together. If this becomes a wide spread method of buying, watch for some dramatic changes coming from the dealers. Even, right now, while in the infancy of this new business model, other changes are taking place that will have the net effect of reducing the number of dealers and manufacturers (acquisitions and consolidations), the impact resulting from car and ride sharing, changes associated with technology and various forms of social media, just to name a few.

A whole new crop of services are being launched by the more aggressive, enlightened dealers and lenders who embrace changes that include:

- An in-house specialist who demonstrates the various car features.
- Leasing Certified Pre-Owned vehicles, heretofore, unheard of.
- Concierge services; post-sale car deliveries and service department-related, pick-up and delivery.
- Digital shopping and a financial tool that's a form of direct lending where the buyer configures and prices the vehicle(s) of choice at the bank, prior to purchase, which, in turn, refers the buyer to a dealership that has the pricing and product in inventory.

Your final stop at the dealer before driving away in your new dream car, is a visit to the F & I Department (Finance & Insurance), whose manager will attempt to sell you on the merits of gap insurance, appearance and weather protection packages, wheel upgrades, and extended warranty/service agreements. If you choose any of these "add-ons", just know that they have the net effect of reducing the amount of money you would have saved on the deal.

Some of the add-ons are deserving of your consideration, many are not. For instance, gap insurance can offer peace of mind, knowing that you have removed a significant risk of loss associated with a possible collision, covering the difference between what your car is worth and the amount of money you still owe on the car. And, maybe, an extended warranty/service agreement might make sense to you because of the number of miles or years you anticipate owning this car. You are under no obligation to purchase any of these products or services and it in no way changes the details of your deal. So, feel free to excuse yourself and drive away. On the other hand, if you change your mind about buying a particular service or product, you can always go back at a later time and make the appropriate purchase. But, know there are some conditions that must be kept in mind if you decide to delay buying an extended warranty. You can't allow the existing warranty to lapse; so, any replacement warranty you might want to buy, must be purchased no later than one day before the current coverage expires.

So, in a nutshell, there are plenty of good dealers out there to choose from. That allows you to take the time to thoroughly check out a particular dealer. The peace of mind it offers is well worth the effort. And, for whatever doubts remain, call me at 602-710-7112 or 866-780-8106.

SOOOOOOOOO MANY CARS

As promised, here's a chapter dedicated entirely to cars...and lots of them. I've compiled and categorized car subjects, placing them in 25 lists, lists that clearly reflect my dreams, passions, preferences, dislikes and the realities I find myself in today.

Much of what you will be reading expresses my opinions with a few facts sprinkled in here and there; facts that won't jump out and bite you, but, by the same token, you'll know the difference between what is and what isn't. I've got to tell you how much this means to me, even at the risk of offending some of you with all of these opinions I am proffering. You luckless creatures, you! You see, these opinions are nothing more than my passions screaming out, begging you to keep reading. So, I just ask that you indulge me a bit longer as we draw closer to the end of the book. I don't want to lose any of you now. Just know that I am making a concerted effort to keep a balanced perspective on the material I am presenting. It ain't gospel, but, it is my gospel. So, don't be overly concerned about the possibility of me stretching your "noodle" beyond your normal limits because it's not going to happen. OK? Let's roll the dice.

My "tiptoe through the tulips," you may recall, all started as a tender-aged little boy, standing by the side of an old, dusty country road, counting and identifying cars coming and going. In time, this would lead to washing cars in the family's Ford dealership at age 12, that should have confirmed for anyone savvy enough to know that cars need refueling of some kind from time-to-time, that I was well on my way to becoming a huge car enthusiast that grew into a love affair that, in time, led to salaried employment with Chevrolet Division, General Motors Corp. Much later, I became a sales and marketing consultant to Mercedes-Benz, this collective experience taken as a whole, prepared me to start my own car-related business, Automobile Buyer Services, some fifteen years ago.

This journey began in earnest at age 16 at the time I bought my first car...a 1956 Ford, Mainline 2-door sedan and the voyage keeps on unfolding. In between, I have bought, leased, sold, traded or collected all sorts of four-wheeled animals: a combination of 30 two and four door sedans, 13 personal luxury automobiles, 5 coupes (no "B" pillars), 7 convertibles, 8 sports cars, 8 collectibles, 1 crossover, 1 muscle car, 6 exotics; and 1 lone, good for nothing, SUV, a GMC Envoy.

Several of these cars are noteworthy for a variety of reasons. However, two of them stand out, justifiably so, in need of some ink to give you a glimpse into the depths of my sacrifice just to get myself through college.

The first of the two was a 1960 Chevrolet Corvair, a literal "death warmed-over" excuse of a car that, in my case, needed a quart of reclaimed oil per day, allowing me to extend its life for, yet, another mile, as it helped get me through school. This car subdued my considerable ego for a time as I was forced to sell the hottest street car I ever owned to accommodate this most basic mode of transportation, all in an effort to make college, financially, doable. Imagine going from a gallon of gas every 8 miles to an imitation of a bathtub on four wheels that required a quart of oil a day! Yes, that gas-loving beast I gave up was a new, 1966 Chevrolet Impala Super Sport, 2-door hardtop. Resting under its hood was a 427 cubic inch, 425 horsepower Ford-eater of a beast, that could "fish tail" in all 4 gears. This was beyond fast, scatting like a 2 year old with a loaded diaper! Present day, I compare that with my current ride, a BMW 7 Series and quake at realizing this transition happened to one man, in one lifetime, and that would be me. Wow...what one does for a college education!!

Upon depleting my budget for buying reclaimed oil more frequently than I attended church, I learned about a 1962 Mercury Meteor. I bet you never heard of that model of Mercury before, have you? Well, neither had I until I bought one. This car, as it turns out, was just one notch higher up the "desirable cars to own someday" list, but it got me over suffering the embarrassment of tooling around town in a 10 year old Corvair that didn"t seem to mind having a quart of oil added ever so many months instead of every day, as I was fully used to. The Meteor wasn't anything to write home about. In fact, it would have made it into "one of the most boring cars I ever owned" category. But, that was OK. I didn't buy it for looks. I could best describe that car as a pulse-elevating vehicle, akin to watching water drip from a leaky spigot. The boredom didn't come at any added expense.

Oh well, enough of this momentary reminiscing as I was, at the time, already dreaming of that next car, a car I would reward myself with, once I got my degree, that would suitably compliment that piece of paper that showed I was now the proud owner of a Bachelor of Arts Degree in Economics. This was in the late 60's where ugly cars were as pervasive as they are today. But, on the opposite end of the spectrum, I found a car to buy that did justice to my sacrifices and that sheep skin that I couldn't wait to hang on the wall. Makes me wonder how Martin Luther felt about hanging his 95 thesis on a church door, probably prouder than a peacock that he did it. On second thought, I don't think proud had anything to do with Pastor Martin's doings but it sure fit mine.

So, after a lifetime of lists, from the "to do's" to either the heralded or dreaded "bucket" list, I thought it only appropriate to air out an accumulation of preferences and give a little organization to all these pent-up opinions, by offering you the "mother lode" of all car lists. Read on and see if you care to agree with me. I promise you one thing, though, it will either be barely tolerable to read, gravitating toward some degree of being entertained, genuinely enjoying the romp through these various categories, or you might become flat-out bored! I'll take that risk. Meanwhile.....you enjoy.

1.) MY TOP TEN LIST; Model Year 2017

AUDI – Best interior designs in the industry; flew by Cadillac in sales as if standing still.

BUICK – Through the first half of 2016, Buick was the industry's fastest growing international brand, this according to Automotive News (09/2016). Buick is preparing to launch a new "sub-brand" in China that, hopefully, will make its way to the U.S. This truly gorgeous car is named the "Avenir" which means "future" in French.

CADILLAC - Working feverishly to reinvent itself as the "standard of the world." Two of their models, the ATS and the

CTS are world-beaters in terms of performance although they haven't lived up to their sales potential, thanks to so many competing cars in this market segment...most notably, BMW, Mercedes, and Audi.

HYUNDAI and KIA – Both sharing a common corporate parent, both styled by Austrian-born Peter Schreyer, who, in addition to being their Chief Design Officer, serves both companies as President, as well. What a talent this man is, bringing much success to these two brands. Through three months of 2016, the combined sales of the two was nearly 320,000 cars, good enough to tie Honda as the fifth largest auto maker. Not too shabby if one takes into consideration that Kia claimed bankruptcy in 1997 and Hyundai was all but given up for dead, thanks to terribly built cars. Who can forget the Hyundai Excel of the early 1990's...what a piece of cra#. Miraculously, today, both Hyundai and Kia can boast of well-built, well-designed, reliable, affordable, fuel efficient automobiles. No small accomplishment, achieved in a relatively short period of time.

JEEP – The Grand Cherokee model is a show-stopping beauty. Just ask my friends Dave Sacks and Bill Burford. Once a stodgy, nearly forgotten model, the car is anything but that today. This is a world-class, luxury vehicle that has successfully repositioned itself in the market other than the one it became famous for...an off-road vehicle.

JAGUAR - Their quality and reliability reputation has been holding back this beautifully designed salon that has, at times, enjoyed a near exotic class distinction among European luxury sedans. Styling was never an issue, but could these luxo's break down easily and often. Early signs point to having much of their quality issues behind them. The only problem is that it continues to haunt them, as the luxury car buyer hasn't fully bought into this huge improvement in quality and reliability in any appreciable numbers, despite record retail sales in Model Year 2017 of one lone model, the Pace crossover model. But, they have a long way to go to catch up to the quality and reliability of Germany's market leading luxury sedans – Audi, BMW, Mercedes-Benz, and Porsche.

RAM – These formerly named Dodge trucks have become a refreshing alternative to Ford, Chevy and GMC makes, thanks to leading-edge styling and optional product content. There is

136

still a quality bug-a-boo associated with this make that will only improve if and when its parent company's (Chrysler) fortunes improve. But right at the moment it is Jeep and Ram that carry Chrysler. This could become a stand-alone company offering just the two brands. One could speculate that the two remaining brands of FCA, Chrysler and Dodge could be spun off to form yet another company. You think China might be interested? If they did, you can bet the price would not fetch a premium any more than they paid Ford for buying Volvo.

TESLA – Their "S" model was given a grade of 99 out of a possible 100 by Consumer Reports in the year it was introduced to the market. This EV continues to define advanced technology, haute styling, and, yes, fuel efficiency in the form of getting nearly 300 miles off of a fully charged battery. Look for this company to become hugely successful with their upcoming Model 3 which will place them in the high-volume portion of the EV market which they are pioneering.

VOLVO – Not everyone has one, right? That's OK as it helps fuel their attempts to build prestige into this once considered "safest car on the road." Today they are building on that claim to gain greater market acceptance for the new model XC 90, which is light years more stylish than its predecessor. Volvo's management is working to gain luxury status for this model, but for this to happen, they have to get some celebrities driving these vehicles for maximum exposure, as Matthew McConaughey has successfully done for Lincoln.

2.) MY ALL-TIME PERSONAL FAVORITES

I get this all the time, surely I have one car that stands out against all the rest as the "one" I would select for this dubious recognition. You know, that's like asking a parent who their favorite child is. But, secretly and with a bit of guilt, you realize that there is or was a favorite.

--My Five Finalists--

1967 Thunderbird – a college graduation present to myself.

1988 Porsche 911 Targa – my first exotic; sorry now that I ever sold it.

2001 Corvette convertible – my first American sports car (which

Sandi totaled); it wouldn't be the last.

2004 Mercedes-Benz SL500 – one of two dream cars I have owned.

2008 Maserati Gran Turismo coupe – my first Italian car; maybe my last.

And the winner is, after stewing over it ever so painfully... the 1967 Thunderbird. My selection is not so much based on the car itself, although it was a beaut and a joy to drive (what wouldn't be after a '60 Corvair and a '62 Mercury Meteor), as it is a reminder of how I rewarded myself for graduating college. What fond memories I associate with graduating and relocating to Chicago as I officially launched my career. This was an incredibly exciting time in my life, and, even today, I continue to associate times with cars. As a matter of fact, I pretty much compare everything with cars and vice versa!

I also want to recognize Cadillac here; a make that has been around for 100 + years, that has tasted their own version of the good, the bad, and the ugly. I hope the limb on this proverbial tree can handle the accolades I am about to thrust on this magnificent luxury car made by General Motors, a car that my heart has had a soft spot for, that has only grown with the years. After owning or leasing thirteen gorgeous examples of this American icon of a luxury automobile, I can unequivocally state, "pound for pound, dollar for dollar," Cadillac, in my opinion, is the best luxury car value in the world today. Period.

Cadillac, what an exciting and glorious future that many car journalists believe is lying just ahead, successfully recapturing the self- proclaimed creed of decades past: "The Standard of the World." I believe they have triumphantly overcome what once looked like a dismal to non-existent future, thanks to years of myopic marketing and overpriced, sub-standard product that was clearly nobody's standard, much less the world. A person could save thousands of dollars by buying a Toyota and get everything that Cadillac had to offer with the possible exception of prestige. Mercedes and BMW felt themselves a cut above, and didn't recognize Cadillac as part of the fraternity known as "luxury". Well, Cadillac is about to massively change that impression under the leadership of their newly named President,

138

Johan de Nysschen, who is now busy changing much of Cadillac's abysmal recent history, which, some say, started with the introduction of the Cadillac Cimmaron. Remember that dog? And I do mean dog!What a deficiently, disastrous dud... dead on arrival, worthy of junkyard status. What a disappointment to anyone who truly expected innovation, highline styling, and quality in a luxury automobile. Actually, it was more like the junkyard went out in search of a Cimmaron and, by George, it found it.

Johan is living proof that it's never too late to become what you could have been; and the will and programs are in place to storm into the current luxury car market that Cadillac has, unquestionably, a right to lay claim to. And, boy, do they have some models coming out of the pipeline that will knock your socks off, to say nothing about their current crop of models which are outstanding! This reminds me of a hymn you might know as well, "once I was lost but now I am found." That would be Cadillac.

3.) MOST BEAUTIFUL CARS AND THEIR COUNTERPARTS – 1950/1960's

Easy On The Eyes:

1954 Mercedes-Benz SL roadster with gull-wing, hinged doors

1956 Lincoln Continental, Mark II – highly collectible even to this day

1957 Cadillac Eldorado Brougham – this car could lay claim to "standard of the world" as far as design was considered; every inch of this car, taken at any angle, is absolutely gorgeous.

1965 Buick Riviera, Gran Sport – GM's finest design effort of that era. Resembled the best taken from Ferrari and Rolls-Royce, all rolled into one fantastic design. A timeless, must-own collector car.

1967 Jaguar XKE – arguably one of the most beautiful cars ever built, in any era. Only problem was they were prone to breaking...incredibly unreliable.

The Uglies:

1950 Nash Rambler – despite its built-in "passion pit" (and a fun little song "Beep Beep" by the Playmates), this car couldn't get admitted into an "ugly shop" (many "beauty shops" should be renamed this).

1958 Edsel – I am compelled to opine that this car far and away was one of the ugliest, failed examples of an American car in my lifetime. They did not have Computer Aided Design automation tools, so the designing of this hideous monster didn't just happen overnight. In typical Ford fashion, they were singing the praises of this meeskait (Yiddish for Ugly of Uglies) to the high heavens as Ford's entry into the mid-luxury market, intended to compete with Oldsmobile and Buick. I will be charitable in describing the front end of the car...it looked a lot like a horse collar. Some said it looked like the remains of a heavily sucked-upon lemon. In any event, this car was a complete, miserable flop. Not restricted just to horrible looks, it failed in about every category one could think of – quality, body fit and finish, just to note a few. Trust me, I am being polite and gratuitously kind by calling this a car...it should never have come to market, and as a result, few were sold. Those that did sell were sold to the type of buyer who would buy tennis shoes for a prosthetic elephant!

1960 Citroen – Another standout choice for this dubious honor would have to go to France's feeble entry in the luxo sedan field. How a country seemingly obsessed with fashion, styling and luxuriating in the good life can come up sooooo empty when it comes to luxury cars...any cars for that matter, is beyond me.

1967-69 AMC Marlin

1971 AMC Matador

1975 AMC Pacer (American Motors sure was busy producing ugly cars in the late 60's to mid-70's)

2001 Pontiac Aztec – This car gets my vote as the all-time ugliest, most embarrassing, poorly-built car in the 100 year history of General Motors. They had other gems, but none tops this one. The model never should have got to market. Even GM focus groups voted down this vehicle, and yet, they went ahead and built it......this on Rick Wagoner's watch. This car has the worth of graduating magna cum laude from Trump University!

2015 Nissan Cabriolet – Finally put out of its' misery in model year 2017. It was long overdue unless you were an over-sexed 90 year old (see my list of "Best Cars To Make Out In").

4.) WORST CARS I OWNED

1960 Chevrolet Corvair – loved oil more than gasoline.

1976 Ford Thunderbird – had no passing gear; even stumped a factory engineer. Car was a born loser.

1999 GMC – my lone truck-like product (SUV); loved gas like the desert loves rain.

5.) BIGGEST LOSERS, FAILURES and NEVER SHOULD HAVE BEEN BUILT (not covered elsewhere)

1971-1980 Ford Pinto/Mercury Bobcat – was a complete me-chanical/design disaster, taking the lives of many people due to rear end crashes, causing the car to explode on impact.

1988 Pontiac Fiero – a plastic-bodied, wannabe sports car. It suffered the same fate as experienced by the Pinto/Bobcat...a fire hazard waiting to happen!

Certain Ford Explorer SUVs – Especially noteworthy was the number of fatalities associated with the loss of control on certain Explorer SUVs due to poor handling characteristics associated with tires manufactured by Firestone that could have set off some serious fireworks between the Fords and the Firestones. It just so happens that Bill Ford (Henry's grandson) recently deceased, and, owner of the Detroit Lions football team, was married to a Firestone.

Mercedes-Benz – believe it or not, M-B doesn't do all things well. Case in point – the Smart Car For Two (make that for "none"). There is positively nothing smart about this casket on wheels. You will need God's intervention if ever rear ended in one of these death traps that rightly belong in a junkyard. I have seen better looking golf carts, no, make that go carts.

DMC-12 – John Delorean's brain child, poorly conceived and built, richly deserving of an ignominious death. The car did, however, enjoy the briefest of fame as it was featured in the Michael J. Fox movie, "Back To The Future." This car was a production disaster with parts falling off during assembly and non-functioning mechanical components that never should have passed the hastiest of inspections. A car with junk status written all over it, which, at best, looked like a pregnant Camaro. To read the popular car literature of the time, one would think this car was destined for star status. Maybe in Antarctica! Just ask Johnny Carson, who invested heavily in this car's development (if you could...he's been deceased for beaucoup years).

1985 Yugo – Who could ever forget the Yugo built in Eastern Europe? This car was a total piece of unadulterated cra#, undeserving of any laudable mention. Calling it a car was a stretch of gigantic proportions. The car was sooooo bad, that exterior parts had a way of falling off, such as bumpers and door handles. Buying it was like showing up at an ugly sweater party without a sweater and telling the world how much you hate cars. Junk yards were reluctant to sell them for spare parts. Despite its name, you "didn't go!" Should have been renamed "Nogo."

Chevrolet SSR – part hot-rod and part pick-up truck with a hard shell, convertible top, of which it was neither. This vehicle couldn't make up its mind what it was or what it wanted to be. With that never determined, Chevrolet wasted no time killing off this model, joining Chrysler Prowler in some discreditable graveyard for failed follies. That GM model was doomed from the beginning; the three initials of that model should have stood for "seriously sick, really."

2001 Pontiac Aztek – I know I am risking beating this dog to death, (see "Uglies" listed above) but it so richly deserves my best chosen adjectives to tell you what I really think... again. Besides it's such fun to beat up on this blatant minivan-in-drag monstrosity. Here goes – the 2001 Astek is, far and away, the worst example of an American-built car in terms of styling and utilitarian features. You couldn't give this car away. Somehow, this poster child for "ugliness" managed to hang around for five long and regrettable years. GM even tried to pass it off as a weekend camper with its pop-up, pup tent features to go along with its laughable, despicable looks. Now, to remove any doubt that I have completely beaten our proverbial dog to death, let me tell you what I really think. The Aztek is so overwhelmingly ugly that a blowfish wouldn't get caught dead swimming next to it! Make no mistake about it, this vehicle was so bad that it should have been arrested for impersonating a minivan. At that, I still can't believe GM brought this pathetic specimen to market. Only God knows, and He ain't telling! Little wonder why GM went bankrupt.

1990-91 Chrysler TC by Maserati – While at Chrysler, Lee Iacocca can rightly be criticized for the disastrous development of a car that goes along with his spotty habit for producing losers from time to time i.e. the Mustang II, in spite of his much vaulted standing as the father of the original Mustang. This time around, his blunder was the Chrysler TC by Maserati....what a mouthful of a name. In its essence, this car was a seriously bad attempt at competing with Mercedes-Benz's world-acclaimed SL roadster. The TC was no more than a rebadged Chrysler LeBaron convertible with a hard shell top with a peek-a-boo, opera styled rear-sided window, reminiscent of a 1956/57 Ford Thunderbird. What an owner ended up with was an over-priced, counterfeit, perfectly good Chrysler LeBaron that in no way resembled a Maserati other than a grille ornament. If you were one of the unlucky ones who forked over some big bucks for this replicar, I hope you liked the color yellow because that was the only color available.

2007 BMW X6 – hard to believe their design studio could come up with such a monstrously styled vehicle. The design team that came up with that harebrain, terribly misplaced design must have endured some serious sleep deprivation with no regard for job security!

2008 Tesla (Lotus-based roadster) – this car wasn't ready for prime-time when it was introduced as an EV sports car. Bob Lutz calls Tesla "the world's biggest cash incinerator."

1996/99 GM's EV1 – GM just wasn't ready to go to market with this colossal failure, another one of Roger Smith's babies. Zero performance – so lethargic it could have passed for a toothless alligator in a Louisiana swamp!

1975-1976 Chevrolet Vegas Cosworth with its unique "twin" camshaft engine that resulted in "twin" realities for their less than happy owners - cost to buy and cost to keep (on the street)...a loser by any comparison with comparably priced vehicles at the time.

6.) COLOSSAL MARKETING BLUNDERS

2010 Chevrolet Volt – It should never have been...at least not a Chevy, given its price. It could have been a Cadillac Volt with the Cadillac ELR never seeing the light of day. The ELR equivalent of the Volt was late to market and terribly overpriced although the ELR may in time become a collector's item. Result? It's gone. Now Chevrolet is readying to launch their new EV, named the Bolt, a less costly, more miles per charge, corral-pal to the Volt. Can Cadillac be far behind with a product I'll jokingly call the Jolt? So, there you have it folks, a new line of EV's from GM...the Volt, Bolt and Jolt...something for every wallet in America. Alfred Sloan (GM's famous former CEO who espoused a hierarchy of GM brands that would suit the rising fortunes of its customers, starting out owning a Chevrolet, progressing upwards to a Pontiac, onwardly upward until the pinnacle was finally reached with ownership of a Cadillac). would have been proud of that statement! And to think you have become part of automotive lore by reading this first...right here, before someone unceremoniously shows me the door! Or, maybe, I should apply for copyright status before GM tries to steal it away from me!

KIA – Has it occurred to you that the brand name "KIA" might be offensive to some? More than likely, few do, but I count myself among them. Maybe it's my military mindset at times, streaming a message of inappropriateness, but this name can (and does) conjure up less than pleasant images and experiences that some might associate with war and loss...KIA as in "killed in action". Why not change the name from Kia to Optima, a present-day, best-selling model that could totally take care of the name and image associated with this public relations-based mine field? After all, Kia has shown that it is not averse to changing a name as they were forced to do so with the naming of their highline model, the K900. That was originally going to be called the K9, when it was brought to their attention that in America, K9 conjured up the image of dogs. That would never work, so they stayed up all night wracking their brains, and came up with K900. See how nicely and easily that got around a probable public relations fiasco? Surely it shouldn't be too big of a deal to go with Optima for their mainstream product, and fire the person who came up with K9...not a very appropriate name for a $75,000 luxury car. And while they're at it, they should give some thought to giving up on the K900 model because that car is not selling, whether part of the dog family or not. LeBron James' endorsement in t.v. commercials creates for me an image of a missed dunk...when he's two feet above the rim!

Cadillac – Few car brands have suffered more marketing reversals and false starts in recent years than Cadillac. That wasn't always so as Cadillac is credited with many industry firsts that date back nearly a hundred years, from the first car to feature an electric starter, to aesthetics like the fins of the fifties. Cadillac simply lost its way, and left it to hiring outside, proven professionals to guide them back on track. That's being done with a vengeance behind the leadership of Johan De Nyschen, former head of Audi and Infiniti where he was widely recognized as a winner, without peer, and is credited as the sales and marketing architect who got both of those companies up on the fast track,the very same track they run on today with Audi deliriously delighted to look in their rear view mirror and seeing a Cadillac! Now, De Nyschen has the task of reversing that role. I like his prospects for doing so.

Looking back to the 80's with their new J-car product, the Cadillac Cimarron...it was nothing but a re-badged Chevy Cavalier. Years earlier Cadillac got away with re-badging the Chevy Nova as the Cadillac Seville, which went on to become a huge success. Can you blame Cadillac for believing they could pull that stunt off a second time? This time, the results were totally different with the Cimarron leaping into the toilet...never to be seen again.

You would have thought by now, Cadillac would have learned their lesson for building poorly conceived, so-called luxury cars, but no, no, no...far from it, as they reserved a little more of their ineptitude for the Cadillac Catera. You remember this one don't you? The one that zig-zagged itself into your heart and out of your driveway faster than you can say "it was an itsy, bitsy, teeny weeny, yellow polka dot bikini"? This was the car that drove (no pun intended) Cadillac loyalists to the doors, many of whom never returned.

Since I am on a roll beating up Cadillac, allow me to remind you of the not-so-famous, Cadillac Allante, the proposed market slayer of the Mercedes-Benz SL. Like everything at Cadillac during those years, despite GM's claim that they had done their homework, the car never caught on as a serious contender to the Benz. Apparently, GM's corporate dog must have eaten the homework, proving once again, Cadillac was not ready to do battle with the big boys! And, then, there was the 2005/09 XLR hard-shell top roadster that suffered the same result. Mercedes owns that market, something that GM's marketing, apparently, wasn't aware of! You can bet your sweet patuty they know now!

1974/78 Ford Mustang II – Lee Iacocca's attempt to do a "one up" on the very car he helped father. As is so typical of car manufacturers, once they bring a winning car to the buying public, they resort to greed by building larger, more costly equivalents of the very successful car that got them to the "dance" in the first place. As such, the original Mustang grew larger and larger over time to the point that downsizing it must have seemed an economic and cosmetic necessity in an effort to regain its former fanfare. Well, in this instance, it didn't work. This product was so bad, even before it was a completed design project, Henry Ford II, our old buddy, got his two-cents worth in, by trying to get the car named the "Mini Bird". This car was destined to failure from the get-go to become an even quicker out-go. And, were it not for retro-styling that made a strong design language for present day designs, the Mustang might not be around today.

General Motors – As part of their restructuring, resulting from their need to claim bankruptcy in order to survive, they chose to drop Pontiac in favor of the company's desire to sell more Buicks in China. That pretty much tells the story behind that move. One of those two brands had to be eliminated. Sadly, it was Pontiac, even though they had a sizable market following, and successes like the Grand Prix, Bonneville, GTO, Firebird, Trans Am to name a few. Although Pontiac was GM's #2 sales producer in the U.S., it was GM's position that the car line did not meet the unique characteristics for the Chinese domestic marketplace. With China, the largest car market in the world, and Buick's established market position in place since the 1940's, the company felt they could support Buick, but not both. The thinking was, why create needless competition for the Pontiac at the expense of an established line that was and continues to do well? Admittedly, this kind of reasoning didn't take into account the unique differences that exist in these two market-

146

places. Personally, I think that line of thinking was full of faulty assumptions, that presupposed Pontiac couldn't make a profit if sold only in the U.S., which it wasn't doing. Interestingly enough, Pontiac's sales in this country, as a division of GM, was greater than several other companies' brands being sold in the U.S...combined! This isn't quantum physics, folks. I just wished that they had checked in with me first (it's ok to chuckle at this time) before they sold or closed down this GM division. What would I have done so differently? I would have set up Pontiac as a stand alone subsidiary (remove their division status) and operate Pontiac as a minor-managed enterprise with a dealer network, also, made up of minorities, all subsidized by Uncle Honey as had happened with Chrysler back in the 80's. As it turns out, GM never found any takers so they left this #2 sales producing division to die. Any operating decision I might have made couldn't have been all bad since their eventual demise reflected the decisions that they made or didn't make. It didn't matter. The result was the same. The shutdown of Pontiac left two stellar performers, the 2008-2009 turbo-charged G8-GXP (their attempted answer to the BMW 5 Series M) and the 2009 Soltice GXP coupe (a wannabe Nissan Z) out of the market, free to die on their own which they quitely did. Watch for the Soltice coupe to become a collector's item in years to come. In my view, these two models could be highly sought after. So, if you already own one, hold onto it! Only 1200 coupes were ever built.

Volkswagon – VW had a couple of noteworthy debacles of their own. The so-called "Dieselgate" scandal cost them billions, depleting the ranks of their executive suites, which emptied out pretty quickly, but, more importantly, the loss of countless numbers of customers and prospects resulting from their dishonesty associated with the intentional, falsified emissions test data they reported, data intended to satisfy a government mandated requirement that they could not meet. It will take years, if ever, before VW will get this ugly chapter out of their history. Prior to that, VWs brought to market a luxury cruiser named the Phaeton, in direct competition with their own Audi A8, an excellent car that would be hard to improve upon. This was the brainchild of the once famously, notorious Wolfgang Pieche, who was unceremoniously shown the door as VW's highest ranking, operating officer. Story has it that he reveled in firing key executives when their performance didn't meet his expectations which, I gather, was a regular occurrence. So, for him to be fired, well, allow me to call that poetic justice...beyond sweet. There was a decided absence of tears in Wolfsburg upon hearing the news that ole Wolfie was a goner. But not entirely, as he could be seen tooling around town nearly daily, sporting his new, north of two million dollar Bugatti Chiron...no doubt on his way to a job interview! It's OK to laugh at that!

Dodge – We can't let Dodge go without some reference to stupid decisions. There is plenty of stupidity to spread around; so why exclude this storied brand? More recently we have their decision to drop the Magnum R/T station wagon with its famed Hemi, V-8 engine. That car was setting the standard for what could have become a "sports station wagon," an alternative to a crossover SUV, but something greater than just a Plain Jane station wagon. Even Cadillac got into the act for a brief time with their CTS wagon with a V-designated, Corvette engine. A decision was reached by Dodge's top management that this model was too much of a laggard to keep, a verdict largely put forth by one member of their product development team. Unfortunately, that one product development member's vote carried the day, snuffing the life right out of that model, much in its infancy, never to be seen again. This market segment, limited though it was and very much under-developed, at the time, was positioned to take off with more products on the way, going further down market with smaller Chevrolet, Buick, Dodge and Chrysler equivalents. In any event, we will never know.

7.) BIGGEST SALES SUCCESSES – 1964 AND FORWARD

Ford Mustang (except Mustang II) – coupe, convertible, and hatchback

Ford F-150 trucks – their management's marketing cry, "Catch me if you can." Apparently, they can't

BMW 3 Series – coupe, sedan, and convertible

Chevrolet Corvette C – 1, 2, 3, 5, 6, & 7 (no, I didn't forget the C-4 – it just didn't make my list)

Toyota Camry – became the #1 best-selling sedan in North America, from market inception until today. No one has been able to catch Toyota despite some terrific, alternative, competitive equivalents from Ford Fusion, Chevy's Malibu, Nissan's Altima and Honda Accord.

Toyota Prius – market leader for a plug-in hybrid. Watch this car's sales drop as the Chevy Bolt, Nissan Leaf and Tesla's Model 3 take hold in the market. I look for this market to explode with buyer acceptance in the coming years, similar to today's market for light trucks and crossovers.

8.) MODEL YEAR 2017's MOST IMPROVED MAKES

Audi
Cadillac
Hyundai
Infiniti
Jeep
Kia
Ram
Subaru

9.) TODAY'S MOST COLLECTIBLE CARS

1951-1956 Ford F-100 pick-up truck – the all-time crown bearer for light trucks then, and now, its successor, the F-150

1955, 56, 57 Chevrolet Bel Air – 2 door hardtop and convertible models and the Nomad station wagons

1962, 1963 Studebaker Gran Turismo Hawk – the last of the Hawk series and the best of the Hawks, that was light years ahead of its time as it combined the best styling cues from Mercedes (grill), Lincoln (trunk) and Thunderbird (top) - $12K to $20K

1963 & 1965 Buick Riviera Gran Sport – if for no other reason than its inherent beauty. Currently, it is Haggerty's #1 candidate for collecting. Today's market - $16K-$30K.

1964 Pontiac GTO – the original "goat", 389 c.i., tri-power, four speed; father to the "muscle cars".

1965 Shelby Mustang GT 350 – this car was just mean.... looking and acting. Featured in some unforgettable movies.
1965 Cobra – even meaner than Shelby's Mustang GT 350 concoction, if that's possible. This car can be seen, auctioned with prices north of $1 million.

1971 Datsun 240Z – successor to the Fairlady SP 1500 and forerunner to the very successful "Z", today known as the Nissan Z.

2005 Ford Thunderbird – Pacific Beach Edition

2009 Pontiac Soltice GXP coupe – my personal top pick of a car to collect

10.) BEST BUILT – within the last 30 years.

Lexus LS, 1989-1994

BMW 2002 and 3 Series, any year

Mercedes-Benz, S Class – any. Arguably, the poster car for elegance and luxury

Toyota's Prius, Cambry, and Avalon models

Tesla's S model, 2016/17

Ford's F-150 pick-up trucks, any year

Any Subaru built after 2012

Honda Civic and Accord models, built whenever

11.) MOST OVERRATED/BIGGEST DISAPPOINTMENTS

VW Bug – ever notice how few men drive this car? Men.... if you want to look like a duck out of water, buy one of these. You'll feel good about yourself...forget the snickers; they're just jealous.

Smart Car – not so smart of a purchase; how did this car ever get its name?

Land Rover – most easily broken car being sold today. If you like going into the dealer's service department frequently, you are going to fall in love with your Rover. Who needs prestige anyhow?

Honda Insight – couldn't compete with Toyota's Prius despite being a "tank-tough" Honda product. Looks didn't help this car either as it looked to be a running mate of GM's EV1, which was a top flop!

Chevrolet Monte Carlo – Downsizing a one-time market leader for a down-market version of a personal luxury car for buyers who couldn't or wouldn't buy the Buick Riviera, Olds Toronado, Cadillac Eldorado, and Ford Thunderbird, was disappointing. Instead, they went further down market taking market shares away from other GM makes, something never intended. Today, this model is a wannabe NASCAR aspirant, and that's all its ever going to be...an aspirant. But, if you can find a cherry 1970 model that's priced right....buy it. The Monte Carlo is a pampered baby just waiting to be a collectible.(not yet on Hagerty's list).

1977-2001 Ford Thunderbird – Ford's decision to progressively downsize this car through 2001 was not a good one. They just tore the guts out of this once famed vehicle that brought us the first "personal luxury car" dating back to 1955. Ford suffered the same richly deserved fate as GM with its Monte Carlo model, although, to the best of my knowledge, Thunderbird found very little time on a race track (Daytona in 1955). When Ford made this decision, I vowed I would NEVER own another Ford product in my life. Fast forward 40 years and, lo and behold, I have compromised my vow and gone out and bought a pristine 2003 Thunderbird....a beauty, but no contest for the earlier model. I don't think I will ever get over the sense of loss I continue to feel for this vaulted marquee. I truly loved Thunderbirds for some rational reasons and some, not so much – but isn't that what love is all about? You didn't have to have a reason; you just felt that way or you didn't.

Studebaker's Bankruptcy , December, 1963 – What a shame this storied manufacturer had to endure. This versatile auto maker had been in business for over 100 years up to the time they claimed bankruptcy, originally supplying coaches and wagons for the Yanks during the Civil War from a southern Indiana location, and, much later, became a market stand-out for their futuristically-styled cars, but, also, produced pick-up trucks and farm tractors. In their heyday, they were the exclusive U.S. distributor of Mercedes-Benz automobiles and were financially able to acquire Packard, a once world-beater of a competitor to Cadillac, Lincoln, La Salle, and Europe's best. All this, sadly, got away from Studebaker as their brand gradually lost its cache over time, forcing their bankruptcy. Their departure from the automotive scene didn't create much mourning out in the marketplace, no small thanks to their management's decision to move manufacturing operations out of South Bend, Indiana, and transplanting themselves into Canada, thus, costing their Indiana-based factory workers their pensions which many accrued over countless years of loyal service. At the time, some could be heard mouthing their total disgust for such a cavalier, shameful act. The rank and file employees couldn't help Studebaker's inability to compete with the Big 3. That was senior management's doing. Why should they have to pay such a price? And, even today, some well-meaning people wonder why labor unions exist!

12.) MOST UNDER-APPRECIATED

Toyota Supra – great sports car that just couldn't compete with Corvette or German/Italian exotics.

Studebaker Avanti & Avanti - a timeless design that only gets better with age and it ain't done aging yet! I would buy a 2001/07 in a heartbeat if only I could find one to buy. A total of 3 were sold in 2016. There is nothing on the market that begins to resemble a 1963 Studebaker Avanti II...and there never will be! There are a few choice '63's floating around out of the 4,663 examples produced. The trick is not to pay too much, for one of these most fabulous of cars ever designed.

Buick GNX (Grand Nat'l) – hope you like black...like the Model T before it, that was the only color made available for this turbo-charged, V-6 entry from Buick that never lived up to its hype, except among collectors, where that's a horse of a different color. This black knight of a car is particularly hot at the moment in the collector market, bringing $60,000-$80,000, depending on condition and miles.

Porsche 928S – Porsche's first V-8, front-mounted motor that was intended to be competition to Mercedes-Benz's grand touring class model, the "SL". Although an able competitor, the styling was a bit over the top with its pop-up, bug-eyed headlamps and the car was ridiculously expensive to maintain. On the other hand, what a beautifully-designed, though compli-

152

cated, car it was, a serious collectors' item in today's market if in pristine condition. Just make sure it is well-maintained before you commit to buying one i.e. no more than 30,000 miles on the cam belt and water pump.

Cadillac – building great cars isn't enough these days, given Cadillac's history of catering to the senior generation. Cadillac is tasked with getting younger people into their dealerships to buy the new XT5 models and the CT6, in particular, featuring an interior nearly on a par with Audi's A8 model; and Cadillac is about to outdo themselves by offering the CT8 model which will be considerably more upscale than the CT6, though built on the same platform. Present moment, the CT8 is a concept car badged as the "Escala" (similar to Escalade in name which continues to be a huge hit for Cadillac). This model will finally give them the opportunity to compete with Mercedes' S Class, the industry's benchmark for world class luxury in a sedan. The CT8 is gorgeous, arguably, the best looking Cadillac in years, if not ever. See Car and Driver Magazine, October 2016, for a feature article and photos.

13.) DISCONTINUED LONG BEFORE ITS TIME

2005 Ford Thunderbird – prematurely taken off the market due to poor sales, linked to a poor market launch, and questionable quality, much of which got corrected by the time they dropped the line. It was too little, too late. Look for that model to resurface. The 2005 (last) model is a serious candidate for future collector status. There's magic in that name...Thunderbird.

Lincoln Town Car – there went Ford's market leadership position with the livery trade and many loyal non-commercial buyers. Just as a throw-in, say goodbye to the municipal market for police cars since they were built on the same frame. This decision, also, killed the Grand Marquis, a favorite with Arizona's and Florida snowbirds.

Dodge Magnum R/T sports wagon – they discovered a market segment with a stellar entry product, ready to leap out of the gates that, in my view, had all of the makings of becoming a market hit, but never had its management's fullest support and, as a result, wilted into an early death. Reason for its death: Under-appreciated, under-promoted, I look for another auto manufacturer to pick up the baton and make a run out of reintroducing this type of vehicle sometime in the foreseeable future.

14.) MOST ADVANCED AT THEIR MARKET LAUNCH

1964 Studebaker Gran Turismo Hawk, the last of the vaulted Hawks (discontinued in December, 1963).

1964 Avanti - and America's only exotic, 4-passenger, performance-rated, personal luxury car; the last model year of the original Avanti, manufactured by Studebaker. The Avanti II that followed was owned by a group of investors, independent of Studebaker and was manufactured by various owners through Model Year 2007.

1966 Oldsmobile Toronado – America's first front wheel drive car.

1989 Lexus LS – Toyota's entry into the U.S. luxury car market – a total success!

2014 Chevrolet Corvette, C-7 model – the best Vette yet; styling, performance, build-quality and interior materials.

2015 Tesla S – first battery-powered, luxury sedan – a car to teach the masses something of the virtues and shortcomings of using electricity as a viable, alternative power source.

15.) MY MOST ENJOYABLE DRIVING EXPERIENCES

1966 Chevrolet Impala SS, 2 door hardtop, 427 c.i., 425 h.p., 4 speed. Hotter than a plate of habanero peppers, the car stickered for $4,002 and didn't even have a radio (highly unusual for Chevrolet's top trim level). Fish-tailable in all four glorious gears.

1985 Jaguar XJ6 –Vanden Plas – what a joy to drive, although not particularly powerful for an inline six cylinder engine. It mattered little, as the handling and looks were extraordinary.

1988 Porsche 911 Targa – driving this puppy into a curve and watching the rear end of the car trying to catch up with the front, borders on an indescribable, joyous driving experience, worthy of more than one unplanned trip to the men's washroom.

2006 Chevrolet Corvette hatchback – just an all-around fun car whose middle name was Torque. Good on gas, great daily driver and reasonably priced, especially, against the likes of Porsche, and the Dodge Viper.

2008 Maserati Gran Turismo – with the beast shifting into "sports mode", making no wasted moves operating the paddle shifters in excess of 6K r.p.m.'s, allowing that Ferrari engine to air out with its mufflers growling, is an experience nearly beyond words

16.) OUTLIVED THEMSELVES

Dodge Viper – the car was originally intended to compete with Corvette, and for a period of time, it did. However, if one were to look at the entire history of this "over-the-top' stylistic performance-based sports car and America's most expensive car ever built in the U.S., it becomes readily apparent that Corvette was the superior choice for an American sports car, dollar for dollar or, as it were, horsepower for horsepower. It would be mentally taxing to justify $85,000 for the Viper when a Corvette priced in the high $50's could get the job done and with a much higher resale value.

Lincoln MKS – never was a viable replacement for the Town Car as Lincoln's primo model that was no more than a re-badged Ford Taurus. The Taurus, as well as the MKS, didn't sell well, either. Now Lincoln is depending on the newly launched Continental to improve its former fortunes but, guess what, this car is still being built on a Ford Taurus frame, featuring a front-wheel drive powertrain. By luxury car standards, this car isn't going to cut it with a discerning luxo car buyer who expects either rear-wheel or an all-wheel drive train, justified to be built on a dedicated platform, specifically, tied to a unique ownership experience. Yes, the Continental, in my view, looks great but that's where it ends. Despite record short-term profits, Ford isn't willing to invest in a new platform that would, truly, re-established Lincoln as an American luxury car. I look for Lincoln to drop the MKS regardless of whether or not the Continental is a marketing success. Count the days...the MKS is a goner!

Acura (cars only) – they were the first Japanese car manufacturer to introduce this so-called luxury make to the U.S. marketplace a full model year ahead of Toyota's Lexus. The momentary advantage held by Acura got wasted away as the car was perceived to be a gussied-up Honda Accord. In addition, Acura made the mistake of launching a couple of other models sporting the Acura name in their intention to go down-market in an effort to build volume for the brand. It didn't happen. One model was the Integra which suffered the same fate as the top-positioned product, the Legend. Both models lacked differentiating identities. But not all has been lost to Acura as a make or brand. Somehow, they have managed to develop a market leadership position for their two crossover models which many people incorrectly refer to as SUV's and should be correctly called CUV's (Crossover Utility Vehicle)....the MDX and RDX. Here, they successfully compete with the market leader, the Lexus RX and the Cadillac SRX (now renamed, XT5, now Cadillac's best selling model).

17.) TODAY'S WORST CARS; requiring mucho repairs

Chrysler 200 – 2017 model

Land Rover – any model and trim level

Tesla X – 2017 model; body fit issues

Fiat 500L – Italy's version to Mercedes' Smart Car. In addition to being dangerous to drive, the car has a history of breaking down regularly.

Mercedes-Benz SL - despite being Daimler's halo car for technology and exclusivity, the fact remains that this model breaks easily and often. Who would believe that would be possible, given a price, typically, something north of a hundred grand.

18.) TODAY'S BEST CARS; Model Year 2017

Audi A 6

BMW; 3 & 6 Series

Cadillac XT5, Escalade, and CT6

Chevrolet Malibu and Corvette

Ford F-150 truck and Mustang

Genesis G80 and G90

Lexus RX and LS

Mercedes-Benz E Class

Porsche 911 and Panamera

Subaru – any 2017 model

Toyota RAV4 and Prius

19.) BEST CARS; by decade (starting in the 1940's)

1949 Ford – Ford Motor's signature car signaling the world that Ford was on its way back from near extinction, although it still didn't outsell Chevrolet, something Ford hadn't done since 1932 and wouldn't again until 1957.

1957 Chevrolet – what can anybody say about this car that hasn't already been said other than the little known fact that Ford outsold Chevrolet in 1957. It's too bad that Ford doesn't share in the same collector class as the '57 Chevy. It seems nearly everyone loves this Chevrolet model, even to this day.

1967 Jaguar XKE – arguably, the most beautiful car ever designed up to that point in time, that according to Enzo Ferrari, who knew something about building beautiful sport cars as founder and head of Ferrari and former design chief at Alfa-Romero.

1974 Ford Thunderbird – this car had all the trappings of a Lincoln Mark series, but significantly lower priced with a comparable ride, a definite alternative and much understated to its big brother, the Lincoln Mark. This T-Bird was one of those rare American-built luxury cars that a young, upwardly mobile male could own without coming off as being visibly ostentatious; it made a statement but not too loudly. In those years, there were not a lot of choices in luxury cars beyond Cadillac, Lincoln, Olds Toronado, and Buick Riviera. Europe's luxury entries hadn't caught on yet in the U.S. marketplace.

1989 Lexus LS400 – easily, the most understated luxury car sold in America in the year of its introduction to the U.S. marketplace in 1989. No one ever accused Lexus as being an overdressed Toyota, though in many respects it was, if you knew what to look for; but, this car went on to considerable fame as a "best value" luxury car that was about as maintenance-free as one can acquire in a lifetime. I mean that car was that good and priced under $40,000, fully loaded! Ford, GM, and Chrysler, collectively, got caught with no new luxury models that could compete with the Lexus when that car landed on our shores. I was fortunate to own a 1990 LS400 and the only repair I incurred was replacing the rubber brake petal cover where the glue used to keep it anchored to the metal, apparently, dried out. Was that enough to keep me convinced that Lexus was and is one special vehicle? See the Appendix in the latter pages of this book, where you'll note the number of Lexus' I have owned.

1990 Toyota Supra – Toyota's sports car answer, competing with what is now called the Nissan Z, Corvette, the lower-priced, down market, Porsche, and Lotus, priced to a market segment that kept them at a considerable distance from Ferrari, Maserati, BMW, Lambo's and upmarket Porsche's.

2003 Chevrolet Corvette Z06 - this was America's answer to competing with Ferrari's at a fraction of the price and cost to operate. This 50th anniversary model could eke out nearly 22 miles per gallon, running on regular, unleaded gasoline! Why more Europeans weren't and aren't today driving Corvettes in significant numbers is beyond me.

20.) WORST CARS; by decade (starting in the 1940's)

1949 Crosley Hotshot – our town drunk owned this midget-sized excuse of a car who seemed to find a way of getting his car lifted from the spot where he last parked it only to find it wedged between two right-angled walls behind the building that housed the local tavern. It was deliriously funny to watch this guy attempt to un-park his car, eventually, giving up the ghost in search of help, just praying a cop didn't see him first because, invariably, he would be "drunker than a skunk" (that's Hoosier-ese for "wistfully wasted.").

1958 Edsel – here's your old friend that embraces any negative description you might choose. Edsel just seems to pop up in so many adverse categories that, after a fashion, becomes a manageable laugh. This so-called "car" was on its way to the junkyard the day it was introduced to the marketplace and was tagged a born loser on the same day, as well.

1960 Chevrolet Corvair – "Unsafe at Any Speed," the title of Ralph Nader's much-read book pretty much sums it up. In practical terms, a driver had better be acutely alert to changing driving conditions because that wannabe "car" that was fashioned after a bathtub (an ugly one at that) with a canopy, was forever surprising its driver with an erratic handling behavior, especially, on wet, curvy roads If not careful, one could find themselves upside down, trapped under this compact-sized, piece of cra#.

1971 Ford Pinto/Mercury Bobcat – a fire trap...says it all. This car should never have made it to market in the first place, a totally worthless piece of sh## that the manufacturer should have included a fire extinguisher instead of a spare tire, which was a waste because the owner might not own the car long enough to use it.

1981 Delorean DMC-12 – this pregnant version of a Chevrolet Camaro got some ink earlier in this chapter. Let's leave it at that.

1997 EV1 by GM – Under-engineered, under-marketed piece of prime bullsh## that one could not buy (one should not have wanted to buy it in the first place); it was offered, exclusively, as a leasable piece of cra# only. What? Why? GM, eventually recalled and scrapped out all of the 3,000 EV1's that were produced in its total production run.

2001 Pontiac Astek – well, golly me, if it isn't our old friend, the Astek, making one more cameo appearance. I hate to beat a horse to death (especially in public) but, in this case, I clearly will, one last time for the record. I hope you weren't expecting some kind of an apology coming from me for being so critical. If you did, sorry folks...this sad commentary sticks like a steroid-filled mosquito on Velcro. In the vernacular of a teenage boy who has just run out of gas, this dog "ain't going to go anywhere, any time soon!" Even in the resale market, one can pay too much for this wannabe minivan. That would be an amount north of $1.00 U.S. Don't let a price less than that fool you. It isn't a bargain even at 50 cents!!

21.) BEST CARS TO MAKE OUT IN

Cars were a gift from Venus for horny, testosterone-fueled teenage boys getting behind the wheel of their "weapon of mass seduction"

1950-52 Nash Rambler – with its back seat folded completely down

1959 Cadillac – trunk or back seat...didn't matter since it was the size of a hotel room!

2001 Pontiac Astek – Lookee here, our old friend is making another guest appearance on this page. OK, I lied...one more shot to shoot at the colossally inept Pontiac product. I've had it...no more ink for this lousiest of losers! OK, but why would I list this most miserable, misfit of a minivan?" Simple....no one in their right mind would come within a country mile of checking this dog out for extracurricular activities. One should, however, feel safe from being discovered in this crème de crème piece of cra#.

Any year Nissan Murano, Cross Cabriolet. People in the know (and I'm not one of them) tell me that this car was made for sex, literally, a mobile sex machine on wheels, thanks to its uniquely designed top that converts readily in a passion pit for its "can't wait" patrons!

2016 Jeep Wrangler Unlimited (I'm sure it has some limits). This Jeep was designed for those adventurous and wannabe lovers who insist on total privacy in secluded areas that can only be traversed by four-wheeling, was (and is) Jeep's claim to fame. To add to one's horizontal comfort, the doors are easily removable permitting one to completely stretch out while enjoying staring at the stars!

2017 Tesla "S" – and you thought its claim to fame had everything to do with ecology, miles driven between plug-ins, looks and status. You would be wrong because, whether parked or leaving the scene of a post-coital event, you would be in total silence except for an occasional whimper. If that whimper becomes an outburst, you'll know how much the occupants are enjoying the car's interior materials and design.

160

An unattended hearse (any model) unlocked and available for recreational pursuits while parked in a funeral home's parking lot. No one is going to bother you unless they are the one who needs to be found inside the funeral home. BTW, why do morticians refer to themselves as operatives in a "funeral home." It would sound friendlier to me if it were called a "funeral parlor" or "funeral salon." But noooooooooooo.! They want to come off as folksy until, of course, they tell you how much there services are going to set you back! OK....back to cars.

Now, I have saved the best for last and its not any car from the past; but, rather it's what future generations have to look forward to. Actually, I'm a bit envious (wasted envy, I might add as that train has left the station for good) of the coming generation that gets first dibs on making out in an autonomously-driven car. Can you fathom the repertoire of things that have full rein to be discovered and experienced? Is this going to become a motel on wheels?

22.) WORST CARS TO MAKE OUT IN

Dodge Caliber (any model year) - Makes my list as the #1 vehicle of my carefully considered choices. Besides ugly, this monster doesn't have enough interior dimensions to please a midget! Having sex in one has the same emotional resonance as trying to have sex in a Goodwill Industries dumpster and, if you do it in Arizona, you may find you have some company!

Mini Cooper – where heavy jolts play havoc with the rear shock mounts (aptly named), thus impacting the ride quality. Heaven knows, we don't want to do anything to affect the ride!

Ford Crown Victoria; with a siren on top – a vehicle choice not normally considered, but in the land of adventurous lovers, a rare yet creative environment to conduct this age-old art. For those select folk, who venture out into this uncharted possibility, how about exercising some playfulness in an unattended police car parked at the police station? One risks getting lost in all of its copious amounts of interior space

23.) DUMBEST THINGS PEOPLE DO WITH THEIR CARS

Despite some people's love affair of their cars, these same

people are capable of treating their prized possessions as toys to be played with in public, while showing a total disregard for the safety of others as well as themselves. e.g. texting or reading something while driving. Mindless stupidity pretty much sums up my view of those idiotic behaviors. And lest I forget, there's another group of drivers out there taking up space on our highways, driving around with reckless abandon, no particular destination in mind, emitting loads of pollutants into the air, thrilled to be paying $2.00 + for a gallon of gas. And then there is the social change that road rage ushers into the driving experience. Picture with me an angry driver going ballistic, expressing his or her ire by elevating both hands, up and away from the steering wheel in unison so they can be seen making a graceless display with uplifted hands, using the, hitherto untried, twin hand gesture featuring the middle fingers of both hands simultaneously! How creative is that?

After the proverbial "dust" settles on these key points, you would be left to conclude that describing the dumbest things people do with or to their cars is a complete and sad commentary on the human experience with a helpless four-wheeled beast that lives to please you, assuming one keeps it in gas, properly maintained and adequately insured. Wrong, wrong! Adjust your attitude (beer helps at times like these). Go show your appreciation by washing her; keep her out of harm's way so she gets the idea of how sincere you are in your love for her and, oh yes, don't forget to pat her on her little a## once in awhile. Cars, even ugly ones, need loving too!

Here's some possible scenarios I offer as further examples of the dumbest things people do to or with their cars, reminding myself there is no known cure for stupidity or elective ignorance.

Washing a rental car! Who in their right mind does that? That's right up there with kissing your sister!

Own a car smaller than its owner.

Buying premium-grade gasoline just because the Owner's Manual says so. I drove Corvettes for years on regular, unleaded, gasoline and never once had a problem with "pinging" or loss of power.

Driving 20 miles per hour over the posted speed limit. That's a felony in Arizona that could get you a free night's stay in the pokey.

Telling a policeman that you didn't know how fast you were going because the speedometer needle doesn't go beyond 160 and due to your alcohol impairment, you forgot you were driving a Ferrari.

Making love in a car in broad daylight, with all your clothes on, while parked at a nudist colony.

Putting on facial make-up while driving.

Picking one's nose while driving, resulting in indiscriminately flipping boogers randomly out the window without any regard to possibly having one land on a fellow driver or its vehicle.... totally classless!

Leaving one's car unlocked while parked at a shopping mall located near an interstate highway that leads to Mexico.

Elevate a truck so high you need a step-ladder to climb into its cabin.

Equipping your car's horn with musical notes.

Honking one's horn to express disdain for something another driver is doing, something that displeases you or it is needlessly being used as a form of salutation. Horn use should be restricted to situations where a need for help is a present-moment necessity like when one runs out of gas or an absolute need to get the attention of someone from the opposite sex. No matter the situation, moderation would be nice.

Installing a set of Rudolph's antlers and red-painted nose on a car's front end during the Christmas season. Who knows, it might attract a wayward deer.... right into a set of headlights.... yours!

Covering the derriere of the car's rear bumper and windows with travel decals or political stickers. Do you really think anyone cares to read those? Am I going to vote for someone just because of a bumper sticker whose words or statements are, many times, juvenile at best? They're like tattoos implanted on human flesh. Since no one is going to read them (of any consequence), why should you? You're too busy driving to take note of these valueless little non-sensical exhibits that attempt to impress you with the owner's vast travels which might include a trip into the nearby county, that's no more than their wasted effort at showing-off. You, as the viewer, are supposed to be in awe of this geographic display of nothingness. To make a believer out of me, I've got to see a "See Rock City" bumper sticker hanging on a new Rolls-Royce and then, I might reconsider my views but it can't be displayed on anything less than a Rolls-Royce!

24.) FUTURE CARS

An observation, as I look to the future, based on what I am reading today, is that cars are going to change big time over what we know them to be present-day. More changes in the next 5 years than in the previous 50, according to Mary Barra, GM's current Chairman, and I don't doubt that for a minute. Future U.S. product offerings will no longer be the exclusive domain of Detroit and its assembly plants scattered around the country. In large part, this is because many of the technological advances behind these changes were developed in Silicon Valley, California, where EVs along with autonomously-driven vehicles and other advanced technologies originated, with many more on the way. Lucky us, huh? Silicon Valley is also the corporate home of Uber, a one company wrecking ball, focused on decimating the taxi industry. Not all is lost if you are one of those people who resist change and go to great lengths to avoid being confronted with force-fed make-overs that you were not consulted on, unwillingly rolling over in reluctant acceptance because you feel you have no choice but to accept it, like it or not. You should get some comfort out of knowing that traditional, evolutionary change will continue to be in play for the immediate future as the auto makers are forced into styling changes every 7 years (sometimes a little less) as they need sales volume to offset the tooling costs that lie behind those exterior body changes. If, however, you don't like the cosmetic changes that you are seeing now, you sure ain't going to like them any better for the balance of that 7 year design cycle! There are, also, sociological changes on the way involving car-sharing, ride-sharing, reflecting changes taking place as a result of social media and mobility needs which are driving (no pun intended) or dictating a whole new ownership/user-ship experience. Let's face it, car-sharing

164

will mean less cars on the road at any given time; thus, freeing up the roads for us car lovers so we can once again enjoy the driving experience.

FUTURE CARS; 2017-2020

Maserati Alfieri – arguably the best looking Maserati ever and priced under the Gran Turismo. It will be priced against the mid-market Porsche 911. Expect a minimum of $85K.

Mercedes-Benz will be launching a new brand, now designated as the "EQ".

Cadillac CT8 – will become the V-8 version of the newly launched CT6; maybe the best looking Cadillac since the late 50's. They out did themselves on this one.

Chevrolet Corvette – finally a mid-engine based model. Cadillac will probably have their own version of this car similar in relationship to what they did when they produced the XLR.

25.) MY PERSONAL LUST LIST

I get this question from time-to-time while viewing an ad on t.v., "what's in your wallet?" A more appropriate question might be, "what's coming out of my wallet?" as far as future car purchases are concerned?   Well, that's always subject to change so I try to keep an open mind; but, when you rarely see a car you don't like, as I, that becomes a delightful chore. With that statement out of the way, I can tell you that I have a serious level of interest in collectibles and cars that are just a hoot to drive, no matter the make or model.

1965 Buick Riviera, Gran Sport as an American collectible; any color except tan. According to Hemmings, an acknowledged expert and publisher of price guides, rates the 1963/65 Rivi as the Number #1 collectible car in the U.S. marketplace for 2018. That hasn't helped keep prices down. As a result, it is difficult to find one in excellent condition, priced to the market. A year ago, a 1965 Rivi Gran Sport could be bought for as little as $16,000. Today, that figure has become $25,000 to $30,000. Who ever said that cars can't be investment-grade products? That statement is partially true but it does not take into account the supply and demand for cars deemed to be collectibles which includes older, well-maintained vehicles in excellent condition with a minimal amount of miles that, more times than not, turns out to be a car produced in small volumes, in its last year of production with a manual transmission. Is your investments in stocks, bonds, or precious metals yielding that kind of return? The major key to making a profit on a sale is buying the car at a significant price level below the going market price so you can sell it at or above the going market price when it's time to unload that puppy. Sounds simple, right? It isn't!

From the perspective of an everyday driver type of vehicle, a more prudent approach to evaluating the value of a car is to minimize the cost of operating (per mile driven) and the ownership cost of a vehicle. Forget about trying to make money on its eventual sale unless, it is a collectible where supply and demand is the tail wagging the dog. The very best that most people can do to minimize ownership costs is to drive that sucker until the wheels fall off. Most people can't do that as they become enticed by what they see on the road and the advertising they get exposed to on TV. To many people, buying a new or late model car is a reward for managing one's finances such that, on paper, they have convinced themselves that they can afford it; therefore, they reward their deserving selves with a purchase or lease of a car that tends to be a little more expensive than they had planned on. However, they will justify it, nonetheless, if for no other reason than reasoning (also known as "self-selling") with the infrequency of buying or leasing that much desired vehicle. I mean, how often does the average person buy or lease a vehicle? BTW, that statement doesn't apply to me as you can obviously surmise.

1979-1985 Buick Riviera – Buick's first front-wheel drive cars The "T" Type, turbo'd V-6, is highly sought after but not yet in the class of a 1963/65 Rivi. I like this model in a gray (similar to BMW's Space Gray) or a light, metallic blue. Besides, it can fit in my garage – the 1963/65 models can't.

1962/63 Studebaker Gran Turismo Hawk – the last of the Hawks whose initial design goes back to model year 1953. The '63, in particular, is the one to buy if you should be so fortunate as to find both a '62 and '63 available for purchase through an auction, private sale, or classic car dealer. The '63 model was the last full year of production of this beautiful European-inspired styling as Studebaker claimed bankruptcy in mid-

December, 1963, while just manufacturing a limited number of 1964 models that, for whatever reason, never caught on with the collector car freaks of this world. The ideal Hawk would be a 1963 model, 289 c.i. engine, with a 4-speed manual tranny, supercharged (R2). Throw on a pair of glass-packed Magnaflow's, and you will have an exhaust system that growls like a mad junkyard dog. The styling of these late model Hawks were years ahead of the styling that existed in the market at the time they were introduced, intended to compete with the Buick Riviera, Ford T-Bird and personal luxury coupes offered by Cadillac and Lincoln with a sticker price around $3,100.

Actually, the Hawks performed favorably with Corvettes at the time but weren't intended to compete in a sports car market segment. Today, a good '62/'63 will, typically, fetch $15,000 to $25,000 These models have been designated as "Milestone Cars" which effectively means, they are a shoe-in to become future collectibles. Right now is the time to buy either of these vehicles before they become roundly viewed as investment-grade vehicles.

2001-2007 Avanti – the last of the Avanti's whose intended market position was to fashion this model as America's lone exotic, styled as a grand touring, personal luxury, performance coupe. No other American car, at the time, could shoe-horn themselves into that precise a description, where this model wanted to call its home. They were beautiful automobiles that never really caught on with the American luxury car buyer despite styling that was widely viewed to be way ahead of its time. If you see one for sale and can negotiate a manageable price, by all means, buy it. I know I intend to. There are not many available for sale and there will be a lesser amount as times goes by.

1956 -1965 Porsche 356A Speedster Spyder convertible – this car is without peer in its position as one of the world's premier, collectible sports cars and the price it fetches confirms that. As a rule, most of the 356's on the market for sale have been well-maintained and are excellent investment-grade automobiles. As to pricing, think Ferrari because that's the sandbox that this particular Porsche model plays in. Don't expect to negotiate a price significantly lower than the market (see Hagerty for their published price evaluation). They are hard to buy "right" but they can be bought, offering their new owner years of unshakable satisfaction and thanking themselves for being wise enough to buy this car, knowing that it is only going to go up in value/price over time. This should be viewed as a long-term hold position; don't even think about buying one to "flip." There are plenty of cars that fit that role but the Porsche 356A is not one of them.

1961 Ferrari Modena 360 California Spider- this car was made famous being featured in the movie, "Ferris Buehler's Day Off." Unless you own a bank, you would be wise to find another car to lust after!

1983 Porsche 928S - the "Risky Business" car driven by Tom Cruise in the movie named the same. Originally, it was intended to complete with Mercedes' SL roadsters but that didn't happen as Mercedes had, and still has, a lock on that market segment in the global marketplace. The 928 was Porsche's first V-8 and, like all Porsche's, has a rear-wheel drive power train. This model is little noticed and, possibly, might become a sound reason to buy this unique German grand tourer. One that is operable (but nothing to look at) can be bought for as little as $7,500 with an immaculately maintained one priced somewhere between $25,000 and $40,000.

2002/05 Ford Thunderbird – an attempt to resurrect the styling of the original Baby Birds of 1955 through 1957. That did not happen as most discerning Bird Watchers weren't convinced this car had intrinsic value of any kind for that matter. Those sentiments might have been true but the one thing that lives on into future is the power of the name "Thunderbird." Mark my words, that "dog is anything but dead." Watch Ford Motor Company reintroduce it sometime in the future. If I were a betting man, I've got to believe the T-Bird will resurface sometime between 2020 and 2025, remembering there was an absence from the market of twelve years between the 2002 model and its predecessor; so a hiatus of 15 to 20 years would seem reasonable. So, for you T-Bird lovers out there, stay tuned. That "bird" is going to live to fly again! Some names just don't go away... Thunderbird is one of them.

2008/09 Cadillac XLR, Platinum trim level was, yet, another ambitious effort to compete with Mercedes' SL roadsters that fell on its own sword as they did with their former Allante model. It was as if Mercedes competed with tanks while the Cadillac warred on with horse-pulled buggies. This was Cadillac's second attempt to compete with the Mercedes SL series. The first was an abysmal failure whose model name is anything but recallable. Do you remember the name "Allante?" If you do, you are the exception because, for most folk, the statement "out of sight, out of mind" became the proclaimed knell for this otherwise, fine automobile that just didn't catch on with the luxury, sports car buyers. Although not a big seller when new, the XLR is a worthy companion for its retirement-based owners, owners who view their cars as timeless. Unlike some of the roadster designs of the past, European or American, the XLR retains its futuristic presence in today's collector marketplace. Like the Studebaker Gran Turismo's described above, now is the time to buy that '08/'09 while few people are paying any attention to this vehicle. This Cadillac model makes most "Possible Collectible Car Lists," ranked in the top twenty cars to consider for an additional horse to put in a collector's corral. It's a "sleeper" about ready to wake up!

New or newer, I would seriously considering buying/leasing a:

BMW, 6 Series, Gran Coupe (4-door similar to the Mercedes CLS 550) or another 7 Series, 740/750Li.

Porsche Panamera – newly redesigned for 2017 which removed the bulbous-appearing rear end that didn't work for a lot of people. The 2017 is a massive improvement in design and is definitely a "head-turner."

Maserati Alfiera – arguably, the most beautiful car my eyes have ever laid on. If a car were being put on a "bucket lists," this would be the one. This car, although approved for production, is not expected to be released for sale until 2021...at the earliest.

BMW i8 – pluggable EV with all the features of a Tesla S plus ability to run on gas if one so chooses. This BMW is a true sports car competing with the likes of a Jaguar, F Type, Porsche 911 Turbo and the Audi RS.

BMW 8 Series coupe – the 8 Series is back for another tour of duty. The photos I've seen would knock your socks off, never to be worn again. "Gorgeous" is a pitifully inadequate word to describe the beauty of this wonderfully conceived design for a coupe which replaces the 6 Series coupe, already dropped from BMW's product line-up to make way for the 8 Series coupe, expected to be launch sometime in a 2019/20 time frame.

2018/19 Mercedes-Benz, E Class convertible – newly redesigned for Model Year 2018. Excellent candidate to buy or lease as a Certified Pre-Owned (CPO) vehicle – great looking, excellent residuals and this model's design should be in place through Model Year 2025. M-B's new design language has the C, E, and S Class convertibles all embracing the same design theme with the major difference between the three being their size and weight. All three pretty much look alike. What a boon to the perception of owners with C and E's, that their car looks just like a S (not an entirely true statement but close enough to make a valid point). Of course, if one owns a S Class, he or she might not take so kindly to a comparison that confirms that their car isn't sufficiently differentiated from the lower priced C and E's, that could be a serious deflating blow to one's ego.

This brings me to the point where, as a once-famous cartoon character so aptly put it, "That's all folks," – my personal version of experiencing life through cars I owned, or wanted to own, ever marching forward . Surely you are getting my message by now. There are "Soooooooooooooooo Many Cars and Soooooo Little Time!"

1929 Chevy Landau
owned by Erik Langhofer

'57 T-Bird -

dream realized,
finally

'77 Vette & '75 Bricklin, both owned by Dave Penn

1953 - Inside garage

*1956 Ford -
my first car*

*1967 Thunderbird -
college graduation
gift to myself*

1953 - New car showroom

*1965
Checker Limo A11E
owned by Ari Garrel*

*1975
Maserati
Merak*

1982 Buick Riviera- my 6 month restoration project

*Aussie friend,
Steve Scott's gorgeous
Maserati GT*

1983 Porsche 928S - what a joy to stare at

*1999
Porsche 911S*

1985 Jaguar Vanden Plas XJ6

*2003 T-Bird -
future
collector
car*

2004 Mercedes-Benz SL500 a dream realized

2015 Maserati - prettiest blue you'll ever see

2014 Beemer - 7 Series

Adoring wife Sandi's 1957 T-Bird

Al Becker's 1999 Plymouth Prowler

*Dad's Award recognizing
his 500th new car sale*

*Buddy Larry Turek
Rolls Royce wannabe -
2016*

Dave Penn's '77 Vette, formerly owned by Vernon Hilderbrand

*Cousin Vernon and wife Lori's
twin 2003, 50th anniversary C-5 Corvettes*

Dave Sacks
2010
Benz coupe

Dave Sacks first Vette

First place showing
2002 local car show

Dave Sacks
2014 Benz ragtop

Grandpa's used car lot Houston, Indiana

Hilderbrand Motor Sales Columbus, Indiana

*Leonard's Drive In 1950's
Bedford, Indiana*

Hilderbrand Ford-grand opening day - 1947, Bedford, Indiana

*My lone muscle car
1966 Chevy Impala SS*

*My first
Corvette
2001*

My first of many Lexus' 1990 LS400

My glorious 1988 Porsche Targa

*Friend Bill Becker's
1973, TR-6*

*My 2017 Vette -
taking 1st Place in a
local car show*

My 2nd of four Corvettes - 2003

My first convertible 1960 Ford Sunliner

Sweet
mother-in-law's
Mustang

Tom and Marina's
gorgeous C-5
Corvette

Doc Maher's
2014 C-7 Corvette

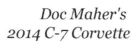

My first Cadillac
1977 Eldorado

My second Cadillac
1981 Eldorado

181

My third Corvette-2006 hatchback

Future conquest - Ferrari 360

CAR INDUSTRY

OVERVIEW

For those of you old enough to remember the rocker, Jerry Lee Lewis, you may recall his song, "There's A Whole Lot Of Shakin' Going On". Well, those words fit perfectly in describing what is happening in the car industry today – that answers the question of how, where, and what we will buy. Worth repeating, Mary Barra, Chairman, GM, put it best when she said that there will be more changes in the next 5 years than the last 50, offering you a snapshot view into the need to prepare yourself for what is coming your way on a lot of different fronts: technological, alternative fuels, cultural, social, emission controls, operating costs and economies, and, of course, the car, itself. Robert "Maximum Bob" Lutz, who I introduced you to in Chapter 4 has gone on record for saying, "The era of the human-driver automobile, its repair facilities, its dealerships, the media surrounding it - all will be gone in 20 years." I might add, a short 20 years. Just look back 20 years ago. Was 1997 so long ago?

Isn't it ironic that the horse and buggy gave way to the automobile as the major means of private transportation for the past 125 years and now, as if by magic, our transportation model will totally change before our very eyes due, essentially, to one technological advance.....the autonomously-driven automobile. Don't try fighting it, folks. It's here to stay, like it or not. Just imagine how annoying the sound of a car engine must have been as cars replaced the sound of horse hooves, 125 years ago. For one, I would trade hooves and dung for a driverless, electric-powered vehicle...any day! Even the word "car" will give way to the term "module." So, in future-ese, "How are you enjoying your new, bright shiny module?"

The future is, largely, about CHANGE, a self-describing word that will give you a whole new perspective for the automotive landscape that "is" changing ("is" as in "now"), before your very

183

eyes, taking place as I put these words to paper and will continue to escalate with time. Car manufacturers, dealers, and buyers are all going to get in on the act, an act, historically, that the industry has not embraced warmly. But, thanks to today's technology, the manufacturers have little or no choice but to accept the advances that technology offers in the making and marketing of tomorrow's vehicles...today.

Much of the technological advance of the recent past came by way of digital-based electronics in the form of semiconductor chips that pack away more functionality into smaller spaces, along with assorted switches, sensors, and embedded devices. It is a much advanced version of this digital-based technology that is ushering in the autonomously-driven car.

Semiconductor circuits, manufactured in the form of "chips" are the conduits that make functionality possible, delivered at a cost that, invariably, goes down as volumes and production yields go up. In practical terms, what does that mean? As with the price for computers, smart phones, and everything else digital-based, the price will drop significantly, over time. That's just the nature of the beast. So, will this find its way into a reduced price that you and I will be paying for a car? I don't know, but, I have the sense that any cost reductions made possible by expanding the use of semiconductors is not going to bring down the price paid at the dealership level, as the manufacturers have a habit of adding more product content and calling it standard equipment. Cost savings will not be exposed as such, but rather, transferred and captured into the overall costs of the finished product. At best, prices will be relatively stable, thus, depriving buyers of the cost savings that should, by all rights, flow to them. Earlier, you might recall the Bill Gates quote made about GM's ability to offer a car for sale, selling for $25.00 and could get a thousand miles off of a gallon of gas...if only GM were forced to compete like a Microsoft!

CHANGES

Why all the changes and why now? In the past, industry changes were pretty much confined to safety and fuel efficiency issues, styling, ergonomics, and planned obsolescence made possible by new model introductions which seem tame by comparison to today's changes.

184

Take a fresh look at what is going on, today. Taken as a whole, these changes are creating a probable answer to a confluence of inter-related social, economic, ecological, mobility, and safety issues...unimaginable a short five years ago. And the industry's collective response to these issues will get played out for the "you's and me's" of the world by answering WHAT, WHERE, WHO, and HOW we will go about buying and driving these cars in the future.

No longer the exclusive domain of the so-called Big Three from Detroit and Japan's version of its Big Three (Toyota, Honda, and Nissan), tech giants by the likes of Google and Apple (who have more cash than God's second cousin!) have entered the fray to become the first manufacturer of a self-driven, electrically-powered automobile. Several of the pieces to that picture are complete i.e. Tesla, and Nissan as far as EV's are concerned. But to combine that technology with autonomously-driven vehicles, while making them economically feasible to the masses, are the challenges being addressed by the development of tomorrow's cars. All of a sudden, tomorrow has become today...already! Heretofore, the unwelcomed trespassing of Google and Apple onto Detroit's turf was viewed as being under siege. And, of course, wherever you find American companies, how far away can the Germans, Japanese, and South Koreans be? And how about the elephant in the room, China? Everyone wants in on the action now that there is general agreement on where the automotive industry is heading. Who is going to get there first? In my view, I wouldn't bet against Google or Apple given their capital, people, and technology. When it is all said and done, it's all about money (or lack of) and the timing that benefits or curses it. Is Detroit threatened by this invasion onto their turf? You can go to the bank that they were but that's all changing now that GM and Ford, in particular, have come to realize that they don't have the expertise to compete favorably with Silicon Valley and there isn't enough time or money to play "catch-up." But, what Detroit has that Silicon Valley doesn't have is marketing and manufacturing know-how for producing automobiles. Bottom line...they need each other. And, there are enough profits to spread around with no real fear of any one company harnessing or monopolizing the financial benefits that these new technologies offer. Technology is advancing at such a torrid pace and will continue chasing off newer technologies, not fully developed! Technology is driving technology (pun intended.)

No question, these changes are going to create a lot of nostalgia but I fully intend to enjoy the here and now, knowing what is coming and, equally so, what is going to be lost...forever! But the seeds of some good news are in place, anticipating the excitement (contained) about what is on the horizon, as I just can't picture stepping into a car that will drive itself...up mountains, across suspended bridges (a biggie for me) and traversing endless miles of barren desert without the benefit of a driver. What a wonderful time to get caught up on sleep!

TECHNOLOGICAL

Easily, the most noteworthy of the technological changes is the autonomously-driven (AD) cars that will soon be a part of our highway landscape...sooner than any of us could ever imagine! Of all the technological advances under development, self-driving cars has to be considered #1 with its far-reaching benefits to the driving public. This technology exploded onto the scene, right out of the lab and onto the highway, literally, overnight, so it seemed. Buck Rogers couldn't have scripted any better the comparison between his science fiction adventures and the soon-to-be-realized...self-driven car, farm tractor, and truck. Picture this with me, will you? Here you are driving down a mountain pass at 70 miles per hour, hands-free. OK, for those of you out there who don't have mountains to drive, try this little trick going down Patton Hill just outside of Oolitic, Indiana. Notice, out of nowhere, how rapidly sweat develops on your brow (and a few other places). I mean, are you ready for this? Will you freely give up control and allow yourself to feel secure, trusting this technology to keep you safe? Here's another imagined scenario...I am traveling down I-10 toward Tucson, when an 18-wheeler goes flying by me (I'm going 70 m.p.h.) and its driver decides to pass me and settle into my lane, while, out of nowhere, a speeding car makes a last second decision to change lanes abruptly, as well, sandwiching his vehicle between the truck and me. After I reflect on my Christian heritage, maybe taking the span of ten nanoseconds (or less), my temper subsides just long enough to realize that everything around me...the billboard signs advertising cheap car insurance, radio ads for accident lawyers...will soon be largely eliminated, thanks to the self-driven car. Just as I am pondering this, I nearly rear-end that car in front of me! Apparently, my car isn't equipped with adaptive cruise control!

There are going to be some major displacements associated with job losses as well as benefits that will be derived from AD's. One such will be the loss of jobs destined for truck drivers, whose numbers approach 750,000, many of whom will experience permanent job losses. But, for a bit of good news that benefits everyone, driverless vehicles are anticipated to reduce traffic-related deaths by 33,000 people per year, this according to a United Nations report (only a reference for me; I did not read it). For the economy as a whole, a loss of 33,000 people translates into a loss of 3% of our Gross Domestic Product (GDP). Who knows what kind of talents and future contributors to the American way of life have been lost to us in the past due to fatal accidents? What if that included an Albert Einstein, Jonas Salk, John Glenn, Bill Gates, Elon Musk or anyone else of your choosing, who has made an immeasurable difference in the lives of thousands? Imagine that loss as if it actually happened...but, it did happen to many talented men and women whose identities and unrealized contributions we will never know. And, think about the impact this technology will have on our soon-to-be-senior citizens (no one is old yet), who, heretofore, had to give up their driver's license because of age and its inherent impairments. This issue will disappear overnight. We are going to have a highway full of 80 year olds, leaving taverns at three o'clock in the morning! DUI citations will plummet, depriving municipalities of much needed revenues through fines, no longer available. They will find a way to make up for that. And, you can triumphantly make your way to the bank on that statement!

Actually, the savings in lives from fatal accidents, though a huge plus for the human potential, amounts to about 50% of the savings being projected by this technological advance in driverless vehicles, this according to a recent article that appeared in Forbes Magazine (4/17). They go on to report a very significant economic benefit as it relates to non-fatal accidents as well as time savings derived from better traffic flow and lower insurance costs. They estimate annual savings of $317 billion from fewer fatal accidents; $226 billion from fewer non-fatal accidents; and $99 billion in time savings from improved traffic flow on urban expressways and what was clogged-artery, intercity streets. Bottom line: Name me one other cost savings medium that offers anywhere near $642 billion in tangible savings...every year! And these statistics don't speak to the trillions of dollars that will flow into Detroit's coffers from the sale of these AD vehicles.

Even with the savings in human lives, accidents, and time through better traffic flow, there is another dividend that this technology makes possible and that is the potential to entertain oneself such as social interfacing with other passengers in the vehicle, taking a much needed nap or, maybe, you would prefer to read a book...anything to take the monotony out of not personally driving the car. Just relax and enjoy this carefree moment. Even the traditional business lunch will be under attack as a restaurant setting will no longer be required. Privacy, alone, will be a huge plus. The lodging industry might, even, feel the impact of what might come to be referred to as the dreaded "AD." The possibilities for self-gratification and relaxation will be limitless, many of which will be legal and moral. It's your choice...use your imagination!

It's little wonder that the auto manufacturers are hustling their collective buns off to get their AD's to market as expeditiously as possible. Henry Ford was the first in this country to introduce an automotive product that was truly revolutionary for the times. That shouldn't be lost on our auto makers of today. The quicker they get to market, the faster they participate in the demand for what appears to be the dominant, future form of private transportation...fully electric, on-demand, autonomously-driven vehicles.

A second technological breakthrough, promising future benefits in the form of lower prices, is the technological march toward the industry's ability to offer lithium-oxide batteries with a much extended life over today's batteries as an alternative to liquid-based fuels. Another dividend comes your way in the amount of time it will take to recharge your EV – from hours to mere minutes.

We were first introduced to this type of battery in conjunction with gasoline-burning fuels in the form of what has become known as a "hybrid" vehicle where one "plugs in" for the necessary electrical charge that the battery provides or one can choose to run on gasoline. Between the two alternatives, gas mileage has been enhanced dramatically. You can either "fill up" or "plug-in"...or do a combination of the two. It's entirely up to you as to which fueling method you choose. Now, here comes along a totally electrical-driven automobile that, as I write this, is getting nearly 300 miles of driving distance between charges. That roughly equates to buying gasoline priced at $1.09 per gallon or, roughly, half the cost of gasoline, with the absence of some pricey automotive mechanical parts that never require replacing i.e. components associated with the car's drive train, transmissions, mufflers, and the like.

<u>ALTERNATIVE FUELS</u>

For openers, gasoline will continue to be the major fuel source for the near foreseeable future. It is estimated that all alternative fuels combined will be less than 10% of all fuels consumed in 2017. Detroit's ongoing effort to meet federally-mandated fuel economy standards coupled with technological breakthroughs coming our way with the internal-combustion engines available today, promises to keep the majority of us buying gasoline for awhile. This is being made possible through producing smaller, lighter, more powerful engines, cylinder de-activation, 8 to 10 gear automatic transmissions, direct injection and turbo-charging all delivering power and torque from 4 or 6 cylinder engines and the rarest of breeds, the much beloved V-8 ...something unheard of 10 years ago.

Longer term and certainly available today is an electric-powered vehicle (EV) that is destined to gradually replace gasoline as our primary source of fuel. Even longer term will be the introduction of hydrogen fuel-cells as a cost-effective alternative to gasoline or electricity. But, it is not without its own unique set of challenges. Despite the giant pioneering efforts made by Bob Stempel, former CEO of GM, who was forced out of GM, founded a company to develop hydrogen fuel-cells as an economically feasible fuel source with its stand-alone attributes, unique to this type of naturally-found gas. Cost effectivity and a lack of dedicated fueling stations kept his company from succeeding. At the time, it was all about venture capital availability, timing, infancy in the development of the technology...none of which were strong enough assets to keep Stempel in the business.

Unique to hydrogen fuel-cells (HFC's) is its lone waste by-product...water. It emits only water. A car can be refueled in as little as five minutes (versus hours for EV's) and has a range slightly greater than the 300 mile range associated with EV's which is comparable to the range one gets from an internal-combustion engine. Up to this point in time, Toyota, Honda, and Hyundai, have become scouts and would-be pioneers for

189

HFC's. But don't bet against Toyota as they have launched 210 cars, designated the "Mirai" in their efforts to compete with Tesla's upcoming Model 3 and Chevy's Bolt with its more revolutionary, hydrogen fuel-cells. At $57,500, the Mirai is about half the price of Tesla's S model. Knock off $13,000 in federal and state incentives and you end up with a car you can lease for around $500 per month. Toyota will, even, buy you 3 years of fuel, valued at $15,000! Last I heard, they were still accepting orders. You can check this out at www.Toyota.com.

According to Forbes Magazine (05/2016), Toyota's product is powered by electricity, but instead of storing energy i.e. the battery, it creates electricity on its own by taking oxygen from the air and hydrogen stored onboard in high-pressure tanks located under the seats that, when released, creates a chemical reaction, thus, generating electricity to power the motor. Right behind Toyota, is Hyundai with its 100 fuel-cell fleet, leased to customers in the Tucson area. Meanwhile, Honda is readying their entry, the Clarity FCV, which goes on sale sometime in 2018.

But without a refueling infrastructure, HFC-powered cars are going nowhere, fast. To help eradicate this challenge, Toyota has loaned a start-up firm, First Element (headed up by our good friend, Joel Ewanik), $7 million to build 19 refueling stations in California and committed funds for another 12 stations on the east coast with Air Liquide. In addition, Honda has also lent money to First Element, twice the amount of Toyota's investment although it is laying the groundwork for the inevitable switch to hydrogen fuel-cell cars with the stated goal of cutting tailpipe emissions by 90% by 2050, this according to Automotive News (07/2016). I'm not going to be around to witness that, but, feel free to tell me all about it when you catch up with me on the other side.

SOCIOLOGICAL

If there is fault to be found in having to deal with sociological issues, you can place them at the doorstep of the Millennials, the largest single age-group in the U.S. Surveys back up the premise that a generational shift is fully underway, moving away from privately-owned cars. "Freedom of the road," a mindset born out of the 1950's, that promoted the idea of physical flight, is being displaced with digital gadgets and a proliferation of social media.

190

There was a study put out by University of Michigan's Transportation Research Institute in recent months, reported by Fortune.com (07/2016), stating that young people between the ages of 16 and 44 (what a spread?) have been in a declining mode as far as car ownership is concerned since 1983 and will become increasingly more uninterested in driving as time goes by. Clearly, this should not be lost on auto makers as they seek to create a sustainable business model that generates enough profits to justify remaining in the business.

Growth of various forms of Social Media, popularized by emailing, texting, postings on Facebook and Twitter, have quietly exploded onto the scene and just, as quickly, have become a way of life, especially, for the Millennials (born between 1982 and 2002). Coupled with smart phones, smart wristwatches, tablet and laptop computers, and every digital-based, Bluetooth device known to man, they have rapidly evolved into a strata of society who use automobiles less and less. This phenomenon has given rise to a new type of transportation service, what some people refer to as "car sharing" which has become an ever-increasing competitive threat to car ownership.

"Car-Sharing" is rapidly making a name for itself in the larger cities where sharing a vehicle makes perfect sense when evaluated in terms of frequency and cost of use that says nothing about convenience and benefits, i.e. no insurance needed; no maintenance expenses; no parking problems or expenses, perfect for weekend trips. Car-rental companies, such as Zip Car, are positioned firmly to take on all comers in their role as the market leader, offering a seamless service that is highly repeatable, works amazingly well, and their service is priced right. Any would-be competitors should think twice before jumping into this swamp full of alligators. There will be imitators with huge amounts of capital behind them that will enter the fray, but much of the early riches of that market will go to the Alpha dog – Zip Car – while the spoils will be fought over like road-kill for a hawk! Personally, I am amazed that the Enterprises', Hertzs' and Avis' of the world haven't already leaped into this bastion canyon of cash presently controlled by Zip Car. Maybe, they don't like alligators, either.

As one settles into getting comfortable with this new car-sharing service, along comes yet another new form of transportation service, referred to a "RIDE-SHARING" that, again, avoids the need for car ownership. But this time, the scope of ride-sharing is significantly different. Ride-sharing refers to a service similar to what taxis provide...more like getting from Point A to Point B while car-sharing is more "event" oriented. No matter how you want to define it, the taxi is going the way of the dinosaur in its inability to compete with ride-sharing fares. It's not uncommon to see a ride-sharing fare 50% less than a cab's fare. Little wonder companies like Uber and Lyft are, literally, running cabs, livery services with their big black Lincoln Town Cars, and shuttle bus services,right out of business. And to think that Uber launched its business during the time that GM and Chrysler were claiming bankruptcy (a short nine years ago),is absolutely mind-boggling! Today, Uber's stock is worth more than GM and Ford combined...by billions, while generating billions less in revenue! Pretty niffty trick,if you can pull it off, don't you think? Meanwhile, let's not lose sight of Silicon Valley's crosstown rivals, Google and Apple. Either one could buy Ford, GM, and Chrysler combined, reinforcing the old adage, "he who holds the gold, makes the rules." The rules are certainly ripe for changing, thanks to technology and that unforgettable, older staple...cash!

In summary, we have looked at the electrification of the automobile and its hybrid derivatives; alternative fuels to gasoline i.e. much extended life of lithium-oxide batteries; the more technologically-advance internal combustion engine (ICE's); hydrogen fuel-cells; and social media's role in ride-sharing/ car-sharing and a few bunny trails in between. I bring this up now to make a point that draws all of these changes into finer focus and its common denominator ...the AUTONOMOUSLY-DRIVEN CAR with its concentric role woven through all of these products, energy sources, and impact on society. That's why I stated earlier that the #1 most significant change we will experience in the next 5 years is the self-driven car. You don't have to take my word for that; but, most, if not all car magazines that I am familiar with (I subscribe to six) and computer search engines i.e. Google, Yahoo, will confirm for you that this is not science fiction, folks. They merely describe and report the inevitable...you and I will soon (relatively so) be "riding" around in a driverless car. Let that statement resonate a bit longer – you would be correct if you are taking away the thought that you will no longer be a driver. It will be a bittersweet, sad reality and at the same time an exciting era to be a part of, knowing those days are, without a doubt, numbered.

EMERGING MARKETS

Much has been written of late about the world's emerging markets for automobiles, namely, because it remains a huge, largely, untapped marketplace. With fuel prices easing and trending downward, the increasing availability of oil and the ever-improving product life of lithium-oxide batteries, is making all of this possible in a relatively short period of time. The benefactors of these positive outcomes are India, Central America, Eastern Europe, and, of course, China. This, the biggest elephant in the room, finds itself doing what it does best... getting pregnant with more little elephants on the way, that puts competitive pressures on anything that stands in its path!

China is now the world's largest marketplace for new cars with everybody and their brother doing everything in their power to address this monumental sales opportunity. VW and GM stand out as the two leading manufacturers who are concentrating on this marketplace. In 2016, the Chinese bought 25 million new vehicles versus the 17.5 million bought in the U.S. According to IHS Insight, a leading automobile consulting firm, that 25 mil figure will grow to 30 million by 2020.

They are now beginning to debunk the earlier self-inflicted myth that they thrive on copying, stealing, and offering their wares at price levels that American and European car makers can't or won't match.....very much like the earlier Japanese marketing model. Sure they copy and steal technologies. You can go to the bank on that as it has become increasingly apparent that, as an industry, the U.S. needs to be standing on constant vigil, guarding its back side, ever on watch for copyright and patent infringement. If you haven't noticed before now, that's the side of the body that the a## is located on! As yet, China, Inc. has not earned any serious level of trust with the American automobile industry, as it surely will, in time. But, their future car models will be more technology-laden which they expect will drive manufacturing costs down to a point where the inevitable result will be lower market prices that will be darn difficult to ignore. They are well on their way toward developing or acquiring technologies that will ease their entry into the U.S. marketplace. What is missing, at the moment, is a design language that distinctly identifies themselves as Chinese with its own unique styles that will be acceptable to the American car buyer. This is sure to change in time as the Chinese hire more and more designers from the U.S. and Europe as the Japanese and Koreans so successfully did in decades past.

Buying a new automobile in China isn't any cheaper than anywhere else in the world, either. According to Automotive News, who recently reported that the cost of buying a license plate in China cost the equivalent of $12,000 (USD) with a vehicle utilization rate of less than 5%. Market research data reveals that car ownership rates grow rapidly when per capita income falls into the $10,000-$20,000 range. That statistic, alone, bodes well for China's domestic marketplace. More up-market, it would appear China can't buy enough Mercedes, Audi's, BMW's, Buick's, or Cadillac's. To meet that pent-up demand, GM has recently built a new factory in Shanghai in support of sales for these two brands.

China has entered the burgeoning market for EV's with an announcement coming out of Chinese-producer Lucid (12/2016), a Chinese-backed U.S. manufacturer of EV's that intends to compete with Tesla's S model with a new car, initially branded as "Atiera." Toward that objective, Lucid is building a $700 million facility in Casa Grande, Arizona, to build upwards of 50,000 cars per year which they plan to have up and running by early 2018 (hiring and training began in January, 2017). According to verbal reports floating around, Lucid can't wait to get started manufacturing U.S.-built EV's as their internally-developed technology, they report, is proven and can be economically manufacturable from day one of production. It's as if they are as frenzied as a puppy in need of a newspaper! Not a lot is known about this start-up other than some transplants came over from BMW, Mazda, Ford, and, of course, Tesla. They are expected to compete, price-wise with BMW's 7 Series and the Mercedes S models, while the physical size will be similar to the BMW, 5 Series.

What can Lucid uniquely offer the market that the Tesla can't? For a couple of things...battery life and something called "lidar," - energy that uses a light source in the form of a pulsating laser. If you have ever noticed a hockey puck look-alike object mounted on the roof of a Google or Uber vehicle, then you have just been exposed to lidar. Lucid has been quoted, stating that it has developed a new battery-cell chemistry without degrading the battery's capacity. Apparently, that claim, if true, boosts the possibilities of using Lucid for high-end, ride-sharing

194

duties that require a 24-hour duty cycle, thus, filling the gap in the marketplace left vacant by Lincoln's Town Car (black car) departure.

LeEco is yet another Chinese company that is attempting to get in on all of the fun but has experienced cash problems of late. LeEco intended to be a major player in the Chinese domestic marketplace as well as the U.S. Neither prospect looks particularly doable at the moment but somehow, some way, the Chinese seem to be able to find a forest made up of money trees, better than most.

On a final note in anticipating the coming Chinese onslaught into the U.S. marketplace, one is left to speculate that if a car is to be enjoyed for its traditional trappings and a badge of hoped-for social status, China is where it's at...as luxury cars are just beginning to establish a toehold in their ever expanding marketplace. American and European luxo car brands are all the rage these days as ownership is perceived as a symbol of success, openly sought. Sounds a lot like the materialistic mirror by which the U.S. luxury car buyer was reflecting it to be...days that are swiftly diminishing.

FAILURES

The #1 issue in the auto industry, today, as in the past, is the product itself. There are/were way too many bad products – design failures seconded by too many cars poorly conceived, clearly, not attuned to the market. At the top of my list (I love lists as you probably have guessed by now), is the Pontiac Astek and its derivative, the Buick Rendezvous. There were lesser known examples of this failed design.....the Chevrolet Caprice Classic, Buick Roadmaster, and a successor to the Oldsmobile Custom Cruiser station wagon, all built in the same, limited number of model years. It is hard to believe that a car company that continues to bring you fabulous products like the Chevrolet Corvette could be capable of products that were colossal, monstrous failures!

Totally out of tune with the market was the DeLorean DMC-12...just a poorly built piece of overpriced metal, destined for the junkyard along with the Yugo. This car could, literally, fall apart if you stared at it long enough or so it seemed!

The balance of my car candidates for not being relative to the marketplace includes Edsel (will that blunder ever die?); Dodge Nitro, Neon, and Dart; Chrysler 200 and PT Cruiser; Chevrolet SSR and HHR; and Nissan's Muro Cabriolet. Little wonder I did not like the PT Cruiser and Chevy's HHR – both were designed by the same guy.

A lack of understanding or care had created a situation where a particular make or model got rebadged. Chevrolet Nova got rebadged as a Cadillac Seville back in the '70's. It stands as an example where the manufacturer chose not to create a new platformed vehicle in an effort to save development costs, masquerading as a truly new product. It was thinly disguised by putting a different model name on it in hopes the would-be buyer wouldn't know or care about the difference. Buick, Oldsmobile, and Cadillac did that for much of their entire life-cyles...year after year after year. And when the design language got a bit stressed as it did in 1985 for GM, one had a hard time distinguishing the differences between a Buick Park Avenue, an Olds 98 Regency, or a Cadillac Sedan DeVille. They were the same car except for badging and some design differences on obvious focal points like the grill, tailights, and side trim. When the manufacturers do the re-badging, they stand to destroy the equity behind what that brand stands for. To use my above example, some people in the "know" would stop buying as many Cadillac's and switch to Buick's to save money on the price of the car, fully believing both cars are one and the same. Guess what? They would be right unless you are a diehard loyalist to Cadillac. Lincoln is another case in point. Sorry, folks, it's still a Ford Fusion or Taurus.

Another monumental failure has been the numerous attempts at covering up poor product and fraudulent data relative to fuel economy claims and meeting federal emission standards. Recent examples include GM's ignition switch catastrophe, the fraud behind VW's "Dieselgate" and Takata's death-inducing air bags.....all examples of greed, immorality, laziness, and needless expediency, none of which needed to have happened. What an assault on a company's integrity at the expense of faulty product, absent any moral concerns for their deliberateness (let's include carelessness) in describing the engineering (or lack thereof) behind these products and subsequent fiascoes. Not so recent, but, quite recallable, were the failures born out of neglect, over-worked egos, and denials. These adjectives make a perfect fit in describing the Ford Pinto recall; Ford's Explorer-Firestone disaster; Ford's transmission defect that took 15 years to fix; and, who could forget the Audi and Toyota's unintentional acceleration debacle? Strong car companies can bounce back but only after years and beaucoup dollars of commitment to right their ships. The weaker companies who don't commit to reinventing themselves with public acknowledgment of past wrongs and product betterment realization goals, are destined to repeat themselves, finding a way as did the Delorean DMC-12, Yugo, Packard (under Studebaker ownership) or doing too little too late as in Studebaker.

Marketing, or lack thereof, is a historical reality that Detroit seems to revel in and continues to hide behind a "sales facade." Can you name one automobile manufacturer who has a Vice President of Marketing? You can't, can you?..I thought so. Car makers fall all over themselves in naming V.P.'s of Product Planning and/or Development, Sales, Sales & Marketing, and the like. But, no V.P. - Marketing, per se. Why? Do they see sales more significant than marketing? In my opinion, I think Detroit has it all wrong. Marketing is a bicycle. Sales is but a wheel on that bicycle. Is sales a significant part of marketing...without a doubt; but, marketing has got to decide what gets produced, at what price, how it is promoted, and how it gets to market. Sales is tasked with "moving the metal" from Detroit to your driveway and all of the things that go into accomplishing that task. I think the roles of sales and marketing get reversed to the point that one can not distinguish sales from marketing or a company places too much emphasis on sales at the expense of marketing.

This time around, tired Detroit is choosing to sell trucks while deemphasizing selling cars for the second time in as many decades. Why? Because there is more money to be made producing and selling trucks than cars. Smart business savvy...yes; greedy...definitely. While the Big Three are busy selling trucks, Japan, Korea, and Europe are busy eating our lunch (called "cars") in terms of increased market share by selling cars (while they are still busy selling trucks, of course) and, when the market turns, as it inevitably and historically does, Detroit's auto makers end up being thrown into the role of selling cars again, but now at a time when its competitors have been busy gaining broader market acceptance, leaving Detroit waiting for the market to turn again in favor of trucks. Just another example of pitting short-term gains against longer-term profits. When this market turn occurs, I am betting the total market share of cars produced by U.S. car manufacturers sold to U.S. consumers will fall into the 35% range which would represent an unheard of loss of market share. And, don't forget the Chinese. They're coming!

Fewer cars manufactured at excessive levels of capacity continues to haunt car makers. I read that it's an ever-recurring challenge to adjust production levels to sales rates (an art in itself?), which has a major effect on labor allocation and the overall ability to run a profitable manufacturing facility.

And finally, why can't Detroit design a battery life gauge that alerts the car's owner of the impending death of a battery? We put a man on the moon, didn't we? What could be so colossally difficult about designing a cost effective device that measures life expectancy? I would think the increased demand for EV's would have something to say about getting this kind of a gauge added to the instrument panel. The topic of battery life is of enormous importance in Arizona as a battery has a life of about 2 years maximum, thanks to a battery's worst friend...the sun.

SUCCESSES

Huge gains have been made on several fronts during the past 15 years. It was as though someone turned on a light switch in Detroit and Korea, awakening them from their slumber, finally realizing their massive problems couldn't be transferred on to somebody else. The need to build significantly better cars was overwhelmingly obvious and the improved models couldn't be developed and produced quickly enough. The market was ready; the auto makers were not nor had they been. That all had to change in a New York minute.

Although bailouts were unpopular with voters, it was bail-outs that helped save General Motors and Chrysler from going out of business, potentially costing the economy - make that, the nation - thousands of jobs and the ripple effect it would have had, vis-à-vis, on suppliers and their suppliers. It would not have been the end of the world but it sure would have seemed that way.

Better products, ones that embraced safety concerns and reliability; more ergonomically-friendly instrumentation; engineering focus originating with greater expenditures on research and development; fuel efficiency, phenomenal improvement on exterior fit and finish, using aluminum and carbon fiber for more exterior parts that lessens weight that, in turn, increases gas mileage where needed. Styling has been drastically improved, particularly on sporty and luxury makes. Examples of better products include: Tesla; Chevrolet Bolt and Corvette; Mercedes "S" Class; Hyundia/Kia; Toyota's Prius, Cambry, Avalon, and Highlander; Lexus' RX Series SUV's (technically referred to as "crossovers") and the good, old world-beater...Jeep Grand Cherokee.

Technology – the development of the autonomously-driven car tops my list as I wrote earlier. This is expected to reduce traffic-related deaths that, today, amounts to 90 fatalities per day! The AD offers several aforementioned benefits but, as an overview statement, the ultimate, meaningful gain is removing the human factor...that can't be overstated. Humans, simply, can't react fast enough to abrupt, unanticipated changes in traffic and weather conditions. And, there are the continuing strides being made to increase the life of a lithium-oxide battery...a huge plus in getting buyers behind the wheel of EV's. Watch that industry explode with acceptance once the driving range off of a single charge hits 400 miles. It's coming, folks.

The industry has made significant, measurable gains in terms of responding to buyers' needs and the marketplace, taken as a whole. Even when mandated by government regulations, meaningful results are being achieved in regards to gas mileage, safety, quality, reliability, and most importantly...communicating with their customers which might include you.

The Hyundai/Kia story – hard to believe that Kia's recent history includes bankruptcy and its parent, Hyundai, has been synonymously linked to terrible quality, as in the once upon a time model, the "Excel" which it was anything but. Despite this company's successes in recent years, today, in South Korea, Hyundai's market share has dropped like a rock...68% plummeting to 57% in one year's time (calendar year 2016). This was largely due to severe labor issues, something South Korea, apparently, is famous for. As hard as it is to learn that this company's market share in their home market has fallen so drastically, this very same company enjoys nearly a 10% market share in the U.S., not bad for a company given up for dead some ten +

years ago. Flirting with a 10% share puts Hyundia and Kia, as a combined name, nipping at the toes of Honda and Nissan. If they surpass these two formidable competitors and it looks like they might, they will become the fifth largest auto maker in U.S. sales – behind GM, Ford, Toyota, Chrysler. In Europe, H/K are enjoying record sales. How is it possible that this one company can thrive in the face of so many competitors with their less than glamorous history? Easy answer – they are giving the customer what he or she is asking for...the first auto maker to offer a 100,000 mile power train warranty, styling, economy, quality, pricing, all coming from a more service-oriented dealer network. Throw in a cadre of talented managers and you have the business model of a dynamic, growing company. It seems so obvious why these factors, taken together, have culminated into a "don't bet against them" kind of company because they, clearly, know what they are doing. Apparently, these factors aren't so obvious to their competition because no one is replicating their business model that has, at its core, a customer orientation, whether service or sales. They all talk as if they do but...they don't.

A tacit acknowledgment that increased budgets for research and development (R&D) is a necessary investment if an auto manufacturer expects to grow is a given, price of admission, if you will. It's interesting to note that VW of Germany leads all auto makers, worldwide, in their allocation of R&D dollars for product development in support of the 11 makes they produce. In fact, VW is in the top 5%

SUGGESTIONS

It's okay to laugh at some of what you are about to read. That was much of the point why I wrote it. So, have at it. But, whatever your reaction, please don't be offended...this is all based on personal observation and jest. You decide what is meaningful or what isn't, trusting all the while you find it amusing. In any event, I would love to get your feedback, either way.

1. Pontiac Astek's should be outlawed if for no other reason than ugliness.
2. All EV's must be equipped with audible exhaust systems. Otherwise, the silence is deafening.
3. Do away with ashtrays and lighters. What good are they?
4. A voice recognition feature that audibly announces that you are speeding in excess of the posted speed limit.

200

5. Require that all vehicles, most especially those driven in Arizona, have to have a "life remaining" gauge, measuring battery life.
6. Outlaw billboard signs – a major distraction. Who has time to read those things, anyway?
7. Make it illegal to flick boogers out the window while driving. One might just land on another car or its driver.
8. All new technologies should be outlawed, period. Technology for technology's sake should no longer be allowed.
9. Courts of law should hand out mandatory prison sentences for anyone engaging a cop in a car chase. The "chasees" have been watching too many movies!
10. Annual model changes should be eliminated that would go a long way toward removing the confusion associated with model year versus calendar year. Put some meaning back into new car introductions, as in the old days, when these were truly exciting events.
11. No preferential treatment given to owners of Tesla automobiles for exhibiting eco-vanity plates. Let's force them to prepay a road-use tax to help offset the lack of tax paid because they no longer buy gasoline. A surcharge put forth by electric utilities might just be the answer. If so, don't forget to buy some stock in your local utility company.
12. No handguns permitted inside a moving vehicle. Use a Taser instead.
13. Have a municipality publish a numerical listing of all license plates issued in its jurisdiction. So, when the next smarta## tears down your street, you merely look up the license plate in your directory, call the police asking that a friendly call be made to the parents of the a##hole who has the gall to speed dangerously down your street. Or, you might want to take this matter up directly with the parent, yourself. No matter what, I can guarantee this works...as it worked on me! Bedford, Indiana, at one time, published such a registry that eventually was discontinued. Privacy invasion, I suppose, caused its untimely demise.
14. Outlaw using handheld cell phones in moving cars. Thousands of people have lost their lives with various forms of distraction...and talking on the phone has got to be near the top of the list. I'm particularly observant of women with their propensity to talk long and often, driving at speeds that would suit a turtle's athletic prowess!

If you own one of those handheld phones, please give some serious thought to curtail using them while driving. Is that so much to ask? It's not exactly like asking a woman for their bra size, weight, or age. Incidentally, my vitals are a 48-AA; 199 pounds (in my dreams), and I'm one day older than I was yesterday. Yep...I'm in a jesting mood but I have to admit my vitals aren't getting me any second looks other than the ones that would tell me the fly on my pants is open!

15. Get rid of needless government regulations that only succeed in spending money that is not theirs to spend. All this in the name of enforcing safety and fuel economy standards? Haven't they got better things to do? Actually, a case could be made that government spending is a form of taxation in that those dollars can only be replaced by more taxable dollars. How grotesque is that? Less spending, less taxes to be paid...there's the answer you weren't looking for.

16. Stop calling "millennials" millennials. That just pi##es them off all the more. They rightly perceive you don't believe they are serious car buyers and are busy doing "selfies" in an attempt to enlighten themselves with their role of using somebody else's mode of transportation as if it were their own. Using the word "millennials" is not meant to be a pejorative description. It's just that their social media orientation belongs, uniquely, to them and the word "millennials" as well as "pejorative" fits...perfectly! That little remark takes care of any possibility of getting this book read by the "you know who's." of all companies worldwide, regardless of industry, for their financial commitment to R&D.

TRENDS

More EV's are on the way. It is a response to the burgeoning marketing for luxury CUV's and other hybridized versions of stations wagons. New market entries will include the Jaguar I-Pace; Mercedes Generation EQ; Porsche's Mission I; and Audi's e-Tron. Why these models instead of more down market entries where there are greater volumes? Money flows to where money dwells - that is to say, auto makers intend to get a price premium for EV's that would be harder to come by with a lower-priced car, where premium money already resides in joining the ranks of luxury vehicle owners. They have already demonstrated their ability to spend bucks on an unnecessary vehicle purchase; so, let them spend some more on technology and prestige while they are at it.

Plug-in hybrids are going to travel down the same path that dinosaurs took in no time flat with the same result. It's like being a little bit pregnant...either you are or you are not,equally applies to car fuels and the technologies that promote alternatives, as well. Hybrids are, at least, a "band-aid" temporary solution, just waiting for the day until electrification technology can become cost-effective and it takes critical mass to make that happen. Without volume to back it up, electrification won't live up to its potential in cost savings and emission controls. By 2021, over half of the vehicles on the road will be electric-based, with a small percentage being hydrogen-based as gasoline consumption will continue to decrease, this, according to Elon Musk, CEO of Tesla. Who knows where the next five years will take us? But, Mary Barra, CEO of General Motors, is stating that there will be more change in the next five years than the fifty years that proceeded it! The lower consumption rate for gasoline is going to show its ugly face at the pump once again, where prices are going to increase dramatically. In economic terms, the supply is there but the demand won't be...so much for the fear we could be running out of gasoline sometime in the foreseeable future, something predicted back in the days of Gerald Ford's presidency (mid-70's). Did you hear that, Prius, you skinny little undernourished, underpowered, piece of sh##? You are destined to be a "goner." Thank you, Thomas Edison.

The marketplace is already telling the auto makers what they want, not what the auto manufacturers could force onto its customers, although admittedly, the customer doesn't always know what he or she really wants. Today, non-gasoline driven vehicles are less than 10% of all the vehicles on the road. That is about to change, big time, and the technology is there to do it today with much refinement on its way so as to make alternative energy sources more cost-effective and user-friendly to the all-important consumer who buys energy in some form or another to get their vehicle from Point A to Point B. Whether we are receptive to these upcoming changes or not...it doesn't really matter because technology is going to wean us off of gasoline, once and for all, whether we like it or not.

The formerly, much-lauded, family station wagon is in the

earliest of a recovery stage and, when full-blown, sales may eat into the standard sized CUV marketplace. Europe appears to be in love with station wagons. Why not the U.S.? But, then again, look what happened to Cadillac's CTS and Dodge's Magnum R/T wagons. Maybe, it was all about needless horsepower and price point or the marketplace wasn't quite ready for these savagely-powered, good looking automobiles. Who knows?

More niche car products will be created as the manufacturers continue to slice up defined market segments into small sub-sets in search of market position uniqueness. This would include the likes of BMW's X6, Ford's Transit Van, and the ever-increasingly popular compact crossovers (CUV's), like the Buick Encore.

Light trucks will continue to outsell cars for the foreseeable future. Light trucks include pick-up's vans, minivans, SUV's and CUV's. Look for more aluminum body and carbon fiber component part content without giving up product strength while improving gas mileage as a result of the truck's lighter weight. We have Ford and Jaguar to thank for their pioneering efforts.

Electric utility companies have got to love EV's as they bill out higher usage rates. Maybe, now is the time to buy some utility stocks?

Banks will be getting more involved in the pre-purchase stage of buying a vehicle that begins with identifying which dealer(s) has the vehicle in stock that you are looking for....all this while visiting your local branch bank which, in turn, will, largely, guide you to the dealer who has in stock the vehicle you are looking for, rather than the more archaic, established custom of starting your vehicle search at the dealer level.

Online buying will become commonplace within the next ten years. The car manufacturers have got to sharpen up their social media skills to address this ever growing trend.

More 4-cylinder engines are on the way. I gasp in dizzying awe that that will include Porsche. In my lifetime? Who would ever have thunk? That word, thunk, is not in the dictionary, but that's OK...sometimes grammatically-correct English just doesn't get it done.

More money will be spent on R & D as a percent of sales. According to 24/7 Wall Street (11/2014), of the top 20 worldwide companies who spent the biggest amount of bucks, 6 of them or 30% were auto makers. VW led the pack not only as a car company but led all companies irrespective of industry., spending $13.5 billion, followed by Toyota's $9.1 billion, GM's $7.2 billion, Mercedes' $7 billion, Ford's $6.4 billion, and Honda's $6.3 billion. Conspicuous by their absence from the list was BMW, Nissan, and Chrysler. Also, interestingly enough, Apple and Google, neither one, made the list, either. Equally clear, is VW's feverish efforts to get "Dieselgate" behind them while they relentlessly attack the Chinese marketplace with their 11 nameplates they have to sell.

Look for availability of leasing as an option in acquiring Certified Pre-Owned (CPO) vehicles. BMW and Cadillac are leading the industry in this direction. Expect to see more used Ferrari's in more driveways!

Payment plans offered by contract financing companies maturing in 10 years from date of purchase will become more commonplace with the norm closer to 5 to 6 year timeframe

Look for more "hassle free" pricing from car dealers in an attempt to build floor traffic and to make the car buying experience less stressful for fear of being taken advantage of. The dealer's efforts to maximize gross profits by overpricing the product has seen its day and....it's gone. A better informed buyer is making the dealers' pricing practices more transparent, thanks to the abundance of information available online that better equips the buyer for the actual purchase long before he or she ever steps foot inside a dealership. The sooner the Roger Penske's of the trade realize and accept this...the better!

More dealership sales personnel will be salary-compensated along with incentive payments in lieu of the long-held tradition of "commission only" compensation model. Dealers have historically opposed a salary model favoring a commission model instead, which afforded them the luxury of only having to pay on the basis of sales performance i.e. dealers only had to pay salesmen/women if they sold a car. This scenario poorly suits the salesperson because he or she isn't being compensated for their actual time spent on the job in pursuit of selling a vehicle. Very typically, a standard work week for a sales person runs 60+ hours a week with one day off every couple of weeks. Do some quick, simple math. If a sales rep sell one car in one week and earns a total commission of $360 (not as uncommon as you might think), that works out to be a tidy little hourly rate for the entire work week of $6.00. Wouldn"t that warm the cockles of your heart knowing you could be flipping hamburgers at the Arizona minimum wage rate of $8.00!! Working a 40 hour work week would be an added plus versus 60 hours a week that doesn't allow for much time off the job.

More product specialists at new car dealerships, demonstrating the vehicle's various product features. Autonomously-driven cars will spur this trend as drivers become more acclimated to the robotic features that must be learned in order to keep the would-be driver and the car's human cargo...safe.

More concierge type services will be offered to get you inside the dealership in an attempt to entice you into buying a car. Really? Would a massage, haircut, pedicure make that much difference? You can bet your sweet, little patronized a## that service won't be offered by a Subaru dealer but, actually, is being offered by Lincoln dealers with their "Black Label" service. Wouldn't you just know that this service has its own trim level which, simply means, you, the buyer, are pre-paying for the concierge type services that Lincoln offers in the price of the car you just bought? Why be so blatant about it...let the buyer think he or she is getting something for nothing. Isn't that the American way?

Just watch someone like Toyota to figure it out how to make concierge services appear transparent and free which, of course, it is anything but.

PREDICTIONS

My success rate for predicting anything, much less the automobile industry stands at exactly zero. With this writing, maybe I can cautiously get you to think I am a bit clairvoyant or merely an unemployed fortune teller, looking for work while trapped in my love affair with cars. Either conclusion you draw might be troubling for my fragile ego but I will suffer it, nevertheless, just to unload some of this unsubstantiated, conjectural, speculation that I have been mentally carrying around inside my head for way too long. So, here we go.

U.S. car manufacturers' market shares will continue to fall in the next 10 years to less than 35% while the U.S. will control 70%+ of the new light truck market. I hope I am still around for you to laugh at or tell me what a sage I am! As I rub my crystal ball, I see GM's market share hovering around 16%; Ford at 12%, and Chrysler around 7% (owned by someone other than FCA).

Chrysler will continue to muddle along in search of a merger or marketing alliance partner as the clock keeps ticking down. Previous attempts to woo GM into some kind of an alliance or friendly merger failed miserably. The train that carried the speculation that Chrysler and VW might get together has left the station and Chrysler ain't on that train! Meanwhile, Chrysler's CEO, Sergio Marchione, is growing antsier about Chrysler's prospects for survival unless a suitable business partner steps up, the sooner, the better.

GM will acquire Jeep and Ram from Chrysler, thus, increasing their light truck lines from 2 to 4. This is the only way they will ever catch Ford with its hugely successful F-150 truck line... the volume sales leader for any vehicle made and sold in the U.S...light truck or car....matters not. GM wants to lead the market in the largest marketplace for light trucks in the world, where U.S. manufacturers will soon control 70%+ of the market.

The Chinese will buy the remaining product lines of Chrysler – Dodge and Chrysler, leaving Chrysler's parent, FCA, with European-built product only – Maserati, Ferrari, Fiat, Alfa-Romero, and Lancia.

Toyota will overtake Ford to become the second largest supplier of new vehicles to the U.S. Marketplace.

Joe Hinrichs will succeed Mark Fields as CEO of Ford in a timeframe that won't be of Mr. Fields choosing. Ford's Class B (voting) common stock is down 40% since Fields assumed the reins as CEO. Something is bound to happen to change that and it won't look pretty on Mark Fields resume.

Car brokers will become just that...broke. As a source for buying competitively priced cars, they will be pronounced dead and will remain so. They are rapidly being replaced by car buying services, online purchasing, with information obtained from the Internet, and social media. These sources are in the process

207

of changing everything we ever knew about buying cars.

Hyundai and Kia will continue to grow toward each other with their identical market entries, the Hyundai Sonata and the Kia Optima, competing at the same price points, selling to the same market segment. This duplication has got to be needlessly costing them retained dollar reserves and lost profits. How to correct that problem – combine the two makes into one brand and, while they are at it, get rid of the Kia name – offensive to some people who lost sons and daughters through KIA or MIA in past wars. Look for one of those two makes to introduce a line of light trucks to the U.S. marketplace.

Japanese and South Korean market shares in the U.S. will continue to grow as they will concentrate on car sales while their U.S. counterparts will keep focused on light truck sales. This is repeating a scenario of the recent past where Toyota overtook Ford to become the sales leaders for all car products sold in the U.S., a lead Toyota fought hard to achieve and isn't about to relinquish .

Thanks to declining market size in part due to age demo-graphics, future utilization rates for the automobile and the growing impact created by various social media, fewer cars will be sold in the next 10 years, thus, forcing auto makers to artificially increase prices to partially offset product development costs that will not be going away in the face of additional, unwanted capacity. This, in turn, will create a need for more high technology product content and lower labor costs that will be realized, not so much from today's practice of using offshore assembly operations, but from a more expanded role for robot-ics and a cooperative labor force. I predict car prices will in-crease on the average of 1.0-1.5% per year for the next ten years. Without technology's critical role in reducing costs, that price increase could easily be twice that much, just to maintain pres-ent-day profit margins much less increase profits as any good, greedy enterprise should seek to do.

Thanks to Mary Barra of GM, concentrating on profits in-stead of market share, this trend is taking hold, especially given the expected change in the size of the U.S. marketplace. Why focus on the present-day 17% share in a mature market with 17 million cars expected to be sold when more money could be made selling fewer cars with more profit per car? GM is in the business of making money, not comparing themselves with the competition. That's what market share statistics are good for! If it were otherwise, it would be like entering a beauty contest and the car with the biggest headlights wins. Headlights make horrible deposits at the bank!

More consolidation and marketing alliances are coming our way. It's less expensive for the manufacturer to align or merge with another company, rather than sustaining the costs to develop the sought-after technology or production in-house. Buy some time and spread the development and marketing costs. This is a situation where competition is a good thing. Why go it alone?

Thanks to product demand being out of sync with production capacity relative to ever-changing market conditions, production capacity adjustments are a constant challenge. Too many assembly plants with excess production capacity, serving a stagnating or declining marketplace, tells only part of this costly story.

Japan supports way too many auto manufacturers, whose numbers, I predict, will shrink within the next 10 years. Today, besides their Big 3 – Toyota, Nissan, and Honda, they count among their numbers, several manufacturers whose products offer little or no distinctive features or benefits. Why do they continue to hang on? Because they have in the past, which is tantamount to no reason at all. The likely candidates to disappear include Isuzu, Suzuki, and Daihatsu, as producers of car products although one or more of these companies may survive as truck manufacturers. However, on the other hand, three other Japanese companies not included, as yet, are Mitsubishi, Mazda, and Subaru, all three of which are doing reasonably well at this writing. Mazda's widely acclaimed styling and quality bodes well for the U.S. marketplace. That same description applies to Subaru as well, who, of late, is on a roll selling cars in the U.S. Mitsubishi, now 34% owned by Nissan, will get some much needed and unaccustomed market exposure in regions where Nissan has enjoyed robust sales, particularly in India.....just one more horse in Nissan's corral.

More advanced technology is on the way, some of which is needless but you will pay for it whether you want it or not. Improved battery life will be welcomed as it will increase the driving range for EV's which, in turn, will increase their popularity among car buyers.

There will be a larger number of older drivers on the road, thanks to autonomously-driven cars. Picture with me, if you will, an eighty-year old, drunken man telling Uber to stick it!

There will, also, be a smaller number of drivers on the road, creating fewer traffic accidents and a smaller number of road-rage acts.

Roadkill will be significantly reduced by using rabbits to train javelinas to look both ways before crossing busy streets. Absent rabbits, maybe lidar will help.

Smaller sized car dealerships look to lose much of their competitive edge which, in the past, was built on service and a more empathetic involvement with their much cherished customer. Fewer cars being sold won't be helping the situation, especially, in the smaller communities who have grown complacent and have taken for granted their tax revenue base, largely, derived from car sales to help fill their coffers in support of public services. Not to worry...all they have to do is raise taxes. That will be about as welcomed as an uninvited rattlesnake in a pup tent! This change will negate the need for maintaining costly new car inventories (the banks are going to hate that) and showroom space. Yep, the small time car dealer is in for some drastic changes and many will be forced to close their doors. After all, for no more often than the average person buys a car, what does it really matter if he/she has to drive 50 miles to visit a larger dealer, where they will have a variety of cars on display to choose from? This larger display can be viewed from a well-lit, comfortable showroom, have a product specialist (salesperson) demonstrate the features, encourage you to test drive the vehicle and, at the same time, get some leverage out of threatening to go down the block to visit another dealer in hopes of getting a better deal. Try doing all this in a time-effective manner in a small town dealership. The one thing the small sized dealer can do is to offer a level of service, previously unheard of. That might include a massage, a haircut, quarterly get-togethers to go over issues while feasting on filet mignon and a bottle of Dom Perignon. OK...that might be a bit of a stretch but something resembling this level of buying your business and staying proactive with you will become a more frequent occurrence instead of the often experienced slap on the back, thanking you for the business and, then, proceeding to disappear until, of course, it's time to buy another car. And, you can bet your old buddy, the car salesperson, is right there pleading for your business like an under-fed dog!

More government regs are heading our way, thanks in part to the increased number of EV's on the road, that have enjoyed a time of not paying a road tax on the electricity they have been using instead of paying their fair share of the tax load that has been falling entirely on drivers of internal-combustion engines. You knew it was just a matter of time. Oops, guess what time it is?

For as long as I can remember (longer than I care to recall), the car has attempted to make a statement in telling your neighbors who you are or, more realistically, who you want to be seen to be. For a teen, it was that euphoric declaration of independence, with a car being so much more than just a car and was held to be sacrosanct. Thanks to technology and socioeconomic factors already presented earlier in this and previous chapters, yesterday has become just that...yesterday! Technology is about to take over steering your car for you. Take a nap...try to enjoy the ride!

TAKEAWAYS

Until pigs learn to fly, a car's purpose won't be changing any time soon. The character behind the automobile, however, will change and change dramatically like caterpillars into butterflies. The automobile will become less of an automobile as we know it today and will become more recognizable for what it truly is...a robotized vehicle of transport, manufactured by robots with the overall purpose of getting us from Point A to Point B safely, in comfort, at an affordable price, with a minimal amount of damage to our ecosystem without the need to physically drive. You will just ride, and like some of the Greyhound bus ads in years past, forget the rest.

The fun factor associated with driving something new, something different, will be largely diminished in the traditional sense. Imagine the impact AD's and EV's are going to have on drag racing. I can just hear it now, "As I settle comfortably into the front or back seat (take your pick) of my race car, (you know,

211

the car without a steering column.) I am amazed at how effort-
lessly I shaved 13 milliseconds off of my best ET (elapsed time)
with my eyes closed!

We can no longer identify ourselves relative to the kind of
car we drive. That special "connectedness" will be lost...kissing
driving skills, prestige and status good-bye. The days of being
in love with your car will be akin to marrying the wrong woman
and is much in keeping with that proverbial train that just left
the station. That train ain't coming back, folks. Contrary to that
view, according to Jay Leno in a statement he made on his "Jay
Leno Garage" TV show, that America is in love with pick-up
trucks and is a part of the American transportation lore which,
of course, will be autonomously driven as well.

Brand equity will be greatly reduced with no minor amount
of thanks to technological changes that will render car styling
to appear more like what happened in the "Tin Lizzy" era. The
Ford Model T morphed into the Model A without a lot of cosmetic changes, but, did change the character of the car, largely,
as a result of technology (mass production) and added functionality, making the car affordable to the masses. That, of course,
all changed over time which I trust, given enough time, will create some semblance of hope that Detroit can find a way to make
the automobile of the future, one that reflects the individuality
of the person who bought it. Time will tell.

AD's and EV's, by design, will grow toward each other and
become somewhat indistinguishable. Car sharing and car riding
will be intertwined in that same mix.

Leasing new as well as certified pre-owned vehicles will com-
prise 35%+ of all non-cash luxury vehicle purchases.

Hydrogen fuel-cells, as an alternative to gasoline or electricity, will make inroads into the EV market, thanks to the elimi-
nation of its singular waste product...water, as more refueling
stations come onboard.

Thanks to buying services, online buying, banking assis-
tance, and the internet, the days of shopping for a car as we have
known them, leveraging one dealer's price against another's
are largely gone. These changes as to how we buy or lease a car
will negatively impact the local, smaller market dealers while

the larger mega-dealers will continue to grow, managing their higher labor costs (salary-based pay) and the changes forced on them by the marketplace and the manufacturers they represent, as they strive to maximize their rewards on capital risked (and spent), in hopes of generating greater cash flow and returns on their investments.

As for emerging markets, China uniquely enjoys the position of being a major player in the global marketplace, but, at the same time, they feed off of supplying their own domestic marketplace, ranked #1 in the world. An emerging, under-developed market is the last frontier for a mature product i.e. automobiles and is, largely, untapped in many third world countries with India standing out as the largest. China isn't going away anytime soon. Who knows what their future product offerings might look like and it may very well turn out to be superior to what Japan and South Korea offer today.

A substantial risk faced by U.S. and European car manufacturers that produce cars built in China to feed that marketplace, is the real possibility that the communist-based Chinese government might up and decide to dissolve the joint venture agreements that are now in place, that require all U.S. and European car producers to enter into as a condition for manufacturing cars in that country. That risk or threat could be minimized by greater market acceptance of U.S. cars built in China and viewed to be superior to their domestic counterparts, a condition that exists today but could change as China's auto makers build more stylish, reliable automobiles. Maybe the answer might be realized if China gave up on communism and adopted a more democratic form of government! Don't go to the bank on that happening anytime soon.

GM's future profitability will be expressed in terms of real dollars of profit as opposed to being measured in market shares, an unbankable number used to make comparisons between competitors, a beauty contest, if you will, this, coming by way of GM's CEO, Mary Barra.

Lastly, I am rounding out my "lists" by offering up one more dish of opinions, sprinkling in a few facts here and there, on specific makes and models that you won't be reading about in The Wall Street Journal. Here goes:

Most improved luxury car – 2017 Porsche Panamera. Panamera married the uniqueness of a Mercedes S Class with an exotic, 4-door sports car powered by superior-performing V-6 and V-8's.

Fastest growing international brand – Buick, thanks to China that buys more of them than their U.S. counterparts. In my view, the 2017 Buick LaCrosse is the best looking car, dollar for dollar, that GM is building at the present time for the international marketplace.

Most innovative - Chevrolet Bolt, a lower-priced version of the Volt. Could even a lower-priced version be coming our way, named the Jolt?

Most disappointing - the 2017 Chrysler 200. This car is so bad that its been decided by Chrysler management to drop this model at mid-year rather than build them out for the full model year. So, if you want one, you had better rush out there and get it bought because, once the dealers' inventory of this loser is depleted, this car is history. Sad to see this formerly named Sebring convertible set out to pasture. Surely, Chrysler has plans to launch another convertible model to replace this present-day, storied piece of cr##.

Worst cars produced in 2016/17 – Fiat 500L; Mitsubishi's iMiEV; Jeep Wrangler Unlimited; Lincoln MKS; Mercedes CLA250, and, you might have guessed it.....the Chrysler 200.

The biggest increase in sales, year-to-date, 2015/-16 – 2016/17 includes Volvo; Jaguar; Audi, Buick, Tesla, and Ram. Notice the absence of any Ford product.

All but given up for dead three years ago and now looks to be on a fast track to recovery is French-based PSA, whose models include Peugeot, Citroen and the DS, a new EV sports car, a product niche they are pioneering in the European marketplace. Very recently (4/17), PSA bought out GM/Europe's Vauxhall and Opel brands; thus, cutting GM's losses in the region while giving PSA two more pigs in the poke. PSA is going to need a huge revival in customer acceptance for these two doggy brands to get profitable again, something GM couldn't do.

And, then, there was the much-celebrated luxury car, Lincoln, a car brand with a glorious past but a bit beaten up of late.

For years, management intentionally starved Lincoln with a lack of cash and plans to keep this once-heralded brand competitive with Cadillac, opting to put their development funds on higher volume horses in their corral i.e. Mustang, F-150 aluminum body trucks, and new powertrains for the Ford brand. They basically showed Lincoln the door. For some time, Lincoln's designs have been passionless. That's what you get...a starved horse can't run very far, or very fast! So, now Lincoln finds itself in the unenviable position of being forced to get this brand growing again without, in essence, a studied road map to guide them toward some kind of planned sales growth that assures the brand's future. Even the famed over-achieving CEO, Alan Mullaly, was all in favor of discontinuing the brand but eventuall, succumbed to his right hand man, Ford's President of the Americas, Mark Fields, who would later go on to be named CEO. With Fields on shaky ground as CEO, witnessing the precipitous fall of Ford's common stock to the tune of 40% (calendar year 2017) since named CEO, this definitely does not bode well for Mr. Fields and quite possibly for the Lincoln brand since he was the #1 cheerleader for keeping this under-nourished, going nowhere, former American luxury kingpin.

Call it what it is and that is, it's "do or die" time for Lincoln. Even with their toes in the fire, so to speak, early 2017 model year sales are up significantly on a year-to-date basis for sales of the newly launched Continental model and refreshened designs for their line of CUV/SUV's, thanks, in part, to featuring Matthew McConaughey in their current advertising campaign. Whether the Lincoln cars used in those ads are an improvement in style, performance, or resale value, only the collective "you's" out there in the marketplace will have the final word. The American luxury car buyer has beaucoup makes and models to choose from...with or without Lincoln. On a personal note, I reminisce back to the time I was a star-struck teenager falling all over myself in awe of the beautiful, largely hand-built 1956/57 Continental Mark II's. It wasn't even called a Lincoln Continental as it was an attempt to build some exclusivity for this car whose roots actually go back to the 1940's with the famed Continental Zephyr model, championed by Edsel, then, President of Ford Motor Company, much to the disappointment of his famous father, Henry. How and why this model got dropped, I wish I knew. What a colossal blunder by a management led by Henry Ford II.

Although there is a much-chagrined view of what we can expect from Detroit in the foreseeable future, I can't help but think there is some basis for hope, hope based on the auto industry finding a way to bring desirable options for transporting ourselves in a fashion that will be fun, safe, ecologically sensible, and stylish as the car manufacturers face the future transportation needs of the American car buyer. As I wrote earlier...time will tell.

CAR BUYING & LEASING

WHY BUY OR LEASE ANY CAR?

Let me begin by pointing out several reasons for buying or not buying/leasing a vehicle, as this topic is getting more attention of late with the growing acceptance of "car sharing." Whatever you do, keep in mind that life is too short to be buying a boring car. So, make sure your decision reflects what you really want in the vehicle that you are about to buy or lease.

Whether to buy/lease is a response to the more basic questions of costs, utility, and frequency of use i.e. how is the car going to be used...basic, livelihood dependence, luxuriant, or a fun-filled form of transportation, how often will it be used and what kind of distances will be traveled? If answered honestly, which can take a serious, candid effort on our part, especially if you are in the throes of falling in love with the car and all you want to do is to get that deal done so you can bolt out the dealership's door in search of friendlier confines, i.e. to relish and to show-off (admit it, its true). The task of buying or leasing a vehicle shouldn't be so daunting and what you are about to read will resolve or help kill most of your anxieties about this second most expensive thing you will be buying in your lifetime.

Why, indeed, do people like you and me go out and buy or lease that special car, a car that you might have been lusting after, always have dreamed of owning or possessing, for a good portion of your lifetime, or, so it seems? Allow me to offer four possible explanations. There are more...some may apply to you, some won't, but seriously consider these reasons with an open mind.

1.) It is a badge to your success and fulfills a long-experienced dream of someday owning. Should that "day" be now? It announces to your world that you have arrived (in more ways than one).

2.) It provides an opportunity to develop some humility skills in response to flattering comments coming from others that, many times, is no more than an attempt at disguising their envy.

3.) It makes a statement, loud and clear (no trumpet necessary), that says, "This car is mine (no matter that it isn't paid for) and it reflects who I am or aspire to become. Really? Oh, come on! People aren't so stupid to fall for that line of thinking. The truth is closer to your FICO score that allowed you to qualify for a loan so you could buy this car and, at the same time, fessing up to the fact that that car really isn't yours as it belongs to the lender who made you the loan. Your retort might be, "I don't care what you or anybody else thinks. This car is going to be parked in my driveway for the next couple of years. Why does it matter how I got it, as long as it's legal and moral."

4.) "Are you impressed yet?" This question never gets asked but if it did, an appropriate response could be, "You should be...I spent some serious money trying to impress you. The least you can do is to openly acknowledge how impressed you are" or "how impressed do you want me to seem to be."

Really, are these the answers you were looking for or are they a little too close to the truth, that makes you involuntarily squirm a bit? Are you a little uncomfortable with the reactions of others? I thought not. Once you think about it long enough, you begin to see just how transparent these responses are, or can be and they don't begin to answer the real questions that need asking i.e." Do I really need that car, does it meet an immediate need, how much will this purchase actually cost me in terms of price, cash outlay, taxes, insurance, depreciation, fuel consumed, and as importantly, what will that car cost me per mile driven, can I afford this without sacrificing my lifestyle?" If honestly answered, you will be well on your way to learning why you should or should not buy that particular vehicle at this particular time. Your personal preferences and genuine needs will all get sorted out by the degree of your excitement or pain inflicted toward your quest for self-honesty and it will be devoid of any negative blow-back that your purchase might create for those jealous-filled souls who only wish that car was parked in their garage. Keep in mind, they are not going to pay for it.....you are!

Seller Scams; "Caveat Emptor"

Welcome to the lion's den! How disappointing to learn that Daniel has left the building but the lions will be returning shortly... to entertain you. Know that you are entering this coliseum (car dealership) at some peril.

Actually, there are no lions left in the building as my friend, Greg Christenson, a former big-game hunter, tidied up the premises nicely so that you are safe to roam, learn, ask questions, buy, walk away, or whatever floats your boat, so you can get at the real reasons why you're visiting that particular dealership.

There is an oft quoted adage attributed to a not-so-modern day economist, Adam Smith (late 1770's) that, simply means (taken from the Latin) "Caveat Emptor" which, roughly, translates into its English equivalent, "Buyer Beware." My personal take on that remark is, "If you're not careful, your a## may come looking for you." Indeed, what you do know about buying a car can have lasting consequences in terms of the correct choice of a car/truck, paying too much for the vehicle, either as over-priced and/or the finance costs offered by the dealer through a third party lender is not compatible with your FICO Score, knowing you have been taken advantage of...again! And, then, there are the outright scams that have been concocted to relieve you of some more dollars in your pursuit of a good deal. BTW, scams are just as prevalent in private party transactions as they are with new and pre-owned car dealers. It is especially bad on CraigsList. I recently nearly got scammed twice in the same day and here's my takeaway – don't buy any vehicle from a private party unless you physically sit down with the seller (don't trust the Internet to do this for you); personally drive the vehicle and have it inspected by a third party inspector. There are plenty of these pre-purchase inspection companies around, charging fees anywhere from $100 to $350, companies such as Road Ready, Carchex, On Guard, and ABS. The expense and peace of mind it offers is well worth the one-time price. When you are spending thousands of dollars on a car/truck that you, typically, only buy every 3 to 5 years, what's another $100-$350? I know what it is. It's call chicken feed. Don't be afraid of spending a few more bucks...thriftiness can have its own penalties.

It is estimated that scams rob car buyers of upwards of 30 billion big ones every year. Some of the more common deceptive tricks that a disreputable dealer might try in an attempt too gain an unfair advantage over you could include:

1.) Bait & Switch – advertise or tell you about this wonderful car that has your name written all over it, only to arrive at the dealership and learn the car has been sold. At this point, the salesperson tries to convince you of the merits of a comparable car that they just so happen to have in stock. But by now, I'm sure you've guessed what's coming next...the price of the car is greater than the price of the car you wanted. Imagine that!

2.) Truth in advertising – the dealer advertises a vehicle that doesn't even exist or there seems to be an error in the advertised price, blaming the advertising source. Some smaller-volume dealers advertise they offer lower prices because their overhead expense is smaller than a mega-dealer. Not so...Large dealers can spread fixed overhead expenses over a larger volume of sales, thus, reducing the dealer's overall costs which can (and many times does) get reflected in the price the dealer is willing to sell the car for...something a smaller dealership can't do.

3.) Yo-Yo Finance – the interest rate has somehow, miraculously, managed to increase between the time you first learned about a particular car being for sale and the time you sit down to complete the deal.

4.) Supplemental Window Stickers (in addition the the sticker price from the factory) – where the dealer places "add-on" items that he has already pre-installed on the car and presents it as if it the "add-on's" are an integral part of the car. Oh, bull snot! That is, simply, not true. This is just another income stream available for the dealer to tack-on more dollars of profit to sweetened his pot. So, turn the tables, and have the dealer sweeten your pot by giving you those "add-on's" as freebies because you are not going to pay for it/them. And, since those items are now an integral part of the car, of course, they can not be removed. So, there you have it....your deal just got a little better at the hands of an avaricious dealer, justice served, richly deserved!

5.) Rebates from the factory that the dealers keep for themselves, that by all rights, belong to you as the buyer which has the effect of lowering the price shown on the window sticker (MSRP). Now, you are ready to negotiate the price down from this net figure.

6.) Getting tricked into a lease in an attempt to get the monthly payment lower than had you financed it. If you hadn't volunteered the amount of monthly payment that you could financially handle, this sale tactic would not have come into play.

These are but a few of the well-worn deceptions that taught me some valuable lessons on the games some dealers try to play. As a result, my expanded knowledge on buying cars now includes detailed measurements of the interior dimensions of a doghouse, where I was detained for days on end, working to forgive myself for being so naive about dishonest practices coming from shady dealers. No more doghouses for me. I have graduated myself into a hard-nose businessman, insisting on my deal or no deal at all, reminding myself, I drive the deal, not the salesperson.

I could go on and on writing on this subject (and love doing it); but, I will work to give you a more condensed version of what you will need to know before ever stepping foot inside a dealer's door. Just know that when that inevitable day comes when you visit a dealer and are confronted by a salesperson face-to-face, remember this little attempt at poetry:

ODE TO A CAR SALESPERSON

Zero percent financing, what a joke!
My ribs can hardly handle such a poke.
Make sure the car's price is right,
otherwise, it's fight or flight.

The deal has got to be fine
if you want that car to be mine
This car needs to scream,"take me home,"
otherwise, this won't be much of a poem.

Let's look at the figures just once more,
keeping you from bolting out the door.
"Maybe," says the salesman, "we can come up with a deal
to kill your anxiety and the way you feel."

"So, what price do you want and I'll do my best
to get you that deal and, please, forgive the BS."

Now that I have beaten dealers to a pulp, I am reminding myself that I need to emphasize that the above references are directed at DISREPUTABLE dealers and, yes, there are more than a few. In fact, the age-old or traditional way for determining a price for selling a vehicle invites deception. I would hazard the guess that if the dealer offered a firm, fixed price that discourages bickering (negotiation is a much kinder word) and the salesperson would get paid with fixed compensation... this would remove many of the dishonest practices experienced by car buyers today. Haggling over price gives the dealer the advantage of, potentially, increasing the amount of profit attainable whereas a fixed price scheme, pretty much, negates that possibility. Attempts have been made to implement both firm, non-negotiable pricing and paying salaries instead of 100% commission-based income but neither has really caught on, something, that I speculate is about to change for reasons I have already presented earlier in the book. But know, that the vast majority of new car dealers are honest (in varying degrees) and work hard to earn your business in hopes he or she will get your service business and sell you more cars in the future.

Did You Get A Good Deal?

Now, let's take a longer look at the car buying process, itself. In this section, we will consider those factors that lead you to a place where you know you got a good deal (could have been a great deal with a little professional help) on the car you chose for yourself, comfortably knowing you can afford it, and can look forward to many satisfying years of enjoying your new loved one safely, reliably, and, if you will, fashionably. We will look at the individual considerations that lie behind the wheel of that dream car. Since you are the helmsman of your own ship, you, alone, must be happy with how you manage the actual buying. At the end of the day, know that the single most important thing can be reduced down to three words...PREPARATION, PREPARATION, and PREPARATION.

When you finish reading this chapter, I trust you will be well on your way to becoming a budding expert on the art of buying a car. You'll know why, what, how, when to buy that dream car and know where to go to get help, should you need it. The answers (there are no secrets) to buying the right car at the right price lies in being well-informed, something the salesman doesn't want you to be. Information is a buyer's best friend while it's a dealer's worst enemy. The dealer doesn't want you to know everything and if you don't ask the right questions, that will be one less thing that the dealer has to fear in getting the deal done to his terms.

So, think of your decision to buy what, when, and how as an enjoyable train ride and that train is about to leave the station. This time, you will be on it, sitting in First Class. So...hop on, here we go!

WHAT?

Now that you've established in your own mind why you want to buy/lease a new or pre-owned car or truck, it's time to tackle the all-important question of what to buy or lease.

What are your preferences for new versus pre-owned, color, and optional equipment choices? Ask yourself again if you can afford it. I know that sounds so basic, but you would be surprised how many would-be buyers don't thoroughly consider that question because they have convinced themselves they can handle a monthly payment of "X" amount. Don't underestimate what the total costs are to buy, operate, and insure that dream machine. Do you know enough about the car to be comfortably prepared to buy it? Do you have a Plan "B" to fall back on if the car or deal doesn't work out? How about having a couple of alternative choices in mind to fend off possible disappointment if, for whatever reason, you can't get the car bought for reasons I'll denote here shortly.

Keep in mind – the right car bought at the wrong price is preferred to buying the wrong car at the right price. In other words, don't let pricing alone sway your better judgment as to what car you buy. Once bought, you and your newly-acquired dream machine are joined at the hip, so to speak. Wouldn't it be a miserable experience to be forced to drive a car or truck that you didn't like (can easily happen after enduring repair bills the size of the Grand Canyon or you realize that you have fallen in love with an EV model while standing in front of a gasoline pump, nourishing what now turns out to be a beast..... that you no longer want? Think – the feckless, untimely lease of a 2009 Hummer, a date that just so happens to coincide with GM's filing date for bankruptcy. That dinosaur, typically, went out the dealer's door with a $1,000 a month lease payment attached to it for, get this, 3 years or more. Compared to this, a purchase of a 2005 Pontiac Astek might have been prescient were it not for the fact that GM stopped producing the Astek in model year

223

2005, thank God. It's punishment enough that you would be driving the ugliest car known to mankind!

Moral to this story: know what you want to buy or lease BEFORE ever stepping inside a dealer's door with a back-up choice or two, just in case. Secondly, the factors that follow need to be at the heart of how you go about deciding what vehicle you should buy or lease.

Powertrain

1.) Internal-Combustion Engines (ICE's) -totally gasoline-powered
2.) Hybrid Electric Vehicles (HEV's)
3.) Plug-In Electric Vehicles ((PHEV's)
4.) Hydrogen-powered
5.) Compressed Natural Gas (CNG) – primarily used in truck products
6.) Transmission types – automatics, semi-automatics, or manual (floor or steering column mounted

Price	You can't always minimize it but you sure can maximize it. What can you afford? The national average as of 11/17 carries a sticker price of $35,000.
Fuel Economy	Always measure it against price of the vehicle, estimate the fuel costs, and miles driven between refueling/recharging.
Styling	Does this speak to you? Do you REALLY like the car's looks? Is this the image you want to project to others? Are you still going to like it 3 or 4 years from now?
Safety	What are the car's safety ratings? How does it handle in various road conditions: Google it to find out or call (don't visit) your questions into a dealer.
Reliability	Learn about product defects, recall history (if any) – use Google and CarFax Reports.
Size	Big enough to transport your human cargo? Roomy enough to be comfortable? Will it fit in your garage or driveway?
Color	Anything but green or brown; those colors

are bad for resale value when it's time to turn the car in on trade or an outright sale by you.

Performance	Powerful enough? How about handling characteristics?
Equipment Options	Expensive to add later as an aftermarket "add-on"; make sure you fully consider your creature comforts and enjoyment needs.
Warranty	Make sure you understand the various items covered by the warranty and equally important, the items not covered. Don't forget the inclusive dates covered by the warranty. If a new car is being purchased, don't buy an extended warranty at the time of purchase.
Availability	Make every effort to buy the car or truck out of the dealer's inventory. To custom order the vehicle from the factory can take up the better part of 2-3 months to take delivery.
Insurance Cost	Shouldn't be an issue unless it covers exotic sports cars; some luxury cars or cars that have a history of being stolen, a poor driving record, or a history of excessive claims.

Post Note: Powertrain choices need to be very carefully considered due, primarily, to availability and the ability to afford a variety of choices. However, if in doubt, your best bet probably falls on the side of internal-combustion engines (ICEs). Know that any powertrain choice in the future will reflect improved performance as technology gets further refined. Cost will always be a serious consideration when comparing the various types. Gasoline, when priced at $3.00/gallon for a $30,000 automobile looks reasonable but compare that with an EV's fuel costs (conversion to gas comparison) of $1.09/gallon...but that might be a $100,000 Tesla S you are comparing it with. Of course, the

Chevrolet Bolt and Nissan Leaf, with their lower price, makes the EV all the more affordable, resulting in an easier decision to make in favor of an EV.

Allow me to clear up a point of confusion that's pretty commonplace when differentiating between Hybrid Electric Vehicles (HEVs); Plug-In Hybrid Electric Vehicles (PHEVs); and Electric Vehicles (Evs). HEVs are gasoline-powered while PHEVs are battery-powered; HEVs are less costly to buy because the energy savings is less than a PHEV. PHEV has the greatest mileage range of the two choices. Contrast this with the EV which is 100% electric-powered and the most expensive to buy of the three. Hydrogen-powered vehicles are just beginning to appear on the automotive landscape. This is a fuel cell-based alternatives with water being its only waste by-product. The tree huggers have got to love this; but, the drawback to hydrogen at this time is a limited amount of refueling stations throughout the U.S., and the cost to produce the fuel-cells that gets passed down to the lucky devils who buy into hydrogen as their fuel of choice.

Anyhow, to you piston heads out there, keep on enjoying your glasspack mufflers. Gasoline is going to hang around for a while as the preferred choice of fuel for the foreseeable future. Availability has long lost itself as an issue, thanks to the technological breakthrough that produced the "fracking" process which allows U.S. oil producers to recover their past market position as the world's largest supplier of crude oil products (yep, we passed up Saudi Arabia for this distinction.) U.S. - 1, OPEC – 0!

HOW TO BUY; the wrong way

How do you go about the actual buying of a vehicle? What are the key things you need to know and how much are you willing to communicate to the salesperson? Should you save some of your questions for your own research, gaining information that might be helpful once the negotiation session takes place, thus, keeping the salesperson somewhat in the "dark," that eventually may turn to your advantage. Do you negotiate the price or have someone you trust to do it for you? Once you acquire the ability to ask and pursue answers to these questions, you will be well on your way to becoming an accomplished car buyer with a buying methodology that is repeatable from car purchase to car purchase. Your buying model is now set for any future car

226

you might want to buy. When you get to that point, I will con-fer you with the honor of being a Certified Car Buyer. Until you become a CCB, watch out and keep in mind that famed Latin expression "Caveat Emptor."

There are a couple of ways to go about buying a car, loosely defined as either the right way or, as you probably guessed, the wrong way. Let's take a look at both.

Picture a man and his wife, neither of whom are in agree-ment as to what they should buy. In this setting, they are defi-nitely combative, ready to fight to get what they want or don't want as the case may be. I can write and speak to this topic as I have accumulated a whole repertoire of knowledge and personal experience, richly acquired through my history of multiple trips into car dealers, many times, just to check out the cars with no intent of buying anything. Well, that might have been the in-tent, but my history says otherwise. Just keep remembering, there are soooooooo many cars, and soooo little time!

Here's how one scenario could play out – The wife's lack of enthusiasm is definitely not contagious when she says, "That car sucks, along with a few other things that I don't want to waste my time talking about." That immediately sets off the husband with his crisply-put response, "what sucks?" In less than a New York minute, she replies, "gas," not expecting to be challenged so boldly, so quickly. After a painful awkward pause, not to be any further intimidated by her spouse, she briskly suggests what he can do with that car..... in his next lifetime. Just as quickly, he asks, "what other things?" After another delayed response, she finally replies with, "that four-wheeled beast is going to break the bank...we can't afford it. Besides, that monstrosity is ugly and I wouldn't be caught dead driving it and for what it's worth, I don't like the freakin' thing. It's not me." The husband promptly digests these muddled words of momentary dismay, which takes all of one tick off of the clock, at which point he elevates his voice to ensure that he is being heard and sarcasti-cally remarks, "That car could have been your new playmate. But, you can thank your pi##y little attitude for robbing you of the joy of owning and driving that dream car. Since you don't like it, you won't mind my driving it since I'm the one paying for it and the one in this family who wears the pants." Wasting no time, she puts her mouth into action by telling him, in no uncer-tain terms, that their future marital arrangement hangs in the balance, all because of one ugly, unaffordable car. This threat brings out the husband's sharpest retort of all when he brazenly says, "Can I help you pack your bags?" I suspect the husband learned one thing from this verbal exchange – asking his wife for her blessing in buying this car is akin to asking a dairy cow for a cold glass of milk! Moral to the story- it is far easier to ask for forgiveness AFTER the car is purchased than to get permission BEFORE the purchase.

Now, if you were married to my wife, Sandi, this whole little episode would have been played out a bit differently. For openers, she would have jumped with glee when telling her that I found this "special" car and "that it won't remain on the market for long, that it is safe, good looking (reflecting the excellent tastes of the new would-be owner), and a great value for the money." Upon hearing this, she exclaims, "What a car! Roger, you should rush out there and buy it before it gets away to another owner.." Rapidly gathering myself up in response to this magnanimous suggestion, I graciously (and gratefully) thank her for her thought-provoking words. I mean, Hallmark couldn't have come up with a better greeting card that would begin to express my joy, befitting the depths of my appreciation for having the smarts for having married this woman in the first place. At this point, I am thinking this is an opportune moment for some kind of conciliatory, witty response (am I up to this challenge?), suggesting that we not lose sight of that special something or occasion that we have been planning for months; thus, attempting to reinforce the pleasantness of these two scenarios that, if I am right, virtually assures her ongoing support for that next car purchase. Imagine the compassion! And, oh yes, one minor distinguishing detail needs a little more ink - .Sandi's undying love of me, despite my love of something that she could care less about, ever reminds me of that riveting truth, "soooooooo many cars, sooooooo little time!

I need to bring this matter of spousal involvement in the car buying process to a head by telling you about two actual incidents that happened to me, involving spousal non-involvement nor support of any kind for buying a car. In both unbelievable situations, I was embarrassed...beyond words. The first incident started out innocently enough. I was invited onto an early evening TV news telecast by the NBC affiliate here in Phoenix. I was asked to answer some questions that the station reporter had prepared in advance of our getting together on this particular nightly news segment, questions she didn't advise me of beforehand. So, here I am "winging" my way through her questions in a time slot that lasted for an eternity, or so it seemed at the time. Actually, it was all of 5 minutes, if that. Anyhow, the reporter wanted to do the interview outside in my office parking lot, rather than, at my suggestion, in a cool, air-conditioned conference room on this typical 105 degree, summer day in Phoenix and would be less distracting if one were to stumble onto our set. So, here we were, the reporter, her cameraman, and me standing in the parking lot with my nerves jangling like a priest in a whorehouse, trying to guess what questions were going to be unfurled on me. My anxiety level must have been off the charts, especially, when she took note of the Maserati Gran Turismo coupe that I was standing next to. I was doing my best to move away from the car so that she wouldn't associate me with it.. But no. That wasn't going to be. She and her cameraman zeroed in on that car like they had just discovered a untapped gold mine with jackhammer in hand, as the reporter immediately went "ga-ga" all over the Maserati, stating how beautiful it was. She went on to remark that I seemed to have some attachment to the car, paused for a moment and asked if that beaut might happen to belong to me. Feeling entrapped, I meekly (something I have to work hard at) answered in the affirmative. Like a colonoscopy, when that interview was over, I mentally jumped for joy, being so glad that the interview was over and done with. Besides a lost opportunity to exercise my hoped-for gift of humility, I was further humbled (humiliated would be a better choice of a word) by a phone call that came not one minute after the TV interview was over, thus, shattering my newly-found television celebrity reverie. On the line was, of course you had to know, my dear, darling wife, Sandi. Well, let me cut to the chase here...I was not about to achieve star status as a television celebrity overnight. This might take a few days! In any event, my airspace time as a television personality was under attack. In fact, any moment now, I might find myself.... dead! Sandi was anything but happy or jumping for joy in seeing her hubby live (a condition about to change) on TV, wasting no time in telling me how disappointed (a much stronger adjective could have been inserted here) it was for her, learning on TV that the newest member of our extended family included, yet, another car. Further, she wanted to know what my plan was for letting her know when I would have made some sort of grand announcement for letting the world in on my buying a car whose name she couldn't even spell! At this point, the fur was flying and the do-do was getting darn deep. Knowing how easily she can fret over anything that involves change, especially, change that she doesn't have a hand in, I pleadingly explain that her feelings were utmost in my mind and that I didn't want to need-lessly concern her. After all, that would be one less thing that she would have to concern herself with, right? Wrong, wrong, wrong...3 words not to live by! But, something good did even-tually come out of this. Sandi came to like that car more than she loved me. Only kidding.....I think. What a change in venue! Moral to the story – don't plan on being forgiven anytime soon, thinking it is easier to forgive than to gain permission. Yes, I know that it worked for the guy in my earlier example, but at what price? Folks, let me tell you, there's nothing like being forgiven! In a nanosecond, I ascended out of a doghouse into a palace...where I can watch over my newly-acquired toy a.k.a. my dream car du jour.

My second situation, which came about a year later, can best be described as sneaky, evasive, and putting oneself at the point of a premature death, all with the same end result - embarrass-ment beyond words, but I'll try. Without Sandi's knowledge, I bought a 2003 Thunderbird in Milwaukee and had it shipped to Phoenix where, you might have guessed, I had no physical room to store it. My three-car garage was full - plus I was using a friend's warehouse to store the overflow my garage couldn't han-dle and now, horror of horrors, he had run out of space to offer me. So, what do I do as I tried to manage my sense of despera-tion? Brilliantly conceived but poorly executed, I asked Shelley, a local real estate guru in our neighborhood and daughter to our good friends, Monty and Barbara, that if garage space were to become available on the house located directly across the street from our house, that she had a listing on, would the owner and former-neighbor mind if I parked my T-Bird in his garage until the house sold? Well, it turns out that not only was it available, he was happy to let me store my car for a short period (until the house sold) and didn't want nor expect a dime in return for his magnanimous gesture. Like all good things, this one had a shorter than desired life and it came to an unplanned, abrupt, shi##y end....one I would have never expected. After the car had been stored in his garage for, maybe, two months, one day Shelley drives up in front of my house, where Sandi, who she didn't have the former pleasure of meeting, is sweeping out the driveway, thinking that she just wanted to introduce herself and say hello, but by total surprise, she told Sandi that her husband

230

(that would be little old me) would soon need to remove the Thunderbird from the garage located across the street, as she points in its general direction. Sandi, instantly startled, reacted by asking, "whose husband?" With the mystery solved as to the identity of the husband, Sandi briskly tears into the house in search of what could have been her former husband (me) with a handful of nails, useful for hammering shut an adult-sized wooden coffin, that I visualized had my name written all over it. As I look back, I have to tell you that it was darn humbling to be put on a spot like that. I finally mustered up enough courage to blurt out, as if my life depended on it (it did), that I couldn't just leave that Bird parked at the curb or overnight in our driveway. That part she understood, and eventually came around to accepting what I judiciously work to maintain, i.e. that car was a short-term proposition with a "sold" sign plastered to the windshield. I flipped it in a matter of weeks and, above all, I would not allow myself to fall in love with it, where it might have come to expect a nice little reprieve from our infamous Arizona sun. Flash forward.....another bit of good news.....I am still alive, that imagined casket vanished, and, yes, I sold that T-Bird within 3 months of the time I bought it and, yes, of course, I replaced with yet another "got-to-have-it" car, a 2014 Cadillac CTS coupe, faster than a pig can scream "Oh sh##" during a guided tour of a slaughterhouse!

CAR BUYING; the right way

This is going to take a little more effort on your part than the examples I wrote about earlier. But, I think you'll agree that what I am about to propose will be well worth your while in terms of saving you time, money, and potential disappointment, while gaining the necessary knowledge to make you more self-confident for your car buying adventures, now and in the future. The fundamentals and ideas that follows are just as valid today as they were on the day that Studebaker decided to stop making those gorgeous Avanti's in late 1963. Learn and practice these time-tested principles today, knowing they are fully transferable into your enlightened, car buying future.

You should:

1.) Have your spouse's blessing for the purchase...BEFORE you do anything!
2.) Determine your true needs and desires and get a rough

idea what these choices will cost.

3.) Decide whether you are going to buy this car entirely on your own or use a buying service.

4.) Determine the maximum amount of money you are willing to pay.

5.) Determine the minimum amount of money you will accept for your trade-in.

6.) Save your questions that you couldn't get answered using the Internet for the dealer.

Use the Internet, googling your questions regarding the car's features, specifications, print their online product brochure; read the reviews offered by other buyers for the same vehicle and use Kelly Blue Book and NADA to get window sticker pricing info. Learn if there are any buyer incentives or rebates available to you and, yes, the dealer is obliged to pass those savings on to you. Occasionally, to the unsuspecting, a dealer might try to keep those rebates for himself. Your job is to keep the dealer honest with you. If he/she doesn't, let your feet do your talking...there's always another deal that can be made elsewhere!

Do the necessary research to learn what the dealer paid for the car; understand the differences between sticker price which is the Manufacturer's Suggested Retail Price (MSRP); invoice – what the dealer supposedly paid the factory for the vehicle; and something called "holdback" which is a term not meant to be commonly known or understood by a car buyer. Holdback refers to the extra profit potential available to the dealer upon achieving certain sales and operations goals set by the manufacturer and, typically, run about 1-3% of the MSRP. The lower percentage gets assigned to a higher priced, lesser-margined vehicle such as Mercedes while the 3% is assigned to lower-priced cars such as a Chevrolet, Ford, Toyota, where sales volume is greater due to the lower price of the vehicle. You can learn the specific holdback amount by make, model, model year, and trim level at website, www/carbuyingstrategies.com. If you stick your dealer's toes in the fire long and deep enough (allegorically put, unfortunately), he or she might be interested in having you share in his/her little bounty but you will never get it if you don't ask for it.

Learn what a typical documentation (doc) fee is in your area. It could range anywhere between $50 to $700, depending on where the dealer is located. In California, the maximum doc fee is fixed by law at $50 whereas, in Atlanta, dealers scalp their buyers by as much as $700 per sales transaction and are totally disinclined to move off of that amount. To clear up any mystery as to what a doc fee is, it is intended to be compensation to the dealer for covering his administrative expense in writing up a completed sales transaction. Isn't that a crock? You have to pay a fee as a condition for doing business with a dealer. With the possible exception of car auction houses, where else, name me one, does a buyer have to pay a fee for the privilege of buying a product from a particular store or vendor? The dealer will fight to the death to hold on to that doc fee and any attempt to get him/her to change their mind is a bit like trying to knock The Ten Commandant tablets out of Moses hands. Good luck with that! You, as the buyer, have the sole recourse of telling the salesman right up front, prior to any negotiating, that you are willing to pay a doc fee in an amount not to exceed "X" amount of dollars. Keep in mind that paying a doc fee has zero value to you...those are "empty" dollars you are paying for nothing. Why should you pay for something that gives you nothing in return?

Just for kicks and giggles, you might want to rehearse your upcoming visit to the dealer, forearmed with all of this nifty information that you have picked-up off the Internet. If he thinks you are better informed than the ordinary bear, you might be forcing him to show you some respect and be less inclined to pull a "fast one" on you. Be prepared to negotiate the price you are seeking...more on that later.

With these questions answered as to how to buy a car, you're ready to tackle the all-important matter of when and where to buy that dream car. You are well on your way to getting that beaut parked in your driveway. So, prepare yourself for the excitement of knowing you bought the car of your choice and on terms that minimized your cost to acquire. Hooray for you!

WHEN; To Buy Or Lease

Like anything else in life, there is a right or best time to buy a car or truck. Surprised as you may be to learn this, there really isn't such a thing as a bad time to buy. Granted, some times are more opportunistic than others. But, just think, "Is there a bad time to pray, a bad time to save money or a bad time to start a business?" The same is true with buying cars – any time is the right time if you are prepared and know what you want to buy and at what price, confident that it fits your budget.

Personally, I think the best time to buy a car is the last weekend day of the month.. My second choice would be to buy sometime between Christmas Day and New Year's Day. Why? The dealer has sales goals to meet that puts pressure on his sales associates to post sales results on a monthly and calendar year basis. The sale he/she makes to you might be just enough to get the dealer to achieve his/her sales goals for the month or year.

There is one notable exception to the right time to buy a car and that is, of course, if you haven't decided on what car to buy, the price you are willing to pay, and most importantly, how you are going to pay for it. Frankly, you shouldn't concern yourself with the question of "when." That's reserved for the person who is set on their choice of a car, color, equipment, where they are going to buy it, the price, and how they are going to pay for it.

Here are some tips to follow that will ease the question of when to buy:

1.) Shop the dealer's showroom and new car lot in the early morning hours, mid-afternoon or a weekday evening on a Monday or Tuesday. These are, typically, the slowest business hours for a dealer, a time when he or she is amiable to spending more time with you because he/she is under less time pressure.
2.) Assuming the role of a father, check out the car thoroughly with no regard to the time it takes to do it, as if it were your daughter's first date.
3.) Test-drive the car to confirm the impressions of your earlier test-drive at the car rental agency.
4.) Ask questions. Remember, the only bad questions are the ones you didn't ask.
5.) If you're not satisfied with the way you are being treated or you just don't feel comfortable for whatever reason, bid the salesperson a "good day/evening" and promptly leave the dealership.
6.) Finally, ask yourself...does this car feel right for you? Styling is one thing, though compelling, but, how do you feel about the car? Is it you? Is this the you, you want to project to others, as far as a car is capable of making this

234

happen? After all, you're going to feel pretty silly having a restaurant valet park your 2005 Pontiac Astek when he informs you that Pontiac Asteks are not permitted on the premises. It creates too much eye pollution! Now, you know you should have bought that bright, shiny Ferrari you were lusting over before you made that fatal decision to buy a pup-tent based van.

I wrote this little squib, "When To Buy A Car," on a lighter note or at least, that was the intent. Any real meaning you might take away from these words will be purely accidental. But just beneath the surface, however, is an attempt at conveying a message relative to time.

Tomorrow has arrived...it's called today.
How amazing it goes unnoticed...as it slips away.

WHEN TO BUY A CAR

Buying a car is a serious business, so you've been told
with so many cars to choose from, you hate being sold.
Just know, there's a seat for every a##.
When you find yours, you're in for a blast!
Or, you are thinking there's an a## for every seat
Take your pick...that's where money and lust come to meet.

This time, it won't be just any old ordinary car,
No siree, this one will set your heart on fire.
How about a bright red Ferrari 488 GTB?
That beauty will most definitely turn some heads, you'll see.

"What are you doing, Roger, smoking another cigar
when you could be busy, buying another car?
I know this is a mental challenge facing you,
buying that beast calls for, another brew.
And, I do hope Sandi likes the color red,
otherwise, you might find yourself among the dead."
Shaken from my reverie, I think about all the love I'm going to bestow on that beaut,
especially, while wearing a British racing cap and driving
  gloves.
Won't I look cute?

It's time to be decisive – enough of these excuses and get out

there and get that car of a lifetime bought
before Father Nature (distant relative to Mother Nature) tells
you, this time, your time is nought!

Like me, you have decided, finally, you are really prepared
Now.....step out there and make it happen, you declared.
OK, OK.....I'm ready to buy, so you cautiously think;
but, what you don't know could place you over the brink,
between loving that new dream machine
or ruing the day you couldn't have foreseen.
That timidity and fear for what you didn't know,
could have done you in, your spirit no longer aglow.

So smarten up, my valued reader and dear friend,
buying a car should be great fun and, not a sin.
All you really need to know, you can easily find
on the Internet or this book, leaving you no binds

Now that you have acquired the needed knowledge and are
ready to go,
get out there, right now, before you spend any more of your
hard-earned dough!

WHERE; To Buy Or Lease

Besides the obvious, a car dealer, where should you go to find
that special car that you want to buy or lease? Where can you go
to get help with locating and negotiating a price?

Let's start with car dealers that come in two flavors, new
and pre-owned. If you don't have a referral or recommendation
from a family member, friend, or associate, lean on the side of
selecting a large volume dealer with their larger variety of cars/
trucks to choose from. With larger volumes, the dealer can accept a smaller profit margin per car sold, while making more total profit by the number of cars sold, whereas, a smaller volume
dealer needs a greater profit margin to make up for the lesser
amount of cars he sells, hence, a higher price for you to pay.
No doubt, you have heard some small volume dealer claim his
prices are lower than his competition because he has less overhead (operating costs) to support. That would seem logical but
the reality is his lower overhead gets you nothing in terms of a
lower price, having a lesser number of cars in stock to choose
from, and his service and parts departments won't have the

236

manpower, equipment, or inventory that a larger volume dealer has to offer. But, what the small volume dealer potentially has is a more intimate level of service. The dealer's visibility in the community dictates a greater ongoing involvement with the sales and service needs of his present-day and would-be customers. And, of course, there is the likeability factor that naturally plays heavily into buying a car. You want to do business with people you like, right?

1. Small and large volume dealers have two major things – the brand or product itself and the warranty as offered by the factory who produced the vehicle. Both small and large volume dealers are selling the same branded product. A Chevrolet or any brand you might choose, whether bought in a rural community where the dealer might sell 50 cars a year, is still the same Chevrolet as being sold with volumes in the hundreds at a mega-dealership on "Automobile Row" (every major city has at least one). The other thing worth noting is the warranty on the car is being offered by the manufacturer, not the dealer. Therefore, any franchised dealer for Chevrolets will honor the warranty that came with your purchase as well as the life remaining on the warranty, no matter where or from whom you bought the car.

2. Private individuals - "Caveat Emptor" that you learned about earlier, really comes into play when buying a vehicle from a private party. This gets discovered, unfortunately, when the vehicle bought does not measure up to the claims of the former owner. Trying to get some recourse on a private sale is darn near impossible to get. The former owner, probably, will tell you that you bought the car "as is" and any defects are the responsibility of the buyer to correct. This scenario assumes you can locate the former owner. In fact, he may have skipped town or is living at an address other than the one used in locating and buying the car. None of this would have happened if you had bought the car from a new or pre-owned dealer. Then, why would you ever buy a car from a private party? There's two valid reasons: the car is available for sale and is exactly or nearly exactly what you have been looking for, that no dealer has had available for sale. That's a valid reason but it doesn't minimize the risk of buying from an individual rather than a dealer. The second reason, which sometimes is not valid but presumed to be,

is there is no sales tax to be paid or collected by either party to the transaction. And, in Arizona, that is a major consideration as the sales tax, depending on where in the state you live, runs anywhere from 8.0 to 9.5%. So, if one can avoid paying that tax, it becomes a major benefit to the buyer. If the seller turns around and buys a new car, he has to pay the sales tax on the entire price he is paying for the car, whereas, if he had a trade, he would be paying the difference between the trade and the net price on the new car. So, if you are a risk-taker and like saving money, a private party transaction might be just right for you. At least, you're going to avoid the expense of paying a sales tax provided the local taxing authority permits it.

3. Warehouse and Travel Clubs - They have a viable service to offer but know that both types of clubs have dealer involvement that could conflict the transaction and end up costing you more money than had you not used their services. The fly in the ointment is the "dealer involvement" which, in practical terms, strongly suggests a potential conflict of interest to your interests. That involvement can, and in many instances, does translate into the dealer compensating the club for bringing them a car deal...yours. Now, the dealer has to get his money back and does so by building it into the price of the car you are buying. So, how much did you really save?

4. Car Brokers – Don't even think about going there. First of all, many so-called car brokers are no more than used car lot operators. But, to avoid the stigma associated with used car salesmen, they choose to take on what might appear to be a more respectable identity, calling themselves a "broker." I am guessing that car brokers have had their day. All I know is, it isn't now. They are a dying breed, right up there with dinosaurs, thanks to the Internet, online buying, and car buying services. And to some degree, the new car dealers have squeezed out a lot of brokers because they represent a cost of doing business that can be easily avoided. Why should a dealer pay a car broker a fee for something the dealer can do for themselves and save paying any fees? I suppose it depends on how hungry the dealer is.

5. Car Shows – It's no place to buy a car unless it is a private party transaction but a great place to go to get ideas for buying a car.

6. Car Auctions – Auctions are rapidly becoming a "tour de force" for buying cars, particularly, collectibles, exotics, muscle cars, sports cars, and late year discontinued models i.e. the Pontiac Soltice Coupe of which only 1200 were ever built. Why? No dealer involvement while buying on auction is viewed in some circles as a prestigious thing to do, enhanced by large television viewing audiences for auctions owned by or featured on Barrett-Jackson, Mecom, Velocity Channel and others.

7. Bankers – Don't forget bankers when it comes to buying a car. If there is money to be made on a buy transaction, you can bet bankers will be there to participate. It's only a matter of time before they get involved with car sales, other than simply car loans and repossessions. Chase Bank has already launched a buying service that pinpoints the location of a specific car make and model, available for sale, that conforms to what you have been searching for.

8. Online Buying/Search Engines – I use the following search engines in my business as they are readily accessible and easy to navigate: Cars.com; AutoTrader.com; Carsforsale.com; Cargurus.com, Google, Trovit,and Craigslist. There are many others, but these work well for me. Online buying, as a defined activity, is very much in its infancy, all of which involve dealer involvement. Dealers would have you believe that you can buy the vehicle of your choice from the confines of your living room, avoiding the price dickering and time consumed in your typical car buying transaction and be confident that you got a good deal. I don't have the bandwidth to deal (pun intended) with that right now - "Give me your best shot Mr. Dealer and know that I am going to shop you. Let's just see how much you can save me. Other online buying platforms are no more than a means to generate sales leads for the car dealers, delivering services to their participating dealer network. One such dealer platform is True Car. True Car gets a fee from the dealer, the dealer gets you for the deal. Again...dealer involvement, fraught with creating a conflict of interest that compromises you.

9. Automobile Buyer Services – My company takes all the guesswork out of locating a car, evaluating the merits of a deal or lack thereof, negotiating the deal, and arranging delivery of the dream car...right to your door. And, what does this cost you?..not a dime as the cost savings obtained in the deal easily offsets the fee or cost of using the service. OK, I admit that I can be rightly accused of promoting my own company's services...Automobile Buyer Services. Can I put my trumpet away, now? We specialize in locating hard to find vehicles. Like a radar-hooked hound dog, if it's out there, we'll find it. Or, put a little differently, if we can't locate it, it doesn't exist in the market on the date that we searched for it.

Your best sources for help with questions are people who genuinely care about you i.e. your family and friends or someone you enjoy a fiduciary relationship with, i.e. financial adviser, lawyer, trust administrator, CPA, or car buying service and information sources such as using Google on the Internet and, believe it or not, new car dealers. Yes, it's time to check in with a dealer(s) with those questions you couldn't find answers for on the Internet or your relationships. Make sure to use them for non-routine type questions and use them as one of the later courses of action you take in going about buying a car. If you make the mistake of contacting a dealer too early in your hunt, that dealer could very well start bugging you with phone calls in an attempt to get you to come to their dealership to get all of your questions answered. In a word, don't.

And for you Millennials out there, use your smartphone. Make it use its name. Check out the various automotive search engines and, of course, do that before ever visiting a dealer. But, when, you do, dress as if you are going to a business meeting. That, also, bodes well as far as a little intimidation is concerned. Chances are, the salesperson will be under-dressed compared to you as he/she is likely to be wearing casual clothing, something comfortable. You ever notice how you almost never see a necktie these days hanging around the neck of a car salesperson? On the rare occasion when you do, it is, invariably, found adorning the neck of a salesperson who's selling a highline car. So, if you see a necktie on a salesperson, watch out. He/she just might have some designs on your neck! That necktie is no more than a prop, disguising his/her demeanor of being pleasant and helpful, a much-practiced art form! So, as the Economist, Mr. Smith so succinctly put it...Beware!.

TRADE/SELL; Your Own Car

Are you going to sell your car in an effort to get more money out of it, more money than a dealer would give you on a trade-in? If you answered "yes," you should be able to get more money for it than a dealer would offer because he/she is going to give you a low-ball price and explain it as a "wholesale" price. But, what do you really gain by selling that former love object of yours, besides, possibly, a higher price than the dealer's of-fer? Yes, there is a price to be paid, by you, that involves more than money. You are going to turn around and give a significant portion of that cost savings back to the dealer by paying a sales tax based on a larger amount of money for a new car purchase (or lease), whereas, if you had traded in your car, the sales tax amount due would be based on the difference between the trade-in allowance the dealer gave you and the amount you would be paying for the car.

Selling your vehicle yourself can get ugly in a hurry. Your would-be buyer now knows where you live (it's on the title and car registration), he knows where to go with his questions or possible desire for retribution (after the sale) if he/she turns out to be an unhappy camper for whatever reason, where the buyer enjoys the benefit of not having to pay a sales tax. No such benefit is available to you as the seller. Bummer! So, is it worth it? Many would argue that it is, especially if you tend to be on the frugal side of a seized dollar (you're out there, you know who you are)! If the amount of sales tax is not an issue, I would opt for selling the car myself, something I thoroughly enjoy doing provided the timing and the numbers are right.

The dealer wants your trade-in for the obvious reason that it is an added income stream when he sells it on his used (pre-owned) car lot. First, he/she makes money on the sale of the new car; secondly, he/she minimizes the trade-in allowance, and gets rewarded with the added profit that comes from the future sale of your former cream puff at an elevated, retail price. Let's face it, what could be easier than having the dealer relieve you of your (now) ugly duckling, thus, avoiding the hassles of selling it yourself, not knowing what price you might end up settling for? Private buyers can be so viciously competitive. By nature, they're looking for a deal (as in a "real deal,") which probably means your selling the car at a price lower than your hoped-for expectation.

BTW, your local CarMax dealer has a standing offer to give you an appraisal of your car at no-charge to you. Throw that number into the mix along with the numbers you got from Kelly Blue Book and NADA and you have given yourself the best, independent estimate of your car's worth on trade-in or outright sale by you.

Hanging around your house on a weekend day, waiting for the phone to ring from a would-be buyer is no way to spend a precious day off from your daily troubles; besides, he might turn out to be a no-show. And, like an overly zealous Tesla owner with a fully charged battery, the dealer is going to go full blast to get you behind the wheel of that dream car...today! Wouldn't you really like that, also? It might take weeks, even months, for you to sell that car. How discouraging would that be, especially, in the face of the dealer's desire to get you off his premises with an under-valued trade that puts more profit dollars in his pocket and, like you, doesn't want any delays in getting that done? In the final analysis, when trading in your car, you are most likely accepting less money from the dealer than if you sold it your-self, which means, you paid too much for your new car that you traded for. But now, flush with the extra money you made by selling the car yourself, you now need to prepare yourself to part with some of that booty by way of paying more sales tax be-cause it will be based on the price you paid for the new car, not the amount of tax you would have paid if you traded the car in, where your sales tax due is the difference between the trade-in allowance and the price you paid for the new vehicle.

Those additional dollars of profit you made possible for the dealer by accepting his low-ball trade-in allowance came by way of your inattention to the details of the trade, in not know-ing the true worth of your trade-in and having an accepting attitude to whatever the dealer offered you. You got so caught up in the moment, that all you could think of was getting that gorgeous car parked in your driveway. As you wipe the drool from your mouth, you realize your best efforts to save money on this purchase just got snookered through a lack of informa-tion, vulnerable to the dealer's tried-and-true sales tactics. The dealer pushed all the right buttons to wear down your resistance so he/she could get what they want out of this deal. Through the dealer's successful sales effort to sell you on those post-sale items I referred to earlier, you know you didn't get the best deal you could have, had you been more patient, better informed, had anticipated the dealer's role in appraising and offering a less than hoped for trade-in allowance. The end result – the dealer took what he wanted, right out of your hide. Unlike Capital One, you now know what is not in your wallet. It's called...cash!

FYI – Once you've decided to trade, don't bring up the subject of a trade-in until your deal is set. Treat it the same way you would by telling the dealer you have changed your mind about buying and are now, only interested in leasing. The dealer is not going to like your unanticipated change of mind. Accomplish this change tactic and the scoreboard will read...Buyer – 2... Dealer – 0. Are you getting the idea that I am rooting for the buyer?

The cruel reality is the dealer holds all the cards and is making the rules. To counter his power, you must have product knowledge, pricing, and financing information at your fingertips, all of which is readily available on the Internet, and you must be mentally ready to do battle to get the best deal out there.

Then, with this background information, why would anyone want to trade-in their car? Worthy of note could include:

- Get rid of the car quickly. You can't match the resources of a dealer and his network.
- Avoid putting more expense into it. Let the dealer do that, a necessity for resale.
- Excessive amount of miles. Let that be the dealer's problem.
- Allows rolling over negative equity into the new car being traded for

Here's a few reasons for not trading in a vehicle:
- Dealer's offer of a trade-in allowance convinces him that he's dealing with someone who is poorly informed, has no stomach for negotiating, is a fool, or all three.
- Your trade is exceptional, relative to the market, and the dealer is trying to steal it from you.
- You don't want to totally let go of the car but you can, knowing where it is and who will be driving it.

As to the true value of your trade, an excellent place to learn how much your car is worth on trade-in, as well as learning the real cost of that new vehicle you want to buy, is Kelly Blue Book (www.kbb.com) or NADA (www.nada.com). You can trust their figures to be fairly accurate for your purposes, showing your make, model, trim level, miles on the odometer and the car's physical/mechanical condition. Actually, the figures offered by these sources are NOT "true" numbers but, rather, are approximations close enough for your negotiating purposes to use as a guide, a figure you wouldn't have had otherwise. The "true" market, on the other hand, is the value mutually agreed upon by the buyer and seller, thus, reflecting a stop-the-clock price that will become a large part of a benchmark for future pricing on an equivalent car in the same geographic locale.

When trading, don't forget to wash the car's exterior, steam clean the engine compartment, remove stored items out of the trunk, vacuum it along with the car's interior as thoroughly as you can, remove any art objects like those highly-prized McDonald's food wrappers from the glove box, console and replace any cracked or broken glass. All of that helps create the illusionary impression that the car has always been immaculately maintained and it breaks your heart to have to part with it. FYI – It's not a bad idea to provide the dealer or a private buyer with copies of maintenance records. If you do all of this, you should give yourself an Oscar for outstanding performance by a, soon to be, Certified Car Buyer.

If you choose not to trade your car and you don't want to sell it yourself, the option of having someone else sell it for you may be just the ticket. Here's a few suggestions you might want to consider.

1. Sell it to a used car lot, also known as the place where some pre-owned cars go to die. Be sure and get at least two independent appraisals of what your car is worth. One of those can come from CarMax which freely offers their appraisals on a no-cost basis.
2. Turn your car over to a consignment dealer. Their fee is, typically, 10-12% of the selling price. They may want to charge you a "storage" fee for the amount of time your car was included in their inventory of cars to be sold. This fee can be painfully expensive, ranging, typically, from $100 to $350 per month!
3. If all else fails, donate your car to a charity in your community. Someone will take that car off your hands and be happy to get it. A donation of this type, normally,

qualifies for an income tax deduction. You might want to check with your accountant before deciding on this alternative.

As you might imagine, trade-in's represent the standard way most new car buyers get rid of their former love object now turned ugly duckling. It's simple, expedient and, OK, so what if the dealer gives me a low-ball allowance? If I had kept the car, I would have had to put $1,200 into it just to keep it running. Its been estimated (source unknown to me) that 80%+ of all new car transactions involve the dealer taking in a trade.

CASH OR MONTHLY PAYMENTS; Overview

In this chapter's section, we are going to take a look at:

- A review of the things you need to do BEFORE you step foot into a dealership.

- The considerations to keep in mind as you step into the dealership.

- The pros and cons of paying cash or financing. It's your choice. Make it a good one.

- Special financing offered by the car manufacturer's

- How to calculate a monthly payment

- How negative equity affects your ability to finance

- Why you shouldn't buy dealer "add-on's" with the notable exception of gap insurance.

Tasks To Complete Before Visiting The Dealer

- It bears repeating.....Get pre-approved on an auto loan BEFORE visiting the dealer. There is an excellent probability that you can get a lower cost loan from a credit union or an online lending source than what the dealer can offer you through one or more of his third-party lenders. Some of those lending sources include: Capital One; Lightstream (Sun Trust Bank); USAA; State Farm, and SoFi. Get your loan request pre-approved in an amount greater than what you actually need. Given a choice, err on the side of being a little high in case you opt, at the last minute, for a higher-priced car than what you originally planned on buying and adjust for any changes in the transaction costs that you might have under-estimated, i.e. the "doc" fee amount, sales tax, and any errors you might have innocently made doing the math behind your loan. When it's time to sign off on the deal, you can always reduce the earlier requested loan amount to match-up with the actual amount of money that you need to borrow.

- Check with your insurance carrier to confirm the cost of coverage is affordable and available for the particular make and model you are interested in buying.
- Shop online to get a lower price than what the dealer might offer you in your upcoming meeting. Check with Cars Direct, Zag.com, Costco, and AAA. You might be mildly surprised at what you learn...that rock might turn out to be a diamond!
- Test drive the car you are planning to buy, but do it first at a car rental agency, provided there is one to rent. This avoids needless pressure the salesperson might be trying to exert on you. And, you can drive the car(s) for a day or two instead of the 15-20 minutes, typically, offered by the dealer.
- Plan on visiting two dealers and get their best deals that, in time, you can leverage one against the other to get the best deal possible. You do NOT attempt to negotiate at this time but rather, listen carefully to what the dealer is offering WITHOUT you asking anything relative to the price of the car. Now, here's an old trick that you can use – know that the first person to talk AFTER the deal is presented will automatically be put at a disadvantage or weakened position before that first attempt at negotiating a price you would feel good about. Whatever the dealer presents to you is not his/her best offer to earn your business. Take some comfort in knowing that the offer is far from what the dealer could offer if forced to do so. At this point, he is merely attempting to avoid leaving any money on the table so to speak, and at the same time, keep you interested in the car.

Let's take a look at financing in terms of whether to finance or not, considering how long it took you to save up all that

246

money in order for you to pay cash. Now, compare that with how much and how long that car is going to depreciate in value. Can you save that amount of money at a faster rate than the car depreciates? Most people can't and that's why 60-65% of all the cars on the road today are either financed or leased; yet, the remaining 35-40% is a big number, showing there are two bonafide schools of thoughts as to which method is preferred.

Another little "I told you so" is the well-known fact that you, as the buyer, will end up paying more for a car if you finance it than if you had paid cash. That alone is a viable reason to pay cash. Financing doesn't always seem like real money. To test that statement's validity, try missing one monthly payment and brace yourself for the fireworks that could follow. The loan creditor could remind you how important it is to your credit score (FICO) that you never miss a payment. What they don't routinely tell you, though, is you have to the tenth day after the payment due date to get that payment in to them without affecting a late payment fee. If you are 30 days delinquent, the lender can report this to the three credit reporting agencies, resulting in a negative notation on your credit record.

But, if you are paying cash, you own that car with all the inherent rights to own and enjoy. Or, to put it another way, "He or she who holds the gold, makes the rules." In buying a car, the gold is your cash. So, go make up some rules of your own and, if the dealer doesn't like them, take them down the street to his nearest competitor! As all things in business, try to find two points of leverage, work one against the other, and sit back to enjoy the fireworks.

Now that you have visited two dealerships (maybe more, it's your time you're managing), confirmed your choice of car to buy and its availability and sized-up the salesperson as someone you can work with, it's time to let the dealer know that you will be taking care of the financing from your own sources or paying cash. Let him talk if he boldly begins telling all about these wonderful lending sources he has available that will meet anyone's budget. He won't waste any time asking you what interest rate and loan term you have in mind. DO NOT answer that question because, if you do, your so-called level playing field just got tilted in favor of the dealer. So, hear out his offer(s). If it's better than what you have pre-arranged...take it. This assumes the deal on the car is sufficiently attractive enough to justify your continued interest in a deal. If, on the other hand, the dealer's interest rate is higher than yours, ask if he would be willing to lower it by 2%? Now, sit back and watch him or her squirm. Chances are, the deal you obtained for yourself is better - that's just the law of averages at work. Up to this point, all talk relative to loan sources and interest rates is just so much "pre-purchase" posturing – things that need to be put on the table before any real negotiations can take place, while keeping that playing field level. There is no reason why that playing field can't be level. In fact, it should be skewed a bit in your favor. After all, you're the one holding the gold!

What about 0% financing that frequently gets advertised in television commercials? Well, it's out there and it's real, despite your cautious thinking otherwise because you're certain money doesn't grow on trees. It doesn't grow any better if you bury dollar bills in your backyard and start pouring water on it, either! News flash...it ain't going to grow!   But on a semi-serious note, be aware that 0% is, in fact, a real deal that gets offered from time-to-time by car manufacturers to spur sales at a strategic time when they can see some advantage in offering it, i.e. a larger than normal television viewing audience such as the Super Bowl, the men's NCAA Basketball Tournament, weaker sales periods when prospective buyers are busy buying things other than cars (Christmas), or possibly, a need to reduce inventories of unsold vehicles that have fallen asleep on new car dealer lots.

Essentially, 0% interest which is the very same thing as saying, "No interest will be charged over the life of the loan," offers the buyer the opportunity to pay the same price as the all-cash buyer; but, the difference is...the monthly payment will, typically, be spread out over a longer period of time. For sure, it's not free money, but it's about as close as you will ever get to it. Personally, I love 0% financing because it means making better utilitarian value of OPM (other people's money) so I can have more money to buy more cars, more often! As for its negative side, the 0% interest rate isn't always what it seems to be, thanks to some slick advertising on the manufacturers' part. The bottom line: You may end up paying for that dream car in the form of a higher than necessary sale price (the manufacturers' attempt to offset the 0%). Acknowledging an economic principal that endures...everything of value costs somebody something. The real cost of that car loan, which you will be paying, is buried somewhere in the price of that car. You can go to the bank on that, sans the former Irwin Union Bank of Columbus, Indiana, who woke up one morning and found themselves bankrupt, thanks to faulty mortgage/consumer loan products. It was as if they believed their own hype on their so-thought position on the costs associated with car loans.

Doesn't it make sense that lending money has its own set of costs? Clearly, it stands to reason that the loan cost is something greater than 0%. In order to qualify for this 0% interest rate loan, usually, you have to have a FICO Score that would put you in the top 10% of potential borrowers. So, obviously, many people can't qualify for this type of loan. Still, not bad, if you take into account that this 0% buyer has no "skin" in the game at this point, so to speak. Bottom line: If a 0% loan comes looking for you...grab it...before it gets away. But before signing anything, wisely check the total cost, verify the cost of each item. And, then, to make an apples-to-apples comparison, compare the total cost of buying from the dealer who features 0% financing with another dealer's price with the same 0% financing. Get the dealers to tell you where the costs of that 0% financing are residing. Once you have identified the better of the two deals, squeeze that OPM for all it's worth, leaving no juice left in that orange!

If you choose to finance, be sure and calculate the monthly payment. That helps clear up the question of affordability. To calculate the monthly payment, see website www.autoloancalculator.com. Merely plug in the net amount you want to borrow, the number of months you choose to pay while selecting an interest rate that is fair in your judgment, manageable, and budget-friendly. An example of a possible calculation could be: You want to finance a car with a sticker price of $32,000 for 48 months at 3.3% interest per year, using a sales tax rate of 8.5%, while the dealer offers you a $10,000 trade-in allowance for your formerly-loved cream puff, now turned older and uglier. The answer - $550.00 per month. FYI – the national average monthly payment for a new car in 2015 was $364.00 per month. Using this example and to get that monthly $550 figure down to $364.00 means putting a significant amount of money down to make that lower payment possible. Using the rule-of-thumb of $22.00 of loan payment for every $1,000.00 borrowed, you can see that the buyer would need to put $9,000.00 down to get to his budget-friendly monthly payment. This example assumes the interest rate and the loan term were the same in both calculations.

NEGATIVE EQUITY

Remember, if you finance the purchase, the very day you take possession of that car, it immediately begins depreciating and like a runaway train without a conductor, there's no stopping it from happening, which puts you immediately into a situation where you owe more money on that car loan than the car is worth.   If you had to get rid of the car to save yourself the monthly payment, well let's just say...you have a problem on your hands. Unbeknownst to you, you have just created something called "negative equity" or more commonly referred to a being "upside down." Even if you paid cash for the car, it doesn't necessarily protect you from losing money involuntarily because the car doesn't know whether you paid cash or are making payments! Rather than creating negative equity, you have merely lost "equity" as the value of the car shrinks over time due to depreciation. So, no matter what, your car is going to lose value, whether it's negative equity made possible by financing, using OPM's or it's positive equity, resulting from your gradual diminishing cash value. Depreciation is such an ugly word.

And now, here comes the typical, undesired scenario that needs to be avoided - If you elect to trade in the car, you have to take the amount of money still owed on the vehicle you are trading in and tack it onto the price of the new, replacement vehicle you are now buying, which effectively means you owe more money than the car is worth BEFORE you the ink dries on your Purchase Agreement (Buyers' Order). Bummer, you say? Indeed. You just bought yourself an over-priced car, negating all the good stuff you learned in this book that would have permitted you to buy that vehicle at a good, competitive price. Now, for a bit of better news (notice that I didn't use the words "good news"). As vicious as this never-ending cycle may become, there is, thank God, a way out and that is to enter into a leasing agreement on the new car, thus, rolling the negative equity (the loan deficiency) into the price of the new car lease. Now, what you have effectively done, is over-priced the lease by the amount of the negative equity. Chances are, with an over-priced lease, you will have a lower payment than what traditional financing offers, even with the negative equity rolled into it. So, you are paying back a little bit of the negative equity with each monthly payment. Another way of offsetting negative equity is to make a down payment on the new, replacement vehicle in an amount equal to or greater than the actual amount of negative equity.

There is a moral to this story. Pay cash if you can afford it and take the lumps associated with depreciation, confident in knowing you have the necessary funds to pay cash for the next replacement car. If that isn't doable, try paying off the car, which kills any possibility of negative equity being carried into the new, replacement vehicle.

DEALER ADD-ON'S

As a rule, avoid dealer add-on's with the possible exception of gap insurance. Add-on's are, by design, expensive to buy, appearing to be a manageable expense if you include it in the car loan. No one in their right mind would pay cash or finance add-on's as a separate item. The Finance Manager, knowing that, will gladly usher you into his office and explain how nominal an add-on expense is and assure you by saying, "don't give it another thought, we'll roll it into the Purchase Agreement. You won't even notice it. It's all about this beautiful car you just bought."

Most add-on items will provide next to no enjoyment in your ownership experience or safety of the vehicle, and, frankly, most of these items are a total waste of money. The add-on items include but not limited to such things as an undercoating treatment, paint protecting coatings, nitrogen-filled tires (are you kidding?), accidental death (you buy that from a life insurance agent, not a car dealer's finance manager) and gap insurance, special performance tires, aftermarket wheels, and on and on.

I have saved one add-on item to tell you about at this point in the chapter because dealers' hawk this product like there is no tomorrow and trust me in what you are about to read here that the dealer makes beaucoup bucks, shamelessly. I would be referring to an Extended Warranty or Service Contract. And, yes, it is a legal contract; make no mistake about that. First things first, why would anyone under the canopy of heaven buy an extended warranty on the purchase of a new car when the car's manufacturer offers a warranty that, typically, runs for 3 or more years, covering 36,000 miles or more. And that warranty will not cost you a dime as it is included in the price of the vehicle. BTW, you can always buy an extended warranty provided the manufacturers' warranty hasn't lapsed. So, the smart thing to do is buy an extended warranty one day before the original warranty expires. And, no, you don't have to buy it from a dealer. And if you do, know that the price you'll pay will likely be twice what you could have bought it for through a car buying service, credit union , privately owned garage, or buying it directly online from a warranty (insurance) company.

As for gap insurance, like an old American Express TV ad, "don't leave home with it." Yes, gap insurance is worth it for its coverage and cost. Simply put (I trust), gap insurance covers the difference between the amount of money you owe on your new car loan and the replacement value of the car.

For instance, if you are in an auto accident, and you still owe $15,000 on the car loan but the car is only worth $9,000, gap insurance steps in and makes up the difference of $6,000. And, the good news, and it is good news indeed, gap insurance is relatively cheap to buy.

LEASE OR BUY: Overview

Basically, a lease is a long-term rental contract with an option to buy. This can be better understood by thinking: LEASE a new vehicle, BUY a pre-owned vehicle, especially, a Certified Pre-Owned (CPO) car, where you get the closest you will ever come to buying a new car-like condition but at a lower price. Purchasing a CPO with a sizable chunk of the depreciation already paid by the car's original owner and a warranty given by the manufacturer, verifies the manufacturer is certifying the condition of the car (not the dealer) meeting the standards they prescribed for that particular automobile.

CPO's are an increasingly popular type of car purchase. Enough so, that leasing a CPO is becoming more and more in vogue as more car manufacturers' sales subsidiaries offer this type of lease. The only way you can lose on buying or leasing a CPO is paying too much for it. BTW, the price of a CPO, typically, is priced 5-10% higher than its non-CPO counterpart.
Just remember,

Whether you lease or buy,
pick the wrong one and you'll surely cry.
That car, new or used, will have one less day
to depreciate but one more day for you to pay.

Are you going to buy or lease? As you study the differences, you will learn that there are distinct reasons for doing either but, in my view, too much is made of making leasing appear to have numerous tax advantages. Please read this carefully. Special tax treatment is a myth of long-standing, perpetrated by the Accounting/CPA fraternity with the intent of creating an impression in the buyers' mind that the uniqueness of their field of expertise requires some tax leveraging in their own behalf. Well, I suppose that worked for a period of time but the public has become wise to this ploy of special tax treatments, supposedly, enjoyed by physicians, lawyers, and, oh yes, lets not forget those bean-counters, themselves,who continue to perpetuate this myth. One could say, "that horse has already run that race and now there are no more races to be run!" Know this – there are few tax advantages in leasing versus buying. They both offer the same tax benefits and the end result, which is, there is always a tax to be paid, no matter what. The only question is, how much and who's going to pay it? You probably have already figured out who that lucky devil is. You can write off certain expenses associated with business usage on a leased vehicle; those very same expenses can be written-off on a purchased car if used for business, just as easily and just as valid. What leasing does offer is possessing (not owning) and getting the use of a vehicle with a monthly payment that is considerably less than buying on time. Think of either form of acquiring a car as an alternative method of financing...you are either financing the "ownership" in lieu of paying cash or you are financing the "use" of the car without the obligatory responsibilities of owning. Think of it this way - In its essence, you are paying rent with the possible option of buying after the terms of the lease have been met. If a lower payment is desired, many times in the 25-35% range, leasing makes perfect sense and might be just right for you. That's one of the reasons why leasing is so popular with young people who, typically, are more strapped for cash than other age groups. Leasing, however, carries with it, certain conditions that have the potential of negating any or many of the advantages that a lease might offer, specifically, as it relates to mileage limits. If you are planning on driving a vehicle 15,000 miles or more per year, chances are, leasing is not for you, as driving more than the stipulated annual miles carries with it a penalty or an excessive mileage charge, i.e. you pay "X" amount of cents per mile driven with 25 cents per mile fairly standard. Under a time-based financing plan, you can drive that beast any amount of miles you choose, treating it as if you owned it already, which you will, once it's paid off.

You can get around an excess mileage fee if you're willing to pre-pay the number of miles you intend to drive in a given year's time. That pre-payment can be rolled into the cost of the lease which, of course, increases the monthly payment. If you choose this type of plan, know that the actual cost per mile driven will be less than the stipulated excess mileage fee that would have applied had you not bought or pre-paid the excess miles you anticipated driving. So, it's worthwhile to buy with this notable exception. Be careful not to over-estimate the number of miles you expect to drive in a year's time because the lessor will not refund the difference between the actual miles driven and the number of miles you bought or pre-paid. So, in a nutshell, if the standard lease specifies an annual mileage limit of, let's say, 10,000 miles and you opt to buy or pre-pay an additional 5,000 miles which you believe will meet your driving needs while avoiding an excess mileage fee, but in actuality you only drove 12,000 miles, the pre-payment excess of 3,000 miles is lost. No refund for you, buckaroo! So, be very careful in considering your mileage needs before ever entering into a lease agreement (contract) that requires monthly payments for, hopefully, no more than 3 years...maximum.

Break out your under-used B.S. Meter (see Glossary for its description) and look at the real picture about leasing versus buying, separating yourself from the false one you get from television advertising where you get the idea that leasing is for everyone.. That's a bunch of cheetah dung...absolutely untrue. If it were otherwise, we would all be running around town in leased vehicles, wouldn't we? For most folks, leasing boils down to the amount of the monthly payment, buying compared to leasing. End of sentence.

Now, if you opt to lease the same car that you might have bought and financed, for the same amount of possession time, same interest rate, sales tax, and trade-in allowance, you need to know:
- The sticker price (shown on the driver's side, front window), also known as the "MSRP" (manufacturers' suggested retail price). The key word in that description is "suggested." It doesn't mean you have to pay that exact amount in order to buy or lease that car. It's merely a guide that gives you a benchmark from which to negotiate while giving you a general idea of what the vehicle will cost to buy or lease.

- The money factor is a term unique to automobile leasing. Those words are totally interchangeable with "interest rate per annum," Why the fancy word when the word "interest rate" is more widely understood? You might have guessed – this might have been a ploy created in the infancy of car leasing to give a certain "aura" of exclusivity to leasing as a form of financing. And, the dealers were counting on you being a bit intimidated by what you didn't know...maybe intimidated enough to be too embarrassed to ask the dealer the meaning of the term.
- The residual value of a leased car – the stated value can be found using Google or the Automobile Leasing Guide (ALG). Residual refers to the remaining value of the car after "X" amount of months from the car's date of manufacture. For instance, many cars have a residual value equal to, roughly, 50% of the MSRP after 3 years. To use the same $32,000 example as a benchmark for a finance-based purchase, the residual value would be $16,000. OK...using a money factor that converts into an annual interest rate of 3.3%, a sales tax of 8.5%, for the same 3 years, and the same trade-in allowance of $10,000, your monthly leasing payment will be...$349/month. That's $210 per month less than traditional financing! To our trumpet players in the band, wake up your instruments and announce with fanfare that leasing is cheaper, in this example, than buying, to the tune of 36%. Not too shabby! To do your own calculation, go to www.edmunds.com/car-leasing or if you want to compare leasing versus buying, side by side, in the same vehicle, go to www.cars.com/car.

CHARACTERISTICS; Likely Traits Of A Car Buyer Versus A Typical Lessee

Car Buyer:
1. Uses the car for every imaginable hauling task known to mankind...dogs to people.
2. Drives more than 15,000 miles per year.
3. Drives the vehicle for 5 years or more.
4. Takes pride in his/her ownership of the car.
5. Not overly concerned about dings, scratches and the normal wear and tear items.
6. Likes to wash his/her own car.

Car Lessee:

1. Wants to stay in a new or newer vehicle every 2-3 years.
2. Drives, typically, 10,000-12,000 miles per year.
3. Wants to avoid the higher depreciation rates associated with the first 3 years of ownership.
4. Abhors the thought of giving up all of that cash for a "depreciating" dream car that, soon enough, will turn into a "depreciated" piece of metal.
5. Less risk-averse in trying out an unfamiliar make or model. If he/she is wrong in their choice, think of it as only 36 months and that monster will be gone. In the scheme of things, that's a pretty manageable level of risk.
6. Having a car paid for has limited value to a lessee. Why own it when he/she can have all the privileges of possession provided the conditions of the lease contract are being met? Further, why tie up all of the purchase price by paying cash for a car when you have full use of the vehicle with your only cash exposure being the "cap" payment you made (think "down payment" when comparing it to financing the purchase). Who's to know the difference other than your spouse or banker? You, of course, and that's all that matters.

LEASING SECRETS; Little Known

1. Down payments don't affect the residual or build any equity. They, merely, lower the monthly payment.
2. Make multiple security deposits – it lowers your monthly and you get it back at the end of the lease (less fees).
3. Begin your lease negotiations by telling the dealer you will be buying the vehicle. After the negotiations are complete and you, presumably, have his lowest price, change gears on him by indicating you no longer are interested in buying that vehicle but now, you prefer leasing it. Trust me, the dealer isn't going to like that end-around play that has the effect of taking some more bucks off the table. End result: you get the car for a monthly payment lower than what you initially negotiated and have, potentially, entrapped the dealer into giving it to you. Score: Buyer – 1   Dealer – 0.
4. Tell the dealer upfront and before any negotiations have begun, that your attorney must approve of the lease document before you can sign it That, many times, forces out ambiguous terms, conditions, and sources of misunder-

standing for the deal itself. If it works per plan, you have just forced the dealer to be a little more explicit with you (I chose the word "explicit" very carefully here).

5. Don't lease a vehicle for a period of time that might exceed the warranty period on the car. Otherwise, you're making lease payment and paying repair bills at the same time. You don't want to do that. Besides, the major portion of the car's depreciation will be realized by the 36th month.

6. The down payment should be within a guideline that you are comfortable with. Too big a down payment (capitalization, "cap" for short) defeats one of the major purposes of leasing – minimal upfront cost to enter into and exit from, without tying up a bunch of bucks

7. Lump sum the total cash outlay of the lease payments into one, upfront payment. Could reduce the total lease costs by as much as 20%. The benefit to the lessee – no monthly payments to make.

8. Lease the cars month-to-month upon the expiration of the lease. It usually can be done for a period of 3 months without having to enter into a new, longer-term lease and, at the same time, takes the pressure off of you to make a move on exercising your option to buy, or turning the car in, or moving into a fresh new lease on a new/newer vehicle.

9. Unlike financing a car where you don't want the dealer to know what your monthly payment budget number is, tell the dealer that your maximum monthly lease payment can't exceed "X" amount of dollars. That should tell you in a hurry if leasing is right for you, thus, making or breaking a leasing deal right on the spot. Assuming that amount is significantly less than the calculated lease payment should be for a particular term,or money factor, ask the dealer to give you the option of a balloon payment midway into the life of the lease, forcing you to pay the difference between your actual payment and the payment amount you should have been paying all along. This gets you a lower initial payment upon taking out the lease, without additional "cap" but, this will create a larger payment until the expiration of the lease. So, if you anticipate your income to increase at a time during the lease, with a balloon, you have the benefit of a lower, initial lease payment with the comfort of knowing that you can handle an increase in the monthly later when your income gets a bump.

10. Lease amounts or payments are not cast in stone. As everything, a lease is negotiable as it relates to payment amounts, payment dates, and money factor. What is not negotiable is the residual value of the car at the end of the lease. You are joined at the hip with that number.

11. To give you peace of mind that you are not being taken advantage of by the dealer, you can buy an inexpensive piece of software, titled "Expert Lease Pro." I use it in my business. It's worth the one-time purchase, knowing you have been dealt with honestly. And, it is relatively inexpensive.

12. Although hardly a secret, but one little caveat to keep in mind is, the lending standard or so-called FICO score for leasing is much higher than for traditional lending. You better be in the mid-700's or higher if you expect to qualify for a car lease.

PITFALLS; Cavaet Emptor (don't say I didn't warn you)

1. Be aware of excess mileage fees than can run as high as 25 cents per mile driven over the annual mileage limit stipulated in the leasing agreement (contract).

2. Getting out of a lease prior to its contractual expiration, can be financially painful for the novitiate unless you are prepared to settle up the balance of the contract or transfer the lease to another lessee through ones own efforts or through a company like SwapaLease or LeaseTrader. This might be the easier and the most expedient way of getting out of a lease, but, know that fees apply. Doing it yourself will be less expensive but the task of finding a qualified lessee to take over your lease could take time you might have. This type of transaction is no different than selling a car directly by yourself with the added condition that the lessor will need to qualify your transfer lessee to their financial standards. If that potential lessee has a FICO less than 700, the sledding could get rough to non-existent.

3. Lease payments can become nearly as high as a traditional car payment if the lease runs for a period greater than 36 months. NEVER lease a car for more than 36 months.

4. Lease payment may or may not include the sales tax. Confirm that BEFORE signing anything.

5. You have to maintain the car as if you owned it. That's to say, it must be serviced to the manufacturers' standards.

This can include the tires on the car, all four of which, depending on the lessor, may need to be the same brand.

ADVANTAGES; Important Factors To Consider

1. You know you'll be driving a new model every 2-3 years without tying up a lot of cash, much of which will be used to pay the largest portion of the car's planned depreciation.
2. You can afford a more expensive car than what would be available to you had you financed it.
3. Take advantage of any "lease special" offered by the manufacturer as they are, in many instances, subsidized such as to offer you a monthly payment considerably less than a traditional lease. These "specials" are easily identified online where they are regularly featured. Google "lowest price leases available in zip code XXXXX".

Are you getting the picture? Leasing, really, is no more than another form of financing.....nothing more, nothing less, but whether you think you're interested or not, it's worth your while to check it out. It may or may not be just what you are looking for. So, lease or buy? As you read earlier, pick the wrong one and you are sure to cry!

NEGOTIATE; Getting The Deal Done

Despite what you might think, this is the fun part of buying/ leasing a car.....pitting yourself against the dealer a.k.a. Goliath, with his presumed power that he thinks he has over you. Why not? His presumed power may have have worked well on the last one hundred victims that stepped foot into his dealership to buy a car. Could you be so different? Mr. Goliath...meet David.

The answer is, "yes." You are different, alright. You know what you want, and you are going to get it. Maybe not at this particular dealership but, without a doubt, you are going to get the deal and car you have been dreaming about. You have prepared yourself for this day... so go get it.

You should see yourself as someone who can haggle SUCCESSFULLY over pricing. I have read various reports that the majority of car buyers who willfully enter into pricing negotiations win price concessions about 65% of the time. Two out three of you readers, right now, fall into that category. So, go for it. If you don't, you will be leaving money on the table for the dealer to scoop up.

Before starting the negotiation process, I set the stage by insisting on complete honesty and the salesperson can expect the same from me. This helps establish a playing field from the get-go and tells the salesperson that you are not a push-over and at the first sign of any questionable comment, you're out of there. Sometimes, this has the effect of mildly intimidating the salesperson which is not necessarily a bad thing. It lets the salesperson know that you, the buyer, are the one who is holding the gold, not him or her. If a deal doesn't work out or it doesn't feel right, there's always another dealer who will welcome your visit. After all, a Cadillac is still a Cadillac...wherever you buy it.

If you follow the pointers presented here, you are well on your way to becoming a car buying pro. Negotiating a buy or lease deal, if done properly, tells the world that 1.) You are no pushover, 2.) You know what you are buying or leasing, 3.) You know what you can afford and how you are going to pay for it, 4.) and now, this minute, you are prepared to do battle with the dealer. The last one standing..... is the winner. (To remove any temptation of sitting down, mentally remove any chairs from the room). Get comfortable standing up to a dealer. Make him/her realize there isn't anyone quite like you and, frankly, he might wish he hadn't met you. You are costing him/her money in the form of less money to be made, no thanks to your trimming fat or excess profit dollars out of the car and the deal behind it, item-by-item.

First of all, keep the negotiation session light and humorous, if possible. Avoid acting the part of Mr. Tough Guy. Any other behavior will likely create a contentious atmosphere, not compatible to working toward a winning deal can be mutually arrived upon. Keep your macho mental strength a secret.

Keep in mind that you are buying a car or truck, not a monthly payment. Thinking about the amount of a monthly payment instead of the price of the vehicle is an ever so common experience, particularly, with young people who are out there trying to find their way in the world. NEVER volunteer your expectations for a monthly payment. Because, if you do, any salesperson worth their salt is going to fashion a payment for you that, more times than not, will be acceptable. They can massage numbers faster than a Gypsy mathematician can rub a crystal ball! He will do his best to convince you that this monthly payment is in line with what you had to have and that his offer is a very good deal for you. And, if you don't take it, there will be someone else out there that's interested in that very same car and it boils down to...he/she with the money gets the car. By saying no to a deal structured around some monthly payment objective, you just saved yourself some money because you didn't commit to that payment.

Allow the dealer to do the talking as you absorb everything he is saying, while standing with this awe-inspiring smile (no smirking) that you are projecting with such self-confidence. About now, you can expect him to bring up the subject of how you are going to pay for it. Cut to the chase by telling him that you are prepared to make an offer at this time. Be as calm and cool as you can muster. This shows your strength of resolve to get what you want and, at the same time, you are telling him, "If your deal doesn't meet my expectations, I'm out of here. Thank you and good-bye." With your offer now on the table, sit back, oh, I nearly forgot, stand up and quietly await his/her response. As stated before, the first person to speak has put themselves into a weakened position, so don't say a word. Words will be flowing soon enough from the dealer's mouth, telling you that he/she can't possibly accept your offer. You respond by telling him/them that you are presenting an opportunity that allows them to remove one more vehicle from their unsold inventory, right now, with a minimum amount of time spent on needless haranguing, that your offer is real and that, in so many words, you have presented them with your best offer, and are prepared to let your feet do the talking as you boldly stomp away to do battle with the next dealer down the street.

Now, you can expect the dealer to give you his/her best parting shot, telling you he/she can't meet your bid and that he/she would sincerely work to get you a price you can be happy with (oh, really?) if only you would raise your offer. Under no circumstances, do not raise your offer UNTIL he/she makes a counteroffer. Now, make a slightly higher counteroffer in a small increment of $50 to $100 (none of this raising by $250 or, God forbid, $500 – leave that to the novitiates to make such a foolish move) . About now, you tell the dealer that this is your final offer and you might want to make a good faith gesture by

261

offering to deposit "X" amount of dollars to help secure the deal and show your sincerity in getting this deal done, but it must be NOW!

Realizing it or not, what has been mentally going on in this bantering exchange of B.S. (some would prefer the word "niceties,") the dealer has been testing your resolve to move off of your offer and onto his; trying to learn how much you know about his less-than-loving tactics and ethics in doing business; learn what the basis is for your negotiating skills (assuming there are some) and try to determine what it will take to break the "camel's back." (I hope that does not need explaining.), How much of a higher bid would you go to get that deal done... TODAY; and at what point can he evaporate your resolve (good luck with that!).

If the dealer doesn't move on price or move enough, say thank you politely and give those shoes of yours some exercise. When it is all said and done, the most powerful tool in your automotive toolbox is your shoes. If you're not pleased with the price offered and/or lack of progress in getting where you want to be on the deal, start walking toward the dealer's front door. You are going to find out in a hurry just how serious the dealer is about striking a deal that would work for you. At this moment, there is nothing more to do. You are done. End of sentence. However, tomorrow is another matter. Take the initiative to call the dealer and tell them you are giving them one more shot at your business. Sometimes, a dealer becomes miraculously flexible about his former price to you and accepts yours. Chances are, your last counteroffer was reasonable and in the realm of acceptability. And, if none of this bears fruit, kick back, relax, confidently knowing there are plenty of automotive fish in the sea!

And, on a final note, just know this should have been fun for both parties. After all, it's only a game. But, as in all games, someone has to win. Just make sure it isn't you doing the losing. And, to think, all of this could have been totally avoided if you had hired yourself an automobile buying service that wouldn't have compromised you. Forget the dealers, brokers, car manufacturers – they all work for themselves. The car buyers' service works exclusively for you.

POST SALE; Avoid Or Minimize

Now that you have satisfactorily negotiated the deal and

262

bought the car, you have one final thing left to do. This is where you pay a visit to the office of the Finance & Insurance Manager (F&I). No buyer leaves the building (obviously not related to Elvis) without sitting in the F & I Manager's office to hear his or her much-practiced spiel on why you should buy any number of "add-on's" offered for sale by the dealer to enhance the beauty and ownership experience that will be coming your way. That could include, floor mats, towing packages, paint protection, window tinting, undercoating, rust proofing, fabric protection, special wheels and tires, an extended warranty, gap, and credit life insurance. Chances are, you don't need any of these. It's overpriced if you did need it, and the F&I guy is taking advantage of you in your celebratory mood. You're so excited about your new or pre-owned car that what would it hurt to buy some special, little something to commemorate the day you bought the car you have been dreaming about, for so long? It's relatively easy to fall into that trap!

The list is nearly endless but all you need to know is one, simple little word..NO. Say "no" to any post-sale item with the possible exception of gap insurance.   Gap insurance is definitely worth its price in the peace of mind it offers in the event you find yourself owing more on the car than the car is worth. If the car is "totaled" in an accident, it will in effect, force the balance of the loan to fall due. Gap insurance makes up that difference. The good news – gap insurance is relatively inexpensive. Credit life insurance should be bought through an insurance agency, not a car dealer. And, as far as an extended warranty is concerned, again, don't even think about buying it from a dealer as its annual cost could haunt you and keep you sleepless, even in Seattle! If you are buying a new car or truck, a factory warranty comes as part of the total price of the vehicle. Why waste your money on buying a warranty that extends the factory's warranty? You can always buy an extended warranty provided the original factory warranty doesn't lapse. So, the day before your warranty expires, assuming you still own the same vehicle, go out and buy yourself an extended warranty that, really isn't a warranty at all. Technically, it would be correct to refer to it as a Maintenance Service Agreement, which can be bought from a credit union, a car repair facility, or directly from the insurance company that provides that coverage.

Much of the money you saved on your hard-earned deal is ripe to be lost. That is to say, the savings you so painstakingly racked up is about to evaporate before your very eyes if you buy into this manager's efforts to sell you on his add-on offerings. It's no accident that the F&I guy is your last port of call before leaving the dealership because it is the dealer's last chance to wring some more bucks out of your bank account or add dollars to the amount of your loan, whichever. So, keep in mind the sage advice offered by our old economist friend, Adam Smith, screaming his lungs out with "Caveat Emptor!"

Oh, Oh.....here comes that pesky salesperson again. Not to worry, as you stand vigilantly in the face of his unexpected, parting remarks, expressed in what is known in the car business as the "battle cry of a starving salesman," which loosely translates into modern English as, "watch out sucker, here comes my best shot."

After what might be several attempts at selling you something, the F&I guy is tasked with getting you to sign the purchase or loan documents that spell out the financial details of your purchase, i.e. whether it reflects an all cash deal or a financed monthly payment amount, when it is due, the interest rate, the final monthly payment date, and so on. Read these documents carefully before signing. If in doubt about their contents, don't sign them - give them to an attorney to review, and if appropriate to your objective, sign and return them to the dealer. Most F&I guys will do their best to dissuade you from taking the documents to an attorney for a sign-off because he knows this deal may go away based on the lawyer's advice and it is crucial to get the deal done now while all the pieces of the deal are in place.

From the salesperson's perspective, he/she wants you to sign those documents, to shake your hand, and bid you farewell as you walk outside to take glorious delivery of your new car. The salesperson will be right there every step of the way until you plant both your feet inside that car, all the while congratulating you on your fine purchase. Again, this is a polished, practiced art, performed by a salesperson who wants to come off as seemingly sincere for he fully knows that your purchase is not a done deal, legally, until you drive away!

CAR BUYING; The Future

In the past one hundred years, the car buying process has been entirely controlled by the dealer. Gradually over time, that has been changing without recognizing the force behind those changes. Now, right now, the car buying process is about to be revolutionized...thanks to digital technology. Yes, if you haven't noticed, it's rapidly becoming a digital world.

Once thought to be the private domain of "product" development, technology is now being applied to "service" development and delivery. This progression started innocently enough with being able to get online and check out a dealer's inventory of new and pre-owned cars and provide facts conducive to getting that person away from his/her computer and get them in front of a dealer's salesperson. It was an honest start but that's about all it ever was...a "shopping" tool, not an actual "buying" tool.

Today, you can not only shop online but apply for a car loan, get an estimate on a trade-in and finalize a price without ever stepping foot out of your house.

In the very near future, you're going to be able to do your own Purchase Agreement/Loan Agreement/Buyers' Order/Application For Title, complete with itemizing the total price of the vehicle, item-by-item (no more "doc" fees), fees, rebates, incentives, document a credit card deposit, schedule the test drive and arrange delivery.

In other words, we're going to move out of shopping online to buying online. Essentially, there will be two sources of help to facilitate the actual purchase of the automobile.....you on a direct, online basis and/or using a car buying service who will assume all the details of the purchase, and in effect replace the interface with a dealer's salesperson, offering products and services that include: gap insurance, interstate vehicle transport, pre-purchase inspections, locating the vehicle to be purchased, evaluating any deal already undertaken; prepare and present a new or recontructed deal, arrange payment and delivery. In effect, the buyer has nothing to do but to tell the buying service what year, make, model, color, and what price boundaries are desired. Sit back and enjoy the anticipation that will come from your purchase. This is something to be truly excited about.

COLLECTIBLE CARS; KEEPERS AND SLEEPERS

Collectible cars are either "Keepers" or "Sleepers." Keepers have earned their pedigree by becoming a near rarity in the car collector marketplace where a limited number were produced either by design or the manufacturer chose to discontinue the model or, just as likely, the market decided it for them. And, ageless styling has a lot to do with maintaining that Keeper status into the coming years.

Some examples of Keepers would be (notice it is "would be" not "could be" as in the case of Sleepers) a Jaguar XKE (any model year); split rear window, 1963 Corvette; 1965 Mustang fastback; a 1957 Chevrolet; any Chevrolet Nomad station wagon; a 1971 Datsun 240Z; any of the baby Thunderbirds; a super-charged 1963 Studebaker Avanti, 1965 Buick Riviera Gran Sport, any Avanti GT convertible, especially the 2001 through 2007; or a 1964 Pontiac GTO convertible. And one of the hottest cars on the planet – a 1961 Ferrari 250 GT that fetched a paltry $17.5 million at a recent auto auction. That beaut was hotter than a shadeless summer day in Phoenix, Arizona, where you can almost fry an egg on your tongue!

Sleepers, on the other hand, haven't quite got out of bed yet, but, they are awake and stirring. Examples could include the 2009 Pontiac Soltice GXP coupe; the 1987 Buick Grand National GNX, the 1967 Mercury Cougar, or a 1959 Ford Galaxie 500 4-door hardtop (no "B" pillar). The passage of time, cost to acquire (while still a Sleeper), and rarity, as recognized by the collector car fraternity, will all work together to ultimately elevate the car into the status of a bonafide collectible car.

But, some Sleepers are destined to remain so because of little demand (forget the supply) for a particular make-model-year, despite the car being in pristine condition. Condition, alone, doesn't make the car collectible. Nevertheless, you sure can still enjoy that automobile for the beauty it is. Case in point – I recently attended a Barrett-Jackson auction in Scottsdale, Arizona, where an absolutely beautiful, 1995 Cadillac Eldorado's opening bid was $5,000. This wasn't just any old Eldorado – the metal top had been chopped off and replaced with a convertible cloth top, custom paint job, pin-stripping by a locally recognized artist, and custom wheels. Clearly, this car was and is a rarity and despite all of these supposed plus's and in spectacular condition to boot, the highest bid was a measly $5,200! Why? This car was doomed not to draw out higher bids because the car had zero collector appeal, and zero demand in the auction marketplace. That's a lot of zeros to overcome just to qualify the car as a collectible which, clearly, it was not. In my view, the person who had the winning bid of $5,200 legally stole that car as it had a probable street value of $10,000-$12,000.

Interestingly enough, Jay Leno offers up some of his own candidates as future collectibles. Some of his Sleepers include: the 1958 Edsel; the 2001 Pontiac Astek (can you believe it?); the 1979 AMC Pacer; and a 2014 Honda Insight. Other celebs have included the 1985 Ferrari Testarossa; the 1957 Oldsmobile Golden Rocket Fiesta station wagon; the 2009 Dodge Magnum R/T station wagon, and the 1959 Cadillac Eldorado convertible.

Car collecting can grow from a hobby (about two-thirds of the market) into an investment-based endeavor. The investment-grade of a particular car is tracked by the Dow Jones Investment Car Index, where you can take note of a particular collectible ROI (return-on-investment) over a specific timeframe. Also, there is the Knight Frank Luxury Investment Index (KFLII) that tracks the annual ROI's on cars over the past 12 months and measures that return against other collectible commodities. For instance, this index reports the following recent ROI's: Wine – 3%; Watches – 3%; Coins – 10%; and Classic Cars – 28%. This index purports that Classic Cars has returned 129% over the last 5 years and 404% over a 10 year period. These findings were reported by the KFLII and are current as of the 1st Quarter, 2017.

Here are some qualities you should keep in mind as you review your plan for buying a collectible:

1. Rarity- the rarer the car and its optional equipment content, the richer the owner.
2. Limited production volume - the smaller the number

produced, the higher the value.
3. Universal, ageless styling – for instance, it looks as good today as it did in 1963.
4. Buy the car in its last model year, if discontinued, and get a manual tranny with a floor mounted shifter.
5. Don't over-emphasize the uniqueness of a car's name-plate at the expense of passing up a pre-established, historical pedigreed automobile. Granted, little known models generate a lot of interest but just know there are risks that come into play that are unique to cars that are viewed to be something less than widely recognized, vintage vehicles. The major risk is the "thinness" of the market, too little demand and could be destined to re-main so.
6. Verify that all serial numbers match – engine block to other drivetrain components, exterior body parts.

The death knoll for collectible cars includes but is not limited to:

1. Rust – a collectible cars' worse enemy.
2. Mismatched numbers– VIN number on title doesn't agree with VIN stamped on the car or there is a variance be-tween the numbers appearing on the engine and its pow-ertrain counterparts..
3. Buying without a pre-purchase inspection and not test driving the vehicle for yourself.
4. An accident history that a CarFax Report (if available) will bring out
5. Use of bondo on exterior painted surfaces in an attempt to conceal body disfiguration or damage to the finish. Place any old magnet on a car's exterior painted sur-face. If the magnet doesn't stick, you know you just got bondo'd.
6. Over as well as under priced. You don't want to pay more than a car can fetch in the marketplace nor pursue buying a car that is under priced or out of sync with the market unless the owner's reason(s) for pricing it such can be substantiated as valid. For instance, maybe the owner is trying to avoid some costly routine maintenance expense that the factory stipulates for a particular mileage level, such as a camshaft belt and water pump. Those mainte-nance items could, easily, set you back $3,000-$5,500, depending on the make of car. But you can expect that

kind of expense if you are considering buying a Porsche or Ferrari. Clearly, there is a reason(s) why a car is underpriced and it's not a reason you want to disregard. Be sure and ask the seller when the last major maintenance items were serviced or replaced and if any items are pending.

7. Lack of documentation – maintenance records are a huge plus when it comes to selling or buying.
8. Impatience – it's a killer. If you can't get the deal done or you can't locate the car you want to buy, sit back, relax, and know that there are plenty of other cars available for sale. Besides, your automotive tastes might change. Patience and persistence are great equalizers for disappointment.

Just as there is a car seat for every a##, there is a collectible or near-collectible car for every budget, taste or stage in your life. It might be a dream car from your high school days or a need to eradicate a mid-life crisis that has been brewing for some time or you might be interested in it as a possible investment. A collectible car can fill any and and all of those needs... simultaneously. If you know that buying a collectible is something you want to do but are undecided on the car to buy, start your search by reviewing car magazines that cater to this market segment, magazines like Hemmings Classic Cars, Hemmings Motor News, Hagerty, American Car Collector, Classic Automobiles, and Autabuy and start checking out ads on the websites for Auto Trader Classics, Classic Cars, and Trovit Cars.   Just for kicks and giggles and furthering your knowledge of what a car is really worth in a "real" time, instant market, go visit car auctions like the Barrett-Jackson (the granddaddy of them all), Mecom, Silver, and Russo-Steele, held regionally throughout the U.S. Those auctions can set you on a fast track to getting collector car savvy in a hurry.

Once you have decided, seriously consider joining a car club for the particular kind and make of car you would consider buying. Review car forums that can be found by Googling the specific car make such as the Corvette Forum, that puts you in touch with present-day owners whose comments on the merits (or lack of) of a particular make or model, gives you platform from which you can pose your questions as a part of getting your questions answered.

In a nutshell, if you are a genuine classic car enthusiast, how can you beat turning a hobby into an investment and enjoy that hobby or investment by driving, maintaining, showing, or just staring at it, knowing it is yours to dote on? Try doing that with stock certificates, silver coins, or financial statements!! And every time you sell one (hopefully, for a profit), you can rightfully get excited about your next classic car conquest. There's always an automotive fish out there in the sea, just itching to be caught and bought!

FAREWELL

About now, you must be wondering when is this book ever going to end? Well, if you hadn't guessed....it's now. Aren't you glad you asked? Some of you, I trust, would have liked more details on specific cars, particularly, as it relates to my opinions, seeing how I have a few. On the other hand, I could have gone on and on about my family and friends whose faith inspired me to take on this writing project in the first place, in hopes that you would come away with something you didn't know but was curious to know more about. And, for you folks who can't entirely get comfortable stepping into a car dealership, maybe now you can see the car buying process as a little less daunting than you originally imagined and can picture yourself looking forward to testing your new-found knowledge on some unsuspecting car salesman. Or, maybe, your take away isn't so much about cars as it is to get to know me better...for better or worse (seems I recall that choice of words with some clarity). Heaven knows I have given myself enough rope here to hang myself, quite nicely. In any event, just know that it has been a real hoot to write and share my thoughts, opinions, and memories with you.

I need to ask,   did you really buy-in to all this hyperbole about "lusting" and "loving" automobiles? If you did, I'm now convinced I made my point. I do, indeed, love automobiles but "lusting" is a bit of a stretch. So, for the record, if you find yourself lusting...stop it! Start buying! You've got to know, by now, that I have taken that advice to heart enough for a couple of lifetimes. I have owned or leased 79 cars and 1 lone truck in the span of 55 years, consuming nearly 1 million miles of driving.   I guess it's a little like eating 1 potato chip...there ain't no such thing, especially, since there's a whole bag in front of you, just begging to be eaten.

And, yes, if you hadn't figured it out by now, allow me to be the first to tell you that there is no known cure for obsessive car buying, best described as terminally addictive, compelling one to go out and buy a car (or two) on a continual, irrational basis. A former spouse had some bizarre notions about how often I should buy a car which, summarily, I dismissed as so much gibberish...an absolute insult to my brain. Of course, I had to tidy up that little disagreement.

I truly hope you perceive me as a person who has left some room in my life for something besides cars. I know...that is going to be hard to believe for some of you. Appearances and opinions can be so deceiving but actions aren't. Thank God. Otherwise, I would be spending my life living inside one of my automobiles, totally consumed with all the comforts of home, i.e. air conditioning, DVD's, music, Bluetooth-paired phone service, secured with lockable doors and a GPS to tell me where I am located....on my way to a place I hope I can find!

But, then again, just thinking about all those cars out there looking for a new owner, keeps me anchored. Think about it, there are literally thousands of cars, like pound-hound dogs, just waiting for a new place to put their food bowl or, in horse lingo, just "biting at the bit to be bought" (how's that for a little alliteration?). For one thing, I don't want to regress into that little six year old boy, standing alongside the road counting cars. My counting days are over; I want to buy them! And, whatever you do, don't get caught up in the false belief that there is always plenty of time to buy that special car. No...there isn't! That special car might be a special car for someone else as well, who is committing to buying it...NOW! Indecision and delay are symptoms of cowardice that produce the ultimate crushing blow, DISAPPOINTMENT, knowing that, that never-to-be-seen-again car got away, finding itself a new home and it isn't at your address. And all of this could have been avoided by allowing two little words to roll of your tongue or brain...BUY IT!!

What a literary journey this has been for me and I hope for you, as well. Did I lose some of you along the way, skipping ahead to get to a chapter you thought might be more interesting? Fair enough...I do the very same thing and sometimes, I don't get back to reading the fill-in chapters. About now, I bet you're feeling a little worn out, right? If so, I hope you enjoyed getting worn down as much as I enjoyed wearing you out! Thank you for indulging me. If, on the other hand, you didn't buy into my extended (I picked that word carefully) love of cars, your common sense should have been screaming at you to get out your B.S. Meter. Much of this must have been an assault on your eyes or brain or both.

It's not every day I get the opportunity to "tell it like it is" (or was), writing in the vernacular of, who gives a rat's aXX who it might offend. Anything less coming from me on the subject of automobiles should be viewed as spineless, given that it's my sandbox which gives me the right to exercise a little power here and there, reminding myself that, "He who holds the gold, makes the rules." Gosh, that felt really good writing that little saying! Thank God my livelihood doesn't depend on my being "politically correct" or writing books. I'll leave that to others. Giving me an outspoken purveyor of unvarnished truth helps make my day and that's exactly how I view my personal hero in the car business and that would be no other than Robert "Maximum Bob" Lutz, who takes no crap from anyone and isn't above judiciously shoveling out a little of his own, when it's "appropriately correct." I hope I don't have to explain that difference. I'm sure Maximum Bob could describe his feelings about "political correctness" more colorfully than I, using what, no doubt, would be a limited number of carefully chosen words that would, roughly, translate into, "Shut the front door on your way out!"

Let's get ourselves focused on the subject of TIME for just a moment.....time you no longer have and time hoped for as we look to the future, if so blessed. On balance, know that

Tomorrow has arrived.....it's called today.
How amazing it goes unnoticed as it slips away,
fleecing its victims of what they thought they had to spare,
thinking there was time to burn.....with ne'er a care.
But victims, we surely are and will remain
as watching that clock tick away drives one insane.
Sometimes, we casually treat time as if it were in our power
    to own,
when we lose sight of God's intent to prepare us for our new
    majestic home.
You see, time stands still for no one, our time on this earth is
    shockingly brief,
where our existence finally falls as if from a tree, leaving one
    less leaf.
As mortals, all we have is the here and now and the past is
    just that.....past.
While awaiting God's glorious and final gift, fulfilling our

lives, joyously, at last!
So forgive and forget.....while there's still time
'cause the day is coming when time will no longer be thine.
It never was ours but a gift to prudently use,
knowing there is a price to be paid, if abused.

So folks, get out and get that special car of a lifetime bought. As Elvis once put to song, "Its Now Or Never." Just go get 'er done!

That dreaded fourth quarter has finally arrived for me as I hoped it would but, equally so, hoped it wouldn't. Before that final timeout is used up, know that when that clock stops...it stops.

One earlier note bears repeating, "Soooooooooooooooo Many Cars, Soooooooo Little Time!" Did you notice the absence of the number of "o's" in my reference to time? That was by design. Like all things, one sad day my love affair with cars will come to a screeching halt as my involuntary, biological brakes lock up, and if they could talk, they would say, "No more, Senior. Those lemons have all been squeezed." What a finish!

GLOSSARY (CONDENSED)

ABS – Automobile Buyer Services; the only way to buy or lease a new or pre-owned car. See autobuyersvc.com.

A##hole – born one, die one.

A##holitis – an unsufferable disease that only gets worse with age.

Athletic Supporter – be one or buy one; it's your choice.

BWM – may the "Best Machine Win"

Bagels – old cars for sale by a car dealer in varying degrees of disrepair. Dealer knows the difference, you don't.

B. S. Meter – a prism that reflects a view that passes through, that attempts to measure "truth" or lack thereof.

Bush-Whacker – on the "giving" side.

Bush-Whackee – on the "receiving" side.

Car Hop – distantly related to the rabbit family; they don't call them "car hops" for nothing.

Car – Passion Pit on wheels.

CARS – Careful Accumulation Requires Savings.

Car Lover – hopelessly lost and soon to be broke.

Car Museum – where cars go to show-off

Character – show some or become one.

Classroom – ultimate competitive threat to the interior of a car.

CPO – Certified Pre-Owned cars for sale by a dealer. Crème de crème when it comes to used cars; usually priced 5-8% higher than its equivalent make, model, and year that is not certified.

Cruising – calculated, repetitive meandering between two or more pre-determined destinations in search of that special "something" that makes the heart race.

Curiosity Meter –measures what you don't know.

Dud – a synonym for Edsel, Saturn and, of course, our old friend, the unmitigated failure that will stand the test of time, the incomparable...Pontiac Astek.

Exhaust Pipes – where automotive opera performs

Expensive – any car financed on a payment plan.

Eye Candy – pleasing to the eye but not edible.

Franchisee – a new car dealer who puts his capital at risk so that others can make money off his investment.

Friend – someone who finds your missing car keys or buys you a tank of gas.

Furious – my Dad laying claim to my car keys, making me angrier than a pixxed-off chihuahua wishing it could be a pit bull terrier for a day.

Future – a concept before its time.

Garage – the keeper of unsold automobiles.

Great Depression – when one ate three meals a day: oatmeal, cornmeal, and skip-a-meal.

Horsepower – under the hood, not under the hoof.

Hyperbole – a nice word for bulls###.

Jock Strap – a basket-like object intended to protect a male's health insurance policy.

Joyous - blissful awareness, knowing that "special" car belongs to you.

Kissology – the study into the delicate art form of passionate kissing; a tongue in search of another tongue.

Lust – passion.

Meeskait – Yiddish for "Pontiac Astek."

Mentally Constipated – a.k.a. "challengi por el stupido" or "writer's block."

Morally Dyslexic – one who losses their moral compass, can't tell right from wrong.

Noise Pollution - a form of automotive opera lacking appeciation.

Passion – actionable lust.

Passion Pit – home away from home.

Pi##ed-Off - when one runs out of gas.

Pontiac Astek – adds a whole new dimension to the word "ugly."

Prank – an unlawful activity masquerading as innocent fun.

Prophylactic – commonly known as "rubbers." (which they better be!)

Repair shops – a hospital for sick cars.

School – an outside activity that gets in the way of automotive pursuits.

Showroom – where dinosaurs go to die particularly in the smaller car markets.

Souped-Up – needless power for a starving wallet.

Sticking The Horn – an acquired art form, when fully exercised, tests the strength of a car battery.

Technology – something ignored until the Japanese came a knockin' on Detroit's door.

Toyota – Japanese for "you bet your sweet a##, we're the best."

Ugly – Pontiac Astek; am I getting through to you?

Used car lot – where pre-owned cars go to die.

Volvo – a luxury car............REALLY?

.Whitney. J.C. (Automotive Catalog House) - where added horsepower and dollars meet.

Woodjatake – an old Native American slang word used by pre-owned car salesmen for "sucker."

NUMBER OF CAR MAKES; by brand

BMW	3	5 & two 7 Series
BUICK	5	3 Park Avenues; 1 Electra 225 Estate Wagon, and 1 Riviera
CADILLAC	13	4 DeVille Four-Door Sedans; 2 DeVille Coupes; 2 DTS's; 1 STS; 2 Eldorados; and 2 SRX's
CHEVROLET	16	4 Four-Door Sedans; 4 Four-Door Hardtops; 4 Corvettes; 2 convertibles; 1 Muscle car; and 1 Corvair 4-door sedan
FORD	9	6 Thunderbirds; 1 convertible; 1 four-door sedan; and 1 two-door sedan
GMC	1	SUV - Envoy
HYUNDAI	1	Four-door sedan – Sonata
JAGUAR	3	1 XJ four-door sedan; 1 Van-den Plas four-door sedan; and 1 F Type Sports car
LEXUS	8	7 four-door sedans (5 LS's; 1 GS; and 1 ES) and 1 SC400 coupe
MASERATI	2	1 Merak; and 1 Gran Turismo coupe

MERCEDES	2	1 E Class four-door sedan and 1 SL grand touring roadster
MERCURY	2	1 two-door sedan and 1 four-door sedan
MITSUBISHI	1	GT Spider convertible
OLDSMOBILE	5	1 Toronado; 2 Custom Cruiser station wagons; and 1 Delta 88 Royale four-door sedan and 1 Aurora sedan
PONTIAC	3	2 Grand Prix and 1 Bonneville four-door sedan
PORSCHE	4	911 Targa; 911 Carrera 4S; 356A Speedster; and a 928S grand touring coupe
TOYOTA	1	RAV 4 crossover

NUMBER OF MAKES; by model year

BMW	2012/2014/2015
BUICK	1978/82/83/85/88
CADILLAC	1977/79/81/82/83/84/2000/02/06/07/11/12/14
CHEVROLET	1965/66/67/68/69/71/72/74/75/78/79
CHEVROLET CORVAIR	1960
CHEVROLET CORVETTE	2001/ 03/06/17
FORD	1956/58/60
FORD THUNDERBIRD	1957/67/70/74/76/2003
GMC	1999

HYUNDAI   2011

JAGUAR   1983/85/2016

LEXUS   1989/90/93/94/95/96/98/99

MASTERATI   1975/2008

MERCEDES-BENZ   1997/2004

MERCURY   1962/88

MITSUBISHI 2000

OLDSMOBILE   1974/76/79/80/97

PONTIAC   1969/73/80

PORSCHE   1956/83/88/99

TOYOTA   2001

NUMBER OF PRODUCT TYPES (12); by category

FAMILY SEDANS   28

SPORTS SEDANS (4-door)   3

PERSONAL LUXURY (2 door)   13

COUPES   5

CONVERTIBLES   4

SPORTS CARS   8

COLLECTIBLES   8

CROSSOVERS   1

MUSCLE   1

EXOTICS   6

SPORTS UTILITY (SUV)   1
STATION WAGONS   3

NUMBER OF CARS; owned or leased/new or pre-owned

I have owned or leased 79 different vehicles in a period of 55 years, categorized as:

NEW 46

PRE-OWNED   33

OWNED   66

LEASED   13

TOTAL NUMBER OF VEHICLES   79

   The number "17" was a figure that kept popping up as I was collecting these data. It would have been one thing if the number showed up once, possibly, twice, but 3 times? Way bizarre... almost beyond my pay grade or math skills to count!

   17   Different car makes I have owned/leased

   17   I owned/leased two or more cars in the same year

   17   Total number of years when I did not buy or lease a car

ACKNOWLEDGMENTS

Writing this book became the most complete expression of my love for those creatures that have four wheels on it...including riding lawnmowers and farm tractors. I am praying that, before that final curtain call, I will have had the opportunity to exercise a John Deere or Cub Cadet riding lawnmower to the extent that it will need frequent oil changes, the tires rotated and replaced because I wore them out. I want to share my mowing experience with my good friend, Larry Turek, who mows seven acres weekly on a riding mower that provides him with hours and hours of entertainment, as if it were a go kart and loving every minute of it.

Yes, writing this book was truly a hoot for me. It all started out to be an essay on marketing automobiles when my sister-in-law, Sandy, (with a "y"), suggested that writing a book about my memoirs relating to cars might be marketable. So, whether it is or not, I, nonetheless, have had the joy of writing something that consumed much of my otherwise free time over the course of the past two years. So, to all of you out there, my valued friends and family, I want to thank you from the bottom of my heart for your prayers and encouragement. I couldn't have done it without you.

I want to recognize several individuals by name who have played a major part in getting this book published, without whose expertise, this narrative would not have seen the light of day.

- Cathy Burford – lovely and loving wife to Bill or "Billiam" as he is known to his friends, who shared some of her literary skills as a novelist that manifested itself in the final editing of this book.
- Bill "Billiam" Burford, the grillmaster and famed father of the Burford Burger. Billiam is a master mechanic extraordinaire. If he can't fix it, it ain't worth fixing...simple

as that. Billiam shares my love of automobiles, ever in search of that once-in-a-lifetime car. Although he hasn't found it yet, his search reminds me of looking for a four-leaf clover. You know it's out there. Hang in there, Bill.

- Jan McLaughlin – for her literary skill as a writer of children's books, who guided me through the graphics formatting , transferring the nearly fifty photos into printable pages that became a significant part of the book you just finished reading.
- Thomas Quentin Lutes, U.S. Navy (Ret.) - my Uncle Quentin persuaded me to believe I could do anything I set my mind to ...including writing this book. I will be eternally grateful for his unshakable belief in me.
- Gary Hilderbrand – more like a brother than a first cousin, Gary has always been there for me. End of sentence.
- Arnell "Arnie" Hilderbrand Standiford – for her magnificent artistry in painting the picture of Grandpa Hilderbrand's general store and used car "market" that appears as a photo in this book.
- Robert "Maximum Bob" Lutz – the automobile industry's marketing guru, par excellence and my personal, professional hero, a man I so admire for his achievements and personal qualities, skills, and talents.
- Tom McClain - Tom is always a joy to talk to about anything having to do with cars, any cars! In particular, he is hugely knowledgeable on Fords and Corvettes. Who do you know who can name the four trim levels of a 1953 Studebaker?
- John "Doc" Maher – Doc's love of Corvettes and his role as President of our local Corvette Club can't be challenged by mere man. His presidency into perpetuity is guaranteed. Of course, it doesn't hurt any that no one wants that job anyhow. As a former college professor of English and an author himself, he has all the tools in his toolbox to criticize my book, had he chosen to shatter my fragile little ego. But, he never lost track of the fact that friends can spar with each other and that's OK. Really?
- Tony Ritz – I have Tony to thank for his guidance and counseling on collectible cars, the ones to avoid and the ones to buy, should they become available, which, of course, 90% of the time they are not. But, old Tony can keep your dreams alive. A nicer gentleman you will never meet.
- David Sacks – Dave is my favorite car enthusiast, busi-

ness confidant, and a swell friend.

- Marvin Siegel – as my cardiologist, he has a lot to do with why I am here today, writing a book instead of pushing up dandelions!
- Ron Thompkins – for his friendship and brilliant witness to Jesus Christ. This man is making a difference!
- The Reverand Susan Ramsey – for her ongoing support in seeing me get this book published.
- Kevin Carson – I want to thank him for his Christian leadership that continues to inspire me.
- Ari Garrel – a car restorer with a limitless imagination and a dear friend who likes to read good books. Hope he like mine!
- Sandra Sue Hilderbrand – a.k.a. "Sandi," (with an "i"). I want to acknowledge my bride and best friend for the many roles she fills in our marriage, none the least is her critique (as in criticize as well as support) of my written work. Without her help and love, this book wouldn't have gotten past page one. So, for the record, thank you, Sugar Booger.

Before I bid you adieu, I have something on my heart that I want to place on yours, if you will permit me. Trusting that I now have your blessing to proceed, here it comes: Praise and glorify God with your actions which will be reflecting your beliefs, knowing He will ALWAYS provide. Yes...always, as He is gracious beyond human understanding, and, here comes the best part of all...God loves you....now and forever!

Made in the USA
San Bernardino, CA
08 June 2018